1972

Many Lappies, Mary & Arthur.

Many Lappies, Mary & Arthur.

£2·50

the
GUINNESS guide
to motorcycling

OTHER GUINNESS SUPERLATIVES TITLES

Facts and Feats Series:

Air Facts and Feats, 2nd ed.
John W. R. Taylor, Michael
J. H. Taylor and David Mondey

Rail Facts and Feats, 2nd ed.
John Marshall

Tank Facts and Feats, 2nd ed.
Kenneth Macksey

Yachting Facts and Feats
Peter Johnson

Plant Facts and Feats
William G. Duncalf

*Structures—Bridges, Towers,
Tunnels, Dams . . .*
John H. Stephens

Car Facts and Feats, 2nd ed.
Anthony Harding

Business World
Henry Button and Andrew Lampert

Music Facts and Feats
Bob and Ceila Dearling

Animal Facts and Feats, 2nd ed.
Gerald L. Wood

Guide Series:

Guide to Fresh Water Angling
Brian Harris and Paul Boyer

Guide to Mountain Animals
R. P. Bille

Guide to Underwater Life
C. Petron and I. B. Lozet

Guide to Formula 1 Motor Racing
Jose Rosinski

Other titles:

English Furniture 1550–1760
Geoffrey Wills

English Furniture 1760–1900
Geoffrey Wills

*The Guinness Guide to Feminine
Achievements*
Joan and Kenneth Macksey

The Guinness Book of Names
Leslie Dunkling

Battle Dress
Frederick Wilkinson

Universal Soldier
Martin Windrow and
Frederick Wilkinson

History of Land Warfare
Kenneth Macksey

History of Sea Warfare
Lt.-Cmdr. Gervis Frere-Cook and
Kenneth Macksey

History of Air Warfare
David Brown, Christopher Shores
and Kenneth Macksey

The Guinness Book of Facts
edited by Norris D. McWhirter

*The Guiness Book of Records,
23rd ed.*
edited by Norris D. McWhirter

© *1974, Guinness Superlatives Ltd.*
Second edition 1976
Filmset by Jarrold & Sons Ltd, Norwich

© *1970, 1976, Editions Denoël, Paris*

ISBN 0/900424/36/2

the GUINNESS guide to motorcycling

christian lacombe

preface by jean-pierre beltoise

guinness superlatives ltd.

2 Cecil Court, London Road, Enfield, Middlesex, England

motorcycles of yesterday and today

summary

2

the sports

racing
motocross
trials
grass-track and speedway
ice racing
sprinting and dragsters
speed records
american sports

3

the motorcyclists

the purists
the show bike (or chopper)

At the time when I made my racing début (about 1960), the motorcycle had neither the success nor the range that it has today. Only the enthusiasts came to watch motorcycle races. One can say that it is thanks to the Japanese that things have changed. When I saw the first Japanese models that drew attention to themselves as novelties, I said to myself that the era of the old machines— oozing oil, and of the design of my father's day—had just died. This is so much the better, both for the motorcycle and for the motorcyclist. The seductive Japanese operation had succeeded, and I was glad to be tempted, because one cannot remain insensible to the attractions of the modern motorcycle. Even if today the motorcycle is the poor relation of the car, it is no longer the spare wheel—and on good days, it proves to be a great rival.

Although today I am a Formula 1 driver, I have not forgotten my origins as a motorcycle racer, and in fact, I am proud of it. One is too inclined to believe that the riders who have given up motorcycles for cars have forgotten their origins. This is not so, and those who, like me, have moved from holding a pair of handlebars to holding a steering-wheel, realise this. These two sports which although very different are, paradoxically, very close to one another. Motorcycle racing is not necessarily the introduction to car racing, but the experience it gives provides a solid foundation of knowledge of the European circuits. The great advantage for a motorcycle racer who becomes a racing car driver is that he has started in a hard school. Everyone, or at any rate all those who have been through it, knows that motorcycle racing is a tougher sport than car racing. When on two wheels one quickly learns, to one's cost, that the smallest error is not forgiven. An error usually means a fall, hopefully not serious, and that makes you watch out. On a motorcycle, even hotheads feel more vulnerable, and conscious of danger. Strengthened by this new wisdom, they learn how to estimate distances, and to fix braking points. In a word, they have learned the technique of riding—which applies just as much to the motorcycle as to the car. So the motorcycle racer who wants to race cars starts with certain advantages. An excellent motorcycle racer cannot be bad in a racing car and, despite what he may think, anything is possible.

Then there are the others, the faithful ones, who remain motorcycle racers. It is these people with whom we are concerned in the following pages. This comprehensive book retraces their history, which like myself, you will have pleasure in discovering, or re-discovering. You will find here the machines of the old days, the ones from which have developed the fabulous machines of today, individual and technically brilliant.

The racing circuits occupy a great part of this book. You will get to know the famous racing champions, the continual hard work of the factories, the arrival of the Japanese on the circuits, the continental circus, the horse-power battle, the frame problem. You will read here names that are immediately recognisable—and discover others, no less celebrated, but perhaps a little forgotten.

If you are fond of precision and a sense of balance, "Trials" will please you. If you prefer the spectacular, look at these chapters: "Dragsters", "Grasstrack", "Ice racing" or "Speed records". If you like endurance, discover "Motocross", or even that awkwardly named race, the I.S.D.T.—the International Six Days' Trial. The motorcycle meetings will hold no more secrets for you. The purists,

probably enthusiasts of the big machines, will talk their hearts out. They are the ones you meet in the winter, in freezing cold weather, travelling hundreds of miles, just for pleasure.

If the legendary Harley-Davidson remains your favourite bike, despite all its changes, then "Show bike" will give you some moments of pleasure.

If you prefer the country, and the woodlands, let yourself be tempted by the cross-country machines that will be shown to you here. You can replace your horse, or your legs, by one of these practical machines, which are easy to maintain, and cost little in terms of hard work. In a word, you will know everything about the motorcycle.

J.-P. BELTOISE

motorcycles of yesterday and today

1

history

To cover the complete history of the motorcycle would require at least ten books, all as large as this one as over 2,000 makes of motorcycle have been in production since the early days. In this history, only the first types, constructed about the beginning of the century, from which the machines of today have been developed, will be discussed. The first motor-velocipede (the name "motorcycle" did not yet exist) was invented in France by Michaux and Perreaux in 1869. A single-cylinder steam-engine, made by Perreaux, turned the rear wheel of the velocipede, made by Michaux, by means of two belts. This machine made a trial run from Paris to Saint-Germain, a distance of 15 km, or nearly 10 miles. Later the steam-engine was used to propel various different kinds of tricycles. Parallel with the development of steam-driven two- or three-wheeled machines there were some particularly original inventions. In 1875 the Frenchman Huret invented the Cynophère, a strange tricycle, in which the two rear wheels were constructed as barrel-like cages, in which dogs were placed. The dogs then ran in the cages, thus turning the wheels, rather like a hamster turns a treadmill. The enthusiast of the large-wheeled Cynophère chose to use Great Danes, and the others, poodles. The Society for the Protection of Animals vigorously protested against this invention, and it was abandoned. A similar scheme appeared in 1906, with the invention of the horse-driven bicycle. For this it was necessary to have a pedalling horse. This is how it was done. A horse was placed between the rear wheels of the cycle, and each of his front feet put on to a pedal. One climbed into the saddle, gave a great cry of "Gee-up", and if the horse felt like pedalling, steered the contraption down the road by means of a pole attached to the front wheel.

In a more serious vein, although no more effective in operation, was the spring-driven bike. It had a clockwork motor, like in a toy train, only larger. Driving this machine, an American, Lybe, in 1893 travelled a distance of some 770 yd (700 m), at a speed of 30 mile/h (50 km/h). After that the spring had to be rewound, something that required more time and effort than doing the 770 yd on foot.

In 1879 an Italian called Murnigotti patented a combustion engine which used a gas mixture of air and hydrogen. However, this patent was never put into production, and the steam-engine continued to develop. In 1884 the American, Copland, produced a steam bicycle which produced 0·25 hp at 1,000 rev/min. This machine was recognisable by an immense rear wheel, and a high driving position.

The year after, 1885, was a historic year. The German, Daimler, constructed the first four-stroke engine, and, in 1886 installed it experimentally into a frame, that vaguely resembled a child's bicycle, equipped with training wheels. The engine was single-cylinder, of 264 cc, and developed 0·5 hp at 700 rev/min. It had one carburettor *à léchage*. The petrol was held in a large tank, where it evaporated, the vapour produced being taken by a tube to the combustion chamber. Before it arrived there, the petrol vapour passed into a mixing chamber where air could be introduced, so as to weaken or enrich the mixture. This mixture was let into the cylinder by an inlet valve, operated automatically by the decrease in gas pressure. The entry valve was reclosed by a very weak spring. Once in the cylinder the gas mixture was compressed, and ignited on contact with a red-hot finger of metal, which was heated by burners. The burnt gases escaped through an exhaust valve operated mechanically by a system of rods and solid cranks from the flywheel of the motor—already at this time enclosed by the gear-case so that for many years this was isolated from the engine.

In 1887 the Englishman Butler patented the first two-stroke tricycle, and in addition, had a rotary valve to regulate the entry of fresh gas into the cylinder. So Butler's valve is in a sense the precursor of the rotary pump. In the same year the Frenchman Millet invented a star-shaped motor of five cylinders. This engine was used to power both tricycles and bicycles. For a tricycle, the star-shaped engine was fitted to the front wheel. On the bicycle, it was fixed to the rear. This cylinder configuration and mounting were used on the Megola of 1921. The ignition of the Millet engine was by electric spark from a Bunsen battery. To assist the evaporation of the petrol in the carburettor the air necessary for combustion was first heated.

In 1892 a motor was constructed that was revolutionary for its day. It was a single-cylinder, air-cooled two-stroke, and was placed on a level with the centre of the rear wheel of the machine, transmitting its power by means of simple gearing. In some ways it was a predecessor to the P50 Honda.

Between 1893 and 1894 more steam-propelled motorcycles were produced, the most interesting being the machines of Von Meyenberg and Dalifol Volta. The first practical motorcycle produced commercially was the Hildebrand-Wolfmüller. To begin with it was constructed in Munich, and then later made under licence in France. The four-stroke motor had two horizontal cylinders, each of 90 mm bore and 117 mm stroke, making a total capacity of 1,488 cc. As on the Daimler, the inlet valve was opened automatically by the decrease in pressure and the exhaust valve was operated mechanically. This motor did not have the same mass of cranks, but instead, used an original system; on each big end a rubber strap was fixed which stretched as the crank descended to its lowest point . . . then contracted again once this point was passed, to bring the piston up again to its highest point. The cylinders and covers were water-cooled. A tank that also formed the rear mudguard held the water. A burner-ignition was fitted to this machine. A finger of metal—either nickel or platinum—ignited the mixture. It was heated by the burners, one end being in the combustion chamber, and the other emerging into a small box which contained the petrol-fed burners. The Hildebrand-Wolfmüller could travel at 25 mile/h (40 km/h), but had difficulty going slowly, as the transmission was very direct—connecting-rod, crank, hub—and this produced a very jerky motion at anything under 3 or 4 mile/h (5 or 6 km/h).

In 1896 the English Colonel, Sir H. C. L. Holden patented his petrol-driven motorcycle. The 1-litre motor had four pistons, but only two connecting-rods. The cylinders operated two by two, and each piston was in three parts. The Holden was fitted with delco coil ignition. The distributor of the delco was mounted above a camshaft, as this machine was equipped with a camshaft that operated the exhaust valve, and which, incredibly, drove an oil pump. This machine developed 3 hp at 400 rev/min and could travel at 25 mile/h (40 km/h). In England, the Excelsior appeared in the same year. This machine was first fitted with a De Dion Bouton engine, and later with Villiers, Blackburne and J.A.P. engines, with capacities varying from 100 cc to 1,000 (J.A.P. V-twin). Excelsior also made their own motors, in particular in 1913, when they came out with one of the biggest singles ever made, an 810 cc.

1897: The Werner brothers were without doubt the greatest pioneers of the motorcycle. They were the people who first coined the name. They were Frenchmen, but of Russian origin. To begin with, before 1901, they mounted their motor, a single-cylinder, on the front wheel, in the fashion of the Velo-Solex. The transmission was belt-operated. After 1901 the motor was switched to fit vertically between the two wheels. The machines were simple, strong and cheap. The most popular of all was the 250 cc which developed 2 hp in 1901.

The Frenchman Pingault built a tandem, with an electric motor, powered by four batteries. Secondary transmission was by chain.

The American E. J. Pennington constructed a twin-cylinder motor which he fitted horizontally behind the rear wheel of his motorcycle. Later, he was to design a small V-twin for motorcycles.

1898: Wait of Great Britain was the first man to use a loop frame, in his Clyde motorcycles.

René Gillet of France made machines that were above all simple and useful. They were from 750 to 1,000 cc in size, and later were used to equip the French Police and Army.

Saroléa, one of the foremost Belgian makes, together with Minerva and F.N., founded. They made all kinds of motors in the single and V-twin layouts, before the First World War. After the war, they made some 350 and 500 side-valve motors, then their 125, 150 and 175 cc two-strokes, and a big 600 cc overhead-valve single. Saroléa raced during the twenties and thirties, using 350 and 500 cc twin overhead-cam motors.

1899: Motosacoche, of Switzerland, made 200,000 motors and motorcycles between 1900 and 1930. Motosacoche motors (M.A.G.) equipped many makes, such as Brough Superior, Matchless and Ariel. The first Motosacoche motor was a 215 cc four-stroke, designed by Dufaux.

The first Laurin and Klèment bikes were made in the Austro-Hungarian Empire, part of which was to become Czechoslovakia in 1918. The very first Laurin-Klèment was fitted with a Werner motor. From 1900 the firm produced its own motors, singles and V-twins, and a splendid in-line air-cooled four, producing 5 hp.

From 1899 until 1920 Matchless in Great Britain used a variety of motors—J.A.P., M.A.G.

The machines our grandfathers dreamed of.

Raglan in Great Britain came out with the three-speed gearbox.

Binks, in the same country, made a four-cylinder motor that could be fitted across or along the frame.

In America, Curtiss, the aviation pioneer, became interested in motorcycles and produced singles and V-twins. To establish a record, he even made a V-8.

In England, Herbert Dennell modified a J.A.P. motor to make an in-line three. As well as this, he used in his machines an air-cooled Franklin-Isaacson four-cylinder.

Harley-Davidson is famous today for its V-twin, but in the 1920s the firm also made a 584 flat-twin.

1904: Roc of Great Britain made the four-speed gearbox common. Formerly, the firm had made a two-speed box with clutch operation.

Zenith of Great Britain produced a four-speed gearbox, which it fitted to its Fafnir motors.

1905: Howard, also in Great Britain, improved his 2·5 hp motor with fuel injection.

Fee, again a British firm, produced the first flat-twin to be fitted along the frame. Later, this motor was to be developed by Douglas.

Grade of Germany, built one, two- and four-cylinder two-strokes, with which it won many motorcycle races of the day.

1907: New Era of the U.S.A. became one of the first firms to adopt a foot-operated gear-lever.

A.S.L. fitted its machine with pneumatic front and rear suspension.

1908: Pope of the U.S.A. constructed V-twin overhead-valve motors of 7–8 hp with magneto ignition, fitted into machines with sprung rear suspension.

1909: Alfred Angus Scott of Great Britain was an inspired designer of two-stroke motors. His 500 and 600 water-cooled twins are famous for all time. In 1911 the Scott racing machine employed rotary pumps. A prototype 1,000 cc three was made as well as a supercharged 1,000 cc V-four.

Wilkinson, again of Great Britain, produced water-cooled in-line fours of 676 and 844 cc, with three-speed gearboxes and shaft drive.

Miyapetex was one of the very first Japanese firms to make motorcycles.

Pierce of the U.S.A. became another firm to use shaft drive.

A.J.S. in Britain began by using singles, but later progressed to using 800–1,000 cc V-twins. In 1927 A.J.S. put into production a

petition for the British makes. In 1920 their 500 overhead-valve machine was considered the fastest 500 of the day.

1910: The British firm, James, produced a supercharged flat-twin two-stroke.

1911: Rudge-Whitworth, one of the most important British firms at the beginning of the century produced 500 and 750 singles, and a 1,000 cc V-twin. In the twenties Rudge produced touring machines with four valves per cylinder, and four-speed gearboxes.

After producing a rather conventional single, Militaire of the U.S.A. built a four-cylinder model, which had a tubular chassis, built car-style, with a gearbox containing three forward speeds—and reverse!

Henderson, also of the U.S.A., was famous for its four-cylinder machines, which had a capacity of over 1 litre. Like the Militaire, they were fitted with reverse gear.

1912: Again in America, Monarch produced a 1,000 cc V-twin with secondary transmission operated by two chains.

Koehler-Escoffier of France was the only European manufacturers to equip their machines (V-twin) with overhead-cams. This was in 1920.

Stallas in Great Britain produced an interesting machine with a vertical-twin two-stroke 784 cc water-cooled motor, two-speed gearbox, clutch and shaft drive.

Senior produced 500 cc overhead valve V-twin motors in Italy, before the First World War.

1913: Rova-Kent, an Australian firm, produced this year several 500 four overhead-valve singles.

Bayley-Flyer produced an extraordinary machine, fitted with a horizontally mounted 3·5 hp twin. It had a two-speed automatic gearbox, shaft drive and crank starting.

Cyclone of the U.S.A. produced the first 1,000 cc overhead-cam V-twin before 1920.

1914. Seal of Great Britain produced an extraordinary side-car outfit. The machine was not steered by handlebars, but by a steering-wheel in the side car, which the passenger controlled. The side-wheel itself was steerable.

1917: In America, Williams produced a single-cylinder motor, which he mounted on the rear wheel of the machine. Secondary transmission was by pinion.

1918: Redrup of Great Britain produced a three-cylinder side-valve motor, and two years later a six-cylinder prototype in two banks of

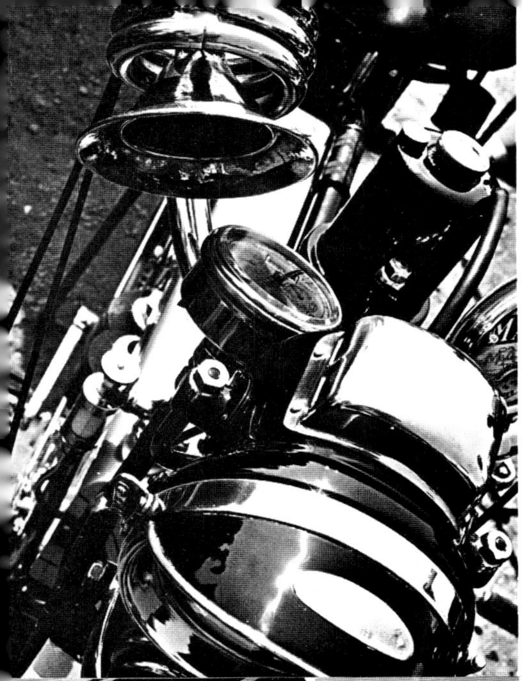

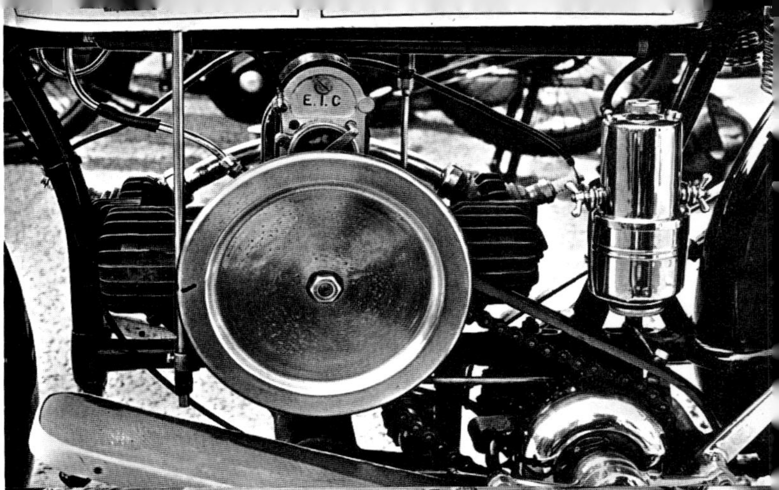
E.T.C

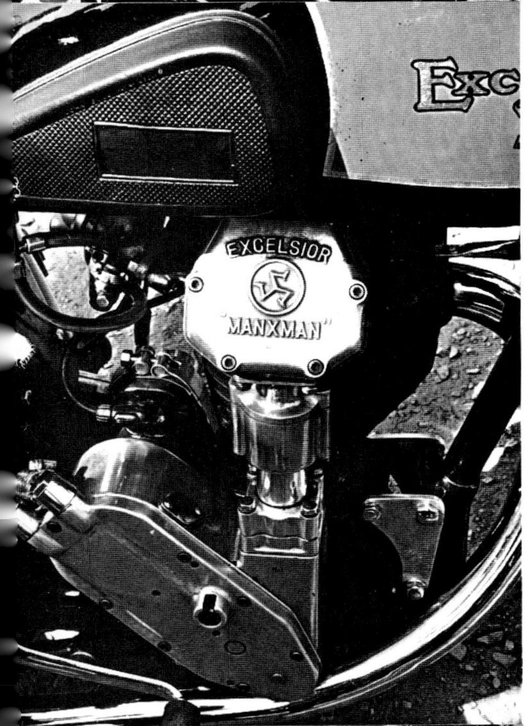
EXCELSIOR
"MANXMAN"

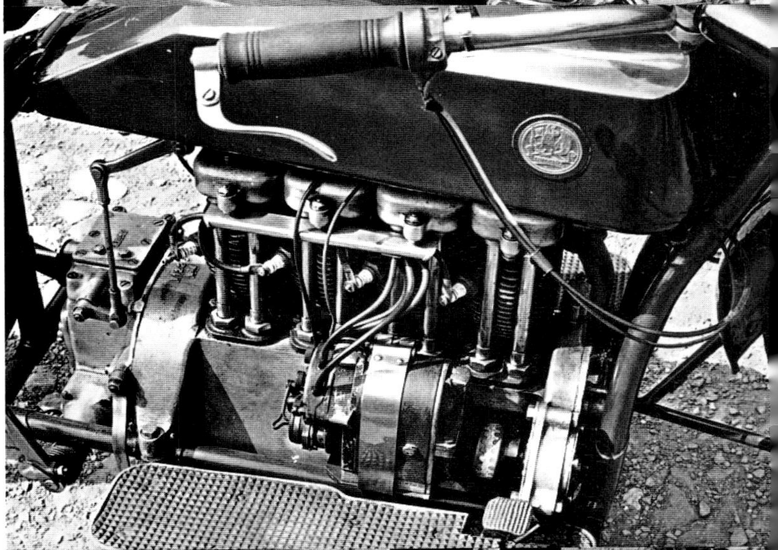

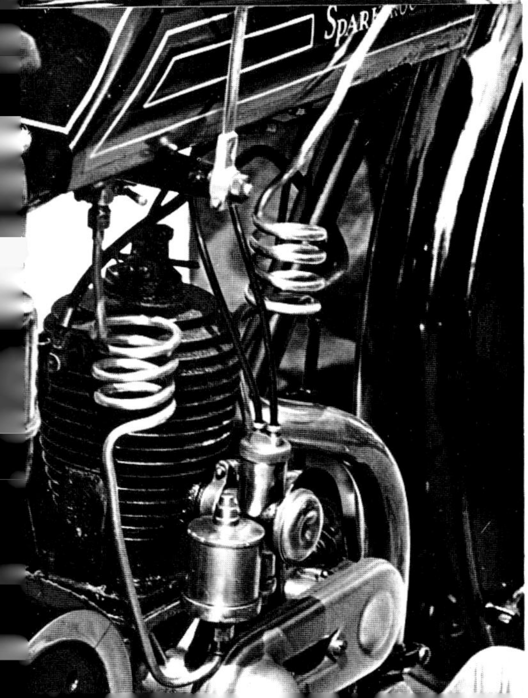

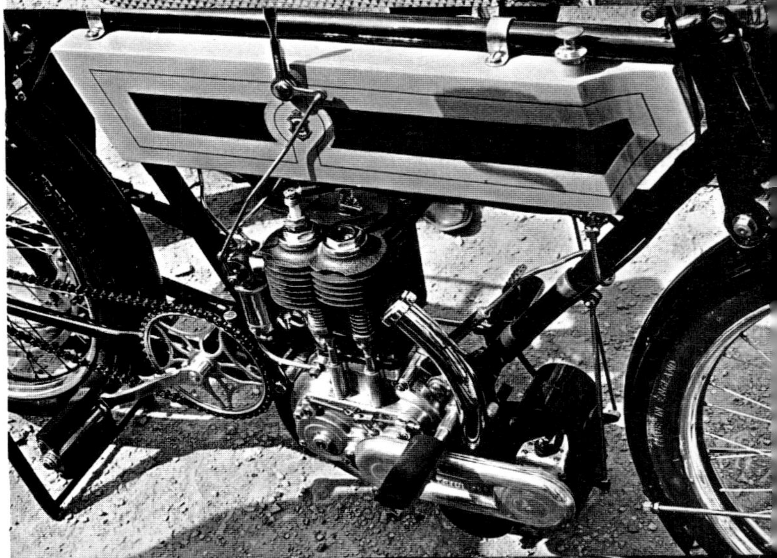

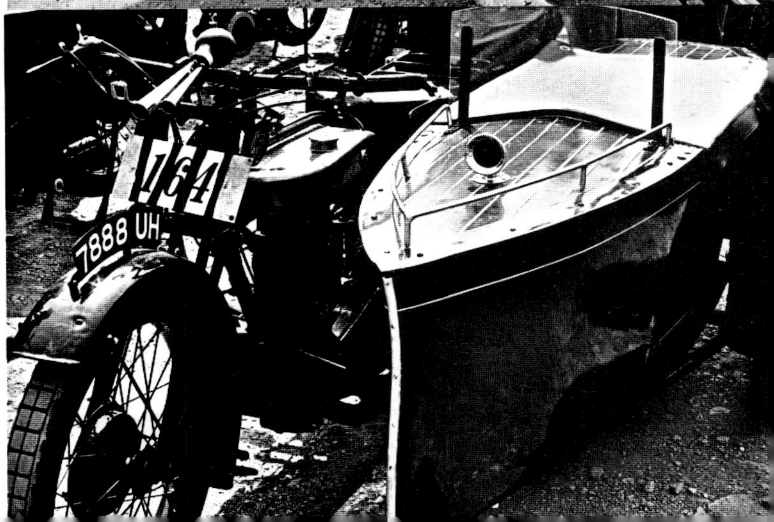
164
7888 UH

sheet metal, and rear suspension.

Gillet-Herstal of Belgium produced a 350 cc two-stroke single with a rotary pump in 1920.

1920: Blériot, the French pioneer pilot, also built motorcycles, the best of which was a 500 cc overhead-valve twin.

Louis Clément of France built a curious 600 cc single overhead-cam V-twin. The magneto was cam operated.

Nimbus, the great Danish firm, produced splendid in-line air-cooled fours. The large upper frame tube was also used as the petrol tank. Because of this, the frame was made of stamped-out sheet metal.

Superb Four, from Britain had, as its name suggests, four cylinders. It was a 998 cc, with a belt-driven single overhead-cam.

Ziro produced a little 150 cc machine in Germany, which had a rotary pump.

Train, in France, built four-cylinder motors, either with overhead valves or single overhead-cam.

1921: Zundapp of Germany, was unique in 1933, when they made an 800 cc flat-four with chain-driven gearbox.

Stanger in Great Britain produced a 538 cc V-twin two-stroke.

S.A.R. of France used oil-cooling on its 350 cc singles.

Lutèce, again of France, fitted its 997 cc vertical in-line twin along the frame, one cylinder behind the other. It was shaft driven.

Megola of Germany produced a more elaborate version of the Millet. This had five cylinders in a star, and was mounted on the front wheel. It was 640 cc, had side-valves, no clutch or gearbox, but in spite of this, the machine won many races of that time.

Moto Guzzi of Italy, makers of the finest flat singles, often applied their racing techniques to their road machines.

Neracar of America fitted its 269 cc two-stroke with a five-speed gearbox.

Brough Superior, the Rolls-Royce of the motorcycle world, and built in the same country, used J.A.P., M.A.G. and Matchless motors. About 1930 Brough Superior produced some four-cylinder prototypes: an air-cooled V-four, a water-cooled in-line four and an air-cooled flat-four fitted across the frame.

British Radial made a three-cylinder 120° radial engine with detachable cylinder heads and enclosed valves.

Chaise the French specialist in overhead-cam motors, as shown by his 350 and 500 singles and 500 and 750 fours, all of which were of this type.

E.T.A. of Great Britain, made another three, this time of 870 cc.

G.S.D., again British, already had a duplex cradle frame.

1922: Arco of Germany fitted a carburettor to the front of its 350 cc overhead-valve water-cooled motor, the exhaust being at the back.

Menos, again of Germany, produced a 618 cc water-cooled flat-twin motor, totally enclosed in a metal frame, painted in black and white stripes like a zebra.

1923: Horex, Germany, began by producing singles of 250 to 600 cc, then, around 1930 made splendid 600 and 800 cc single, central chain-driven overhead-cam twins.

The birth of the B.M.W. factory. B.M.W. used flat-twins.

D.A.W., Germany. They built a 405 cc two-stroke single.

D.A.R.T. of Great Britain produced a 350 cc single overhead-cam motor producing 17·5 hp.

Garbello, in Italy, made a 1,000 cc water-cooled four.

Grote, of Germany, was the first firm to produce a three-cylinder two-stroke.

1924: Motobécane, of France, before building their 49 cc Mobylette, was a great producer of large motorcycles. They even made a 750 cc single overhead-cam four.

M.W. in Germany built a small two-stroke twin, only 145 cc.

1926: Gazda, of Austria, on their 250 cc two-stroke used a supplementary piston, working in an opposite direction to the main one.

McEvoy of Great Britain produced the prototype of a single-cylinder motor having two inlet valves, and a single exhaust valve.

W.M.R. of Germany built a three-valve, single overhead-cam 500.

1927: W.G. of Great Britain had a 490 cc vertical twin two-stroke.

Windhoff of Germany produced an extremely beautiful, oil-cooled four.

Schliha of Germany produced two-strokes with an exhaust valve.

Freyler of Austria replaced the conventional valves of its 350 single overhead-cam motor by a rotary-valve system.

1928: The Ascot-Pullin, which was British, had a 496 cc overhead-valve engine, mounted horizontally in the frame, a gear-case with a sealed secondary chain, hydraulic brake and spoked wheels.

The D.P.R.A. motor was designed by the famous Italian engineer Rémor who produced the four-cylinder racing Gilera. The 500 D.P.R.A. had one of these four-cylinder motors.

1936: Galbusera of Italy, made more for prestige than to sell—a 250 V-four, and a 500 eight . . .

The 1884 Copland.
The 1,000 cc V-twin Vincent.

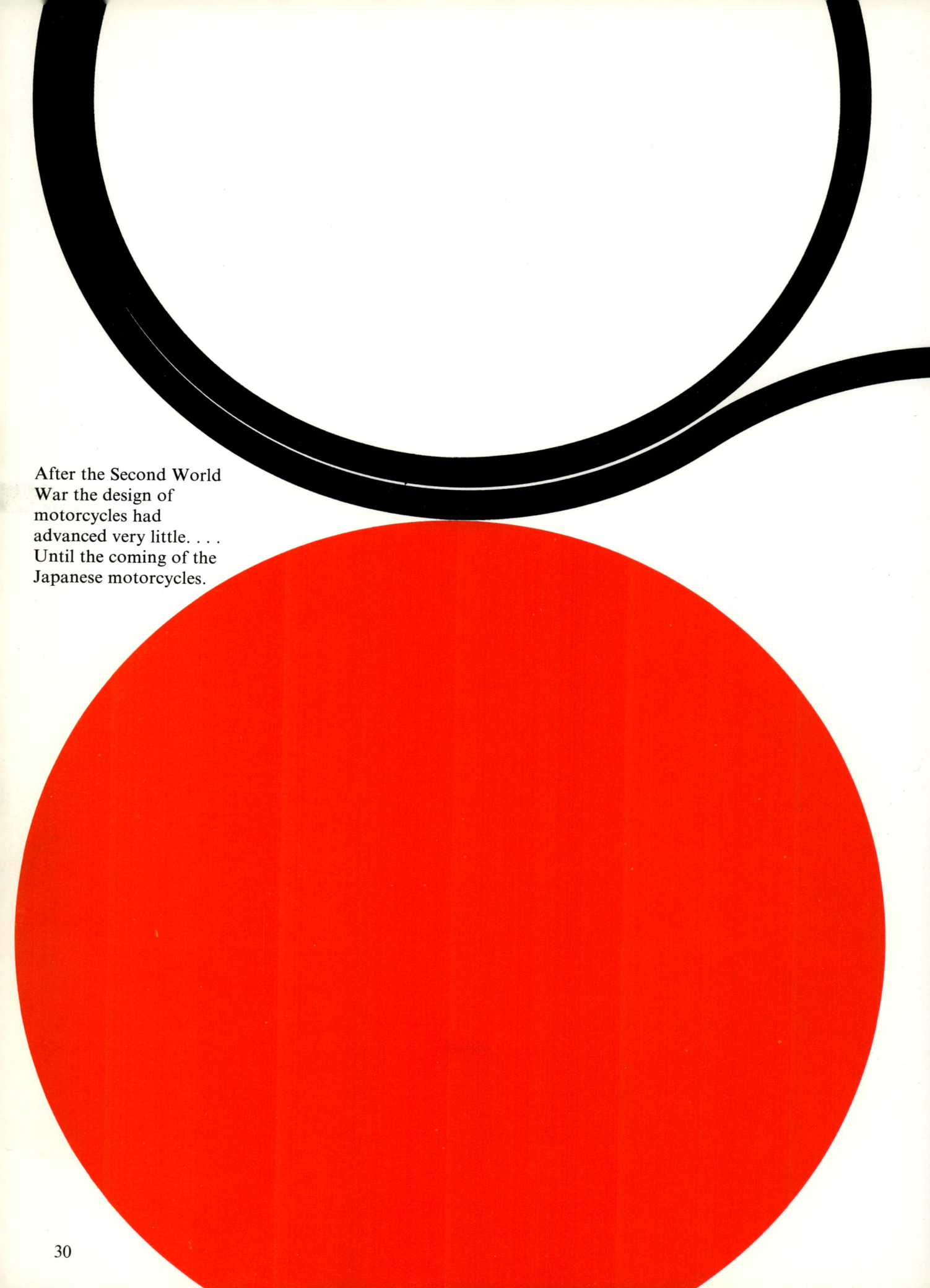

After the Second World
War the design of
motorcycles had
advanced very little. . . .
Until the coming of the
Japanese motorcycles.

motorcycles of today

the 125s

A motorcycle worthy of the name must really be of above 125 cc. Below this, it is a motorised cycle, though still capable of speeds equal if not better than some of the motorcycles of say, ten years ago. Because of this, they can be considered as real, small motorcycles. One can even find even smaller motorcycles than a 125, still having all the characteristics of a real motorcycle. They have the line, the equipment and a performance approaching the real thing. However, to simplify the problem it is better to divide up the bikes into the five most common capacities, 125, 250, 350, 500 and above 500. There are very many makes in the world, and to discuss them all would take too long. Therefore only the best—either the best known, or the best made—will be dealt with. According to the temperament of the rider he may choose a sports machine, or a touring model. It depends on the use to which he is going to put it. In town, the big machines are inadvisable, but on the open road they are ideal. There is also a compromise between the two—the machine that behaves well both in town and out in the country. For those who are thinking of buying their first motorcycle another problem arises: where to begin. For a beginner, a small motorcycle is advisable. However, if one feels capable of controlling it, a 250 may prove the answer. Many people would like to own a 500, because they can ride their 125. They should perhaps be more cautious. They should try the 125 first, then progress in stages, rather than frighten themselves on a big machine. It is possible to start on a 500, but it is difficult to ride and the beginner will not exploit its potential to the full.

At the moment the 125s occupy a considerable portion of the bike market. The 125 is a true motorcycle but still retains all the advantages of the motorised bicycle. For example, a 125 has equal, if not better acceleration than most saloon cars, and is therefore ideal for use in town. A 125 is, therefore, far less dangerous than a motorised bicycle. For a beginner, it is an excellent machine to learn on, and one on which he feels immediately confident as it is just as easy to handle as a bicycle.

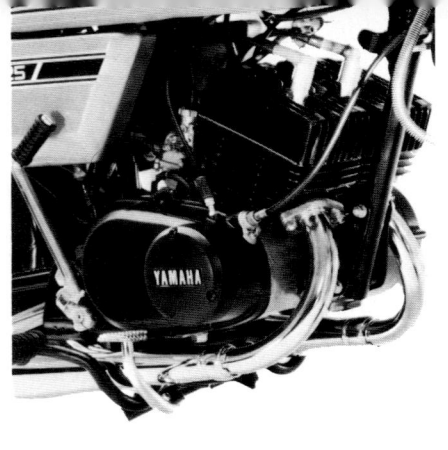

125 HONDA JX

125 YAMAHA RDX

125 SUZUKI GT

This is the smallest of the 125s. It is perfect both in size and equipment, and in addition is very attractive. The motor of this 125 revs very high (over 10,000 rev/min) without risk of breaking. Moreover, a Honda motor revs quickly for its power. Both the braking system (disc brakes) and the comfort are excellent. The JX has a more supple engine than the old Mk5 and is the most sporty of the 125 Hondas. Touring models are also produced: the CB125S3 is a very robust, cheap single-cylinder machine.

As it is a little smaller than the Honda, it weaves between the traffic even better. Its small two-stroke twin-cylinder motor is incredible, and very sensitive. Take care not to take-off with a wheelie. . . . It is a machine that one would like to ride flat out. More praise for the comfort and brakes. Like the Honda, the finish is impeccable. It is well equipped, and has a rev counter. Not a drop of oil on the gearcase, and breathtakingly beautiful. Disc brake. The Yamaha 125RS is the equivalent of the Honda CB125S3.

This new Suzuki has replaced the T125 to good effect and is in direct competition to the Honda JX and the Yamaha RD. Aesthetically, it is a better machine than its rivals and is fully equipped throughout. The old T125 was not renowned for either its comfort or its braking. With the GT125, everything has changed: it is very comfortable for a 125 and, thanks to its hydraulic disc brakes, has a very effective braking system. The engine, which is fitted with the Ramair cooling system, is as powerful as the Yamaha unit, but slightly less supple. It has excellent roadholding ability. There is an inexpensive touring version of the Suzuki: the B100P.

Technical notes

Engine: Four-stroke twin.
Petrol supply: Two carburettors.
Power: 15 hp at 11,000 rev/min.
Gearbox: Five-speed.
Weight: 267 lb (121 kg).
Speed: 78 mile/h (125 km/h).

Engine: Two-stroke twin.
Petrol supply: Two carburettors.
Power: 17 hp at 9,500 rev/min.
Gearbox: Five-speed.
Weight: 324 lb (106 kg).
Speed: 75–80 mile/h (120–130 km/h).

Engine: Two-stroke twin.
Petrol supply: Two carburettors.
Power: 15·5 hp at 8,000 rev/min.
Gearbox: Five-speed.
Weight: 238 lb (108 kg).
Speed: 80 mile/h (128 km/h).

125 KAWASAKI G7T

125 MORINI

125 CZ

The last of the Japanese machines is a 125 with many useful characteristics. This little two-stroke single has a carburettor and rotary valve, and is said to be unbreakable. The 125 Kawasaki is no bigger than a 50 cc and no heavier, which accounts for its excellent performance. An irreproachable finish, and usefully equipped.

A very pretty Italian four-stroke machine, intended particularly for the young sporting market. The Veloce is fast, holds the road perfectly, brakes well, and is reasonably comfortable. The touring version loses the name Veloce, but gains a certain number of accessories, which make it more civilised.

In Czechoslovakia, CZ and Jawa are two separate factories, but for export purposes, they present a common image: CZ builds the small machines and Jawa the large ones. Obviously, this machine has been built for export. The design is not revolutionary, but tailored to the taste of the day, and one has a good, useful little machine with what is rare on a non-Japanese model —separate oil supply for the two-stroke mixture.

All the speeds given are those announced by the maker or importer. Between these two sources of information there is sometimes a surprising difference. When two speeds are given, for example 85/90, this means that, depending on the final gearing, the machine is capable of either 85 or 90.

Engine: Two-stroke single.
Petrol supply: One carburettor.
Power: 11·5 hp at 8,000 rev/min.
Gearbox: Five-speed.
Weight: 174 lb (79 kg).
Speed: 75 mile/h (120 km/h).

Engine: Four-stroke single.
Petrol supply: One carburettor.
Power: 13·5 hp at 9,000 rev/min.
Gearbox: Six-speed.
Weight: 236 lb (107 kg).
Speed: 80 mile/h (130 km/h).

Engine: Two-stroke single.
Petrol supply: One carburettor.
Power: 11 hp at 5,250 rev/min.
Gearbox: Four-speed.
Weight: 265 lb (120 kg).
Speed: 68 mile/h (110 km/h).

125 M.Z. TS

125 MOTOBÉCANE LT1

This is a utilitarian bike. It is not very attractive, rather heavy and is designed to be ridden for long periods, in all weathers, without problems. The M.Z., coming from East Germany, which is renowned for its bad roads, has a particularly comfortable suspension, and super-efficient brakes. Another point—it is very cheap.

The biggest French, or even European, constructor has taken a while to realise that the machines today have changed. Now the LT1 proves it. Seeing that the majority of the 125 clientele prefer Japanese machines Motobécane has given its 125 a Japanese flavour, both aesthetically and technically. It is the only European 125 to have a twin-cylinder motor, fed by twin carburettors. The power obtained is as good as Suzuki, Yamaha and Honda outputs. As regards equipment, the LT1 is almost as good as its Far East competitors. The LT2 is even equipped with a separate lubrication system and the LT3 also has a disc brake.

To finish the 125 section, one or two 50 cc machines, which deserve inclusion in the mini-section, by virtue of their performance should be discussed. There are three special German mopeds. They are all two-stroke singles, but with five gears, developing 5 hp. Zundapp, Kreidler and Hercule are the machines, and on them it is possible to travel at a steady 50 mile/h in complete safety. It is not unusual to see a Kreidler that has done over 60,000 miles. For its part, a Hercule has covered a distance equal to the circumference of the globe, and probably at over 50 mile/h.

Technical notes

Engine: Two-stroke single.
Petrol supply: One carburettor.
Power: 11hp at 6,000 rev/min.
Gearbox: Four-speed.
Weight: 240 lb (109 kg).
Speed: 65 mile/h (105 km/h).

Engine: Two-stroke twin.
Petrol supply: Two carburettors.
Power: 15 hp at 7,500 rev/min.
Gearbox: Five-speed.
Weight: 203 lb (92 kg).
Speed: 74 mile/h (120 km/h).

the 250s

By comparison with the 125s, the 250s are more comfortable. They are honestly and squarely motorcycles, with everything that that signifies, including aggressiveness. The performances of most of the 250s are such that they stand good comparison with bigger machines, and from this the 250 rider can discover the pleasure and advantages that a big machine gives.

Moreover, the power of a 250 allows a passenger to be carried, although, of course, the machine will go better without. It will go well on the open road, and in town will behave like a 125, in other words, it will be just as good in the traffic jams.

250 HONDA CB250G

An undeniably attractive motorcycle, with elaborate mechanics. The motor is a single overhead-cam twin, that revs happily to 10,000. Comfort is one of its strong points, as well as the flexibility of the motor, which makes it very pleasant to ride in town. By contrast with its two-stroke rivals, it is perhaps slightly slow in acceleration. In addition, it is one of the heaviest of the 250s and is fitted with an electric starter and a disc brake in the front.

250 YAMAHA RD

Like its little 125 sister, the 250 Yamaha is a nervous machine. Its acceleration is vivid, and the motor peaks quickly. The comfort and road-holding are both excellent and it is the most sporting of the touring 250s. Add to this a fantastic, harmonious noise—don't forget that Yamaha is the foremost builder of pianos in the world. Disc brake.

Technical notes

Engine: Four-stroke twin.
Petrol supply: Two carburettors.
Power: 27 hp at 9,500 rev/min.
Gearbox: Six-speed.
Weight: 364 lb (165 kg).
Speed: Approx. 95 mile/h (150 km/h).

Engine: Two-stroke twin.
Petrol supply: Two carburettors.
Power: 30 hp at 7,500 rev/min.
Gearbox: Six-speed.
Weight: 304 lb (138 kg).
Speed: 93–99 mile/h (150–160 km/h).

250 SUZUKI GT250

250 KAWASAKI S1

250 M.Z.

At the moment the most powerful of the 250s, the one with the most gears, and the one which, logically, should be the fastest. It is a totally satisfactory machine, and very attractive. The roadholding and brakes are excellent, but the comfort leaves a little to be desired. The equipment and finish are perfect, like all the other contemporary Japanese machines. Disc brakes.

This is the first 250 with three cylinders. Having three cylinders—technically more elaborate—gives some advantages: originality, smoothness and pulling power. Otherwise, this 250 is based on the 350 Kawasaki three (the same low-slung motor), which gives it strength. It has excellent roadholding, but it is perhaps a little heavy for a 250, and the brakes are marginal. However, it looks very good.

This is the big sister of the 125, and has been tested over the years, and now fulfils its role as a useful, utilitarian machine. It is not very fast, not too pretty and does not accelerate all that quickly, but it never fails, and is very comfortable. It is also the least expensive of the 250s.

Engine: Two-stroke twin.
Petrol supply: Two carburettors.
Power: 33 hp at 7,500 rev/min.
Gearbox: Six-speed.
Weight: 337 lb (153 kg).
Speed: 90–100 mile/h (140–160 km/h).

Engine: Two-stroke three.
Petrol supply: Three carburettors.
Power: 32 hp at 8,000 rev/min.
Gearbox: Five-speed.
Weight: 326 lb (148 kg).
Speed: 105 mile/h (168 km/h).

Engine: Two-stroke single.
Petrol supply: One carburettor.
Power: 21 hp at 5,300 rev/min.
Gearbox: Four-speed.
Weight: 344 lb (156 kg).
Speed: 75 mile/h (120 km/h).

the 350s

For some time the 350s have been considered somehow as bastard motorcycles and most riders have tended to graduate from 250s to 500s. It must be admitted, too, that the 350s (for five or six years) have had a job to keep up with the completely new Japanese 250 machines. Motorcycles have developed quickly, and many modern riders are people who ride little on the open road, but a lot in town. Even so, they may well want a machine capable of good performance for an outing at the weekend. In fact, the ideal would be the power of a 500, in the frame of a 250, to maintain manoeuvrability in town. In some ways, this ideal motorcycle is the 350, revised and corrected by the Japanese, who have understood the problem, the other manufacturers following suit. All the 350s shown here are no larger than 250s.

350 SUZUKI T350

The T350 is the smallest of the Japanese 350s. The styling is remarkable. To ride it is a real pleasure: it is easy to handle, has good brakes, holds the road, and the six-speed gearbox is a joy. The performance is fantastic, the acceleration is powerful and the top speed high. Against this, it is not very comfortable, and very noisy.

Technical notes

Engine: Two-stroke twin.
Petrol supply: Two carburettors.
Power: 39 hp at 7,500 rev/min.
Gearbox: Six-speed.
Weight: 341 lb (155 kg).
Speed: 95 mile/h (152 km/h).

380 SUZUKI GT380

360 HONDA G

400 HONDA FOUR

The 350 Suzuki is now to be backed up by the 380 three. Even more sophisticated technically, but also larger and heavier, which means that the performance is the same as the twin, but with more comfort and flexibility. Disc brakes.

This machine is the 250 with a motor bored out to 350 cc. The flexibility of the motor is amazing. It has a good braking system (disc brakes). The silence and comfort of the machine are perfect. A good all-purpose machine for everyday or sporting use, although its roadholding could be improved. It has an electric starter.

Completely new, and far more attractive is the 400 Honda Four. This little four-cylinder machine is marvellously flexible, comfortable and silent, and incredibly beautiful. This machine is much more expensive than the twin, and is aimed at a clientele of enthusiasts who like sophisticated bikes which are not too clumsy.

Engine: Two-stroke three.
Petrol supply: Three carburettors.
Power: 38 hp at 7,500 rev/min.
Gearbox: Six-speed.
Weight: 377 lb (171 kg).
Speed: 105 mile/h (169 km/h).

Engine: Four-stroke twin.
Petrol supply: Two carburettors.
Power: 31 hp at 9,500 rev/min.
Gearbox: Six-speed.
Weight: 364 lb (165 kg).
Speed: Approx. 100 mile/h (160 km/h).

Engine: Four-stroke four.
Petrol supply: Four carburettors.
Power: 34 hp at 9,000 rev/min.
Gearbox: Six-speed.
Weight: 373 lb (169 kg).
Speed: Approx. 100 mile/h (160 km/h).

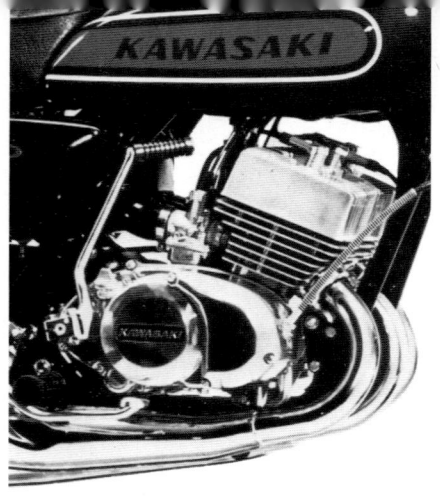

400 YAMAHA RD

400 KAWASAKI S3

350 DUCATI

Beautiful as a lotus-flower, sensitive as a bee, swift as a racehorse, and supple and comfortable as a carpet of pine needles, this 400 Yamaha is a poem. It is not excessively aggressive, but one only has to go a few yards on it to realise its temperament. Many motorcyclists consider it to be the best of the 400s. Its famous competition model, the TZ, confirms this reputation. Disc brake, front and back. It is also the first motorcycle to be fitted with alloy wheels.

This, the most powerful of the 400s, is powered by a three-cylinder engine and its performance is equivalent to a good 500. The power curve of the motor is such that it allows two styles of riding: the touring rider can have a fairly flexible motor when revving between 2,000 and 6,000 rev/min; the sporting rider will appreciate the kick in the back over 6,000 rev/min. It has excellent roadholding and is originally styled. Disc brakes.

The Ducati twin is much less sporty than the single of the same make. That is, the new Ducati 350 (and 500) resembles the Honda 360 (and 500). Except for the electric starter Japanese machines have nothing to envy. Front disc brake.

Technical notes

Engine: Two-stroke twin.
Petrol supply: Two carburettors.
Power: 43 hp at 8,000 rev/min.
Gearbox: Six-speed.
Weight: 311 lb (141 kg).
Speed: 100–105 mile/h
  (160–170 km/h).

Engine: Two-stroke three.
Petrol supply: Three carburettors.
Power: 42 hp at 7,000 rev/min.
Gearbox: Five-speed.
Weight: 351 lb (159·5 kg).
Speed: 112 mile/h (180 km/h).

Engine: Four-stroke twin.
Petrol supply: Two carburettors.
Power: hp (figure unavailable).
Gearbox: Five-speed.
Weight: 366 lb (166 kg).
Speed: 90 mile/h (145 km/h).

350 JAWA CALIFORNIAN 4

350 MOTOBÉCANE

400 KAWASAKI KZ

Everything turns up in time, and Jawa, like CZ, has modernised its machines. Its styling has lost its old-fashioned roundness, and the motor has gained some horsepower, as well as a separate oiling system. The comfort remains the same, that is to say, excellent, something necessary on an essentially practical machine.

The French designer wanted to compete with the Japanese on a market which has developed a great deal in the last ten years. The 350 Motobécane presents some really modern improvements such as the three-cylinder engine, the disc brakes, quartz halogen headlights. . . . On the other hand the 350 loses some points as it is not so well finished; this would not be so important if the sales price was lower than that of the Japanese machines. On the whole, however, it is an encouraging result.

This machine is a direct competitor to the 360 Honda. It has a moderate capacity, but is adequate for the type of use intended for it. In order to reduce the natural vibrations in the vertical twin, a counterbalance system is fitted to the lower motor. It has an electric starter and a front-wheel disc brake.

Engine: Two-stroke twin.
Petrol supply: One carburettor.
Power: 28 hp at 5,750 rev/min.
Gearbox: Four-speed.
Weight: 346 lb (157 kg).
Speed: 78 mile/h (125 km/h).

Engine: Two-stroke three.
Petrol supply: Three carburettors.
Power: 38 hp at 8,500 rev/min.
Gearbox: Five-speed.
Weight: 375 lb (170 kg).
Speed: 96 mile/h (155 km/h).

Engine: Four-stroke twin.
Petrol supply: Two carburettors.
Power: 35 hp at 8,500 rev/min.
Gearbox: Five-speed.
Weight: 375 lb (170 kg).
Speed: 90 mile/h (145 km/h).

the 500s

A 500 is not a toy, it is a big motorcycle with a surplus of power. If a 350 can stay with the biggest sports cars in acceleration, a 500 leaves them standing still. These are machines for riding fast, whether on one's own, or in company. When in town they are relatively heavy to handle, especially when wheeling them through the traffic. On the other hand, the motorists have respect for big motorcycles, perhaps they think that the bigger the machine, the stronger the man!

500 KAWASAKI MACH 3H1D

The most powerful 500 cc touring machine ever made, this three-cylinder two-stroke is capable of performance that equals the best 750s. It is also very good-looking as it is long, slim and distinguished, and it is the opinion of everyone, including its rivals, that the Kawasaki is the queen of the 500s. To be honest, the motor does not have enormous flexibility, but this does not worry the sporting rider, who is the normal client of the 500 Kawasaki. It has disc brakes.

Technical notes

Engine: Two-stroke three.
Petrol supply: Three carburettors.
Power: 60 hp at 7,500 rev/min.
Gearbox: Five-speed.
Weight: 384 lb (174 kg).
Speed: 125 mile/h (200 km/h).

500 HONDA T500

500 SUZUKI T500

SUZUKI RE5

This model has very modern mechanics. It is the only touring machine with double overhead-cams. These permit the motor to rev high. With a 500 one can travel at 8,000 rev/min for thousands of miles—it is a motorway machine. It has an electric starter. Disc brake.

A wicked little two-stroke twin that does not need to envy bigger machines. Up to 5,000 rev/min the big Suzuki is calm and gentle. Above this, the T500 is transformed into a formidable and sporting machine. Good styling, excellent roadholding, very comfortable, it has carved for itself a reputation of strength, while remaining one of the most economical of the 500s. Disc brake.

This is the first mass-produced rotary engined motorcycle. Technically it is a work of art, but practically it is a little disappointing. The rotary action functions badly at low revs and petrol consumption is high. It has two disc brakes and an electric starter.

Engine: Four-stroke twin.
Petrol supply: Two carburettors.
Power: 45 hp at 9,000 rev/min.
Gearbox: Five-speed.
Weight: 388 lb (176 kg).
Speed: Approx. 105 mile/h (170 km/h).

Engine: Two-stroke twin.
Petrol supply: Two carburettors.
Power: 45 hp at 7,000 rev/min.
Gearbox: Five-speed.
Weight: 403 lb (183 kg).
Speed: 110 mile/h (175 km/h).

Engine: Single rotary.
Petrol supply: One carburettor.
Power: 62 hp at 6,500 rev/min.
Gearbox: Five-speed.
Weight: 507 lb (230 kg).
Speed: 112 mile/h (180 km/h).

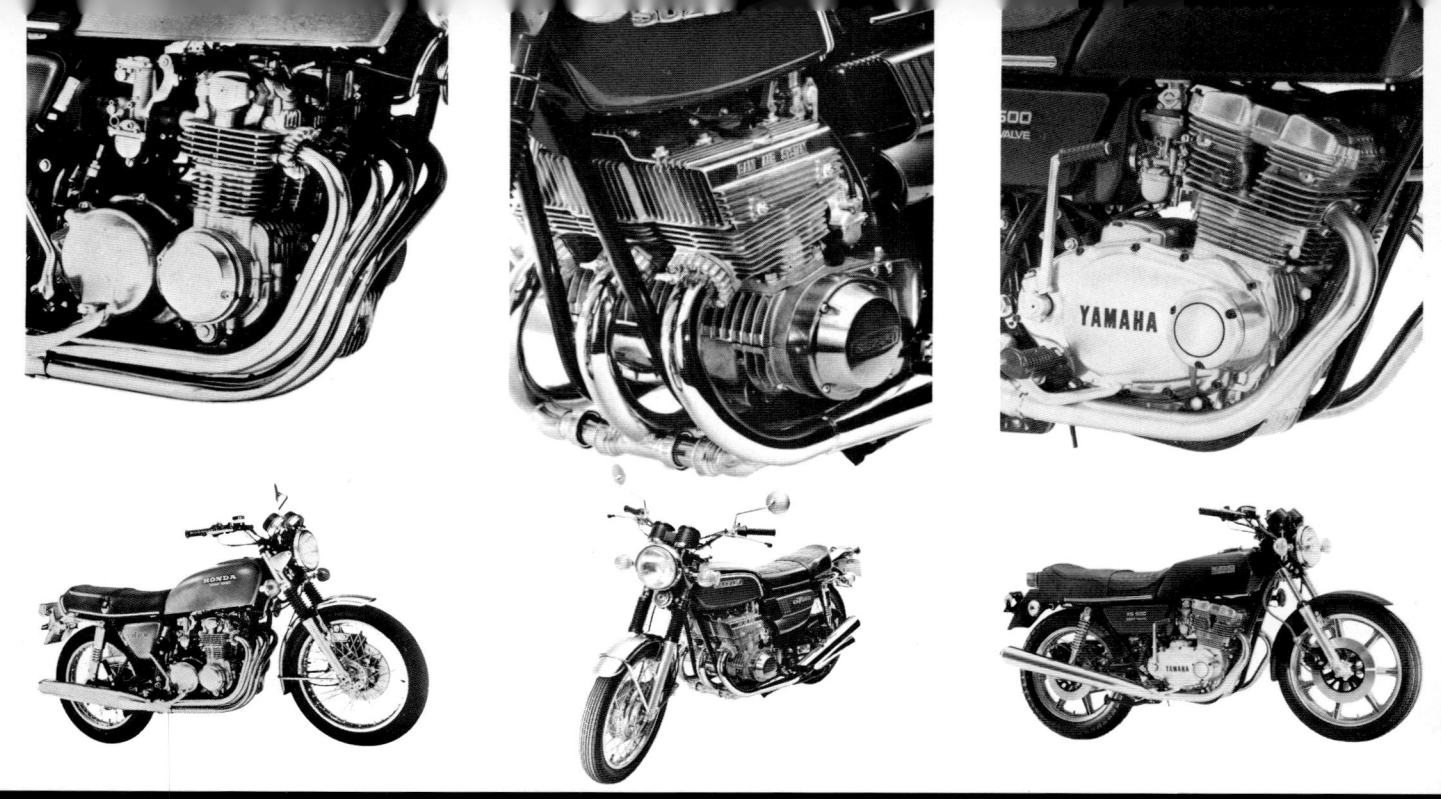

550 HONDA

550 SUZUKI GT550

500 YAMAHA XS

It is very difficult to talk about what is the ideal motorcycle as everyone has their own idea. Anyway, the 550 Honda Four has the maximum of good qualities. It is beautiful, not too big, very flexible, quite powerful, super-strong, distinguished, and behaves itself equally well on the open road or in town. It is of course equipped with an electric starter and disc brakes.

To back up the T500, which had begun to date, Suzuki produced the GT550 three, which from this moment one must consider to be the principal rival of the Honda 550 Four. It is an elaborate machine, pleasant to use, and with astonishing flexibility and acceleration. Electric starter. Disc brake.

This is the most sophisticated twin on the market. The cylinder-head contains twin overhead camshafts and eight valves (four per cylinder). To eliminate the inherent vibrations of a twin there is a counterbalance system. The result is a machine with performance, yet tractability. Disc brake, front and back. Alloy wheels. Electric starter.

Technical notes

Engine: Four-stroke four.
Petrol supply: Four carburettors.
Power: 50 hp at 8,500 rev/min.
Gearbox: Five-speed.
Weight: 423 lb (192 kg).
Speed: Approx. 112 mile/h (180 km/h).

Engine: Two-stroke three.
Petrol supply: Three carburettors.
Power: 50 hp at 6,500 rev/min.
Gearbox: Five-speed.
Weight: 412 lb (187 kg).
Speed: 112 mile/h (180 km/h).

Engine: Four-stroke twin.
Petrol supply: Two carburettors.
Power: 50 hp at 9,000 rev/min.
Gearbox: Five-speed.
Weight: 441 lb (200 kg).
Speed: 112 mile/h (180 km/h).

the 750s and over

These are the really big machines churning out horsepower and capable of incredible speeds. They are the kings of the road, capable of averages that would make a sports car driver pale. In fact, for most riders, the 500s represent the ultimate, the top of the ladder, the pinnacle of the machines. The only reasonable use for these machines is on the open road, on the highway, and not in town. It is certainly possible to occasionally ride through the jams on one, but to use it constantly for this purpose is really a sacrilege. Those who really love motorcycles will understand this.

750 SUZUKI GT750

A two-stroke three, we know—the Kawasaki, for instance—but a three-cylinder two-stroke that is water-cooled, has not been seen since the famous Scotts. With this new beautiful monster Suzuki takes on in a direct fight the queen, the Honda Four (to support this image the three exhaust pipes are fed into four silencers, just like the Honda). The 750 Suzuki uses methods taken from automobile technology, for example the radiator, which is automatically regulated to control the temperature of the water, and other gadgets are to be found on this superb racing beast. It has an electric starter. Double disc brakes.

Technical notes

Engine: Two-stroke three.
Petrol supply: Three carburettors.
Power: 67 hp at 6,500 rev/min.
Gearbox: Five-speed.
Weight: 507 lb (230 kg).
Speed: 116 mile/h (186 km/h).

750 HONDA

The most beautiful, the most powerful, the best balanced from all points of view. . . . In a word, the machine of the century until something better comes along. Comfort, acceleration, braking, roadholding, top speed—all are superior, and make one forget its small faults, for it has some all the same. For many, the CB750 is the realisation of a beautiful dream. Electric starter, disc brake, front and back.

750 DUCATI

This is a 750 sports machine, low-slung, elegant, narrow – ready to leap forward. The engine layout is a 120 degree V-twin. While the engine is entirely new, the cylinders and heads (single overhead cam) resemble the 250 and 350 singles. Less sophisticated than the Japanese models it is rather like its Italian contemporaries, the Laverda and MV 750s. Disc brake.

900 KAWASAKI

When the 750 Honda appeared on the market it had a fantastic reception. The 900 Kawasaki is like a 750 Honda, but better. She is not heavier or larger, but rather less high. Roadholding qualities and brakes are at least as good. The double overhead cam engine is powerful, supple, flexible and can propel the machine at 127 mile/h (205 km/h). Disc brakes.

Technical notes

Engine: Four-stroke four.
Mixture supply: Four carburettors.
Power: 67 hp at 8,000 rev/min.
Gearbox: Five-speed.
Weight: 463 lb (210 kg).
Speed: Approx. 115 mile/h (185 km/h).

Engine: Four-stroke twin.
Petrol supply: Two carburettors.
Power: 67 hp at 8,000 rev/min.
Gearbox: Five-speed.
Weight: 397 lb (180 kg).
Speed: 124 mile/h (200 km/h).

Engine: Four-stroke four.
Petrol supply: Four carburettors.
Power: 82 hp at 8,500 rev/min.
Gearbox: Five-speed.
Weight: 507 lb (230 kg).
Speed: 127 mile/h (205 km/h).

750 B.M.W. R75/6	**750 KAWASAKI KZ**	**900 B.M.W. 90/S**

As long as the competitors fight with each other for more horsepower and higher top speeds, B.M.W., contenting itself with making grand touring machines, can remain king of this field. The R75/6 has the same qualities as the R50/6, with, of course, a higher performance. For example, it is possible to cruise all day at 100 mile/h. There is also a more economical model, the 600 R60/6. Electric starter. Disc brake.

This belongs to a new breed of motorcycles. Classic in conception (twin cylinder, twin overhead camshafts) but very pleasant to ride. Its chief attributes are high torque and flexibility at low revs. An antivibration system improves the ride, and disc brakes, front and back, aid safety.

This is a superb B.M.W. model which greatly enhances the name of the marque. Technically it is identical to the 750, but the increase in capacity improves the pleasure of riding it. The 900 B.M.W. 90/S belongs to the 125 mile/h (200 km/h) range of motorcycles. Even so it is very comfortable and easy to ride. It holds the road well and has excellent stopping ability due to its double disc brakes. It is also the only motorcycle to fit a clock in the fascia and a streamlined handlebar fairing, which is most useful at high speed. The 90/S is backed by the 90/6 which is less powerful, but has similar performance and is much cheaper.

Engine: Four-stroke twin.
Petrol supply: Two carburettors.
Power: 50 hp at 6,200 rev/min.
Gearbox: Four-speed.
Weight: 463 lb (210 kg).
Speed: 110 mile/h (175 km/h).

Engine: Four-stroke four twin.
Petrol supply: Two carburettors.
Power: 85 hp at 7,000 rev/min.
Gearbox: Five-speed.
Weight: 481 lb (218 kg).
Speed: 106 mile/h (170 km/h).

Engine: Four-stroke twin.
Petrol supply: Two carburettors.
Power: 67 hp at 7,000 rev/min.
Gearbox: Five-speed.
Weight: 419 lb (190 kg).
Speed: 125 mile/h (201 km/h).

850 NORTON COMMANDO INTERSTATE

850 GUZZI T3

750 LAVERDA 750SF

A prestigious make, and no less so a machine. Completely classical in its design, the Commando's motor does not lack any power, and the machine has an extremely good power-to-weight ratio. It is a machine designed for the sporting rider, and requires extremely careful upkeep. Aesthetically remarkable. Disc brake and electric starter.

The great rivals of B.M.W., and intended for the same type of clientele. Technically, with its big car-style motor and shaft drive, it compares with the B.M.W. Aesthetically, it is better balanced than the B.M.W., but is larger. Electric starter. Disc brakes, front and back. The photo shows a 1,000 Guzzi with automatic transmission.

This latest model from the dynamic Italian factory is a sports machine with a single overhead cam. Low, comfortable, sensitive, quick, but very noisy. The racing-style saddle is not really suited for two. Those who want to ride two-up can choose the normal 750 which has a comfortable double saddle. Electric starter. Double disc brake. The 1,000 cc three-cylinder model deserves to be better known.

Technical notes

Engine: Four-stroke twin.
Petrol supply: Two carburettors.
Power: 60 hp at 5,900 rev/min.
Gearbox: Four-speed.
Weight: 419 lb (190 kg).
Speed: 112 mile/h (180 km/h).

Engine: Four-stroke twin.
Petrol supply: Two carburettors.
Power: 68·5 hp at 6,500 rev/min.
Gearbox: Five-speed.
Weight: 507 lb (230 kg).
Speed: 120 mile/h (193 km/h).

Engine: Four-stroke twin.
Petrol supply: Two carburettors.
Power: 66 hp at 7,300 rev/min.
Gearbox: Five-speed.
Weight: 481 lb (218 kg).
Speed: 115 mile/h (185 km/h).

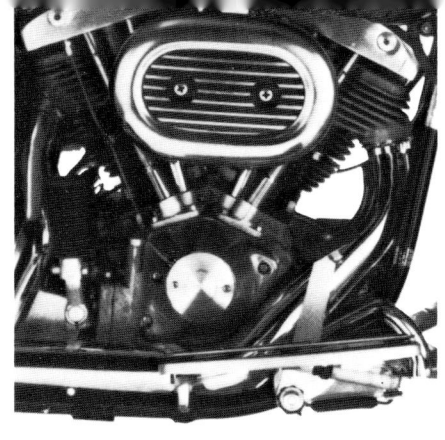

750 BENELLI

1200 HARLEY-DAVIDSON FLH

750 GUZZI SPORT

This is a phenomenon of its type. A motor with six cylinders in line. The exhaust note is certainly pleasant, and despite an engine which is wider than the fuel tank it remains manageable. As with a car the six cylinders give a bonus to the pleasure of riding.

Everyone has heard of the Harley, and many think that it is the fastest, the most sensitive, the most. . . . In fact it is a very big, utilitarian machine afflicted by too great a size, and one capable of carrying a number of incredible accessories, each one chromed more than the one before. Apart from this though, it is certainly comfortable, but only with one up, and not above 90 mile/h. Above this the 1,200 cc V-twin vibrates. The machine is unbreakable. The 900 Sportster is closer to being a real motorcycle, and is capable of better performance. Electric starter. Double disc front disc brake.

It is only recently that the 750 Guzzi Sport with five gears has been in production. It is specially made to travel down the motorways at speed. The 750 V7S is small, manageable and holds the road extremely well. All Guzzi V7s have shaft drive. Electric starter. Disc brake, front and rear. The rear brake pedal applies both the front and rear discs simultaneously.

Engine: Four-stroke six.
Petrol supply: Three carburettors.
Power: 76 hp at 9,000 rev/min.
Gears: Five-speed.
Weight: 485 lb (220 kg).
Speed: 124 mile/h (200 km/h).

Engine: Four-stroke twin.
Petrol supply: One carburettor.
Power: 66 hp at 5,200 rev/min.
Gearbox: Four-speed.
Weight: 772 lb (350 kg).
Speed: 105 mile/h (170 km/h).

Engine: Four-stroke twin.
Petrol supply: Two carburettors.
Power: 70 hp at 7,000 rev/min.
Gearbox: Five-speed.
Weight: 454 lb (206 kg).
Speed: 128 mile/h (206 km/h).

1000 HONDA

650 YAMAHA

750 KAWASAKI

This is the motorcycle of 1975: four water-cooled horizontally opposed cylinders and shaft drive. This new Honda directly competes with the B.M.W.s. It is very quiet and very much a touring machine, which borrows greatly from car engineering. Despite its weight, the 1000 Honda handles well: the centre of gravity has been lowered by placing the petrol tank under the seat. A contra-rotating device turns in the opposite direction to the crankshaft, so eliminating the couple effect common to flat engines. It is the first machine of the Honda range to be fitted with three disc brakes (two at the front and one at the rear). Electric starter.

Until Yamaha market their 750 three-cylinder four-stroke motor, they have fallen back on a completely new 650 four-stroke twin. It is a very fine machine, superbly equipped (electric starter), with excellent roadholding. Double disc brakes. The main quality of this machine lies in its lively engine.

The Kawasaki is the most powerful 750 in the world. The three-cylinder two-stroke motor never pushes out less than 74 hp. The acceleration of this bike is like a dragster, and the top speed takes one's breath away. Not a machine to be put into the hands of the foolhardy. Good-looking, whether painted Bugatti blue or in gold.

Technical notes

Engine: Four-stroke four.
Petrol supply: Four carburettors.
Power: 80 hp at 7,500 rev/min.
Gearbox: Five-speed.
Weight: 573 lb (260 kg).
Speed: 130 mile/h (209 km/h).

Engine: Four-stroke twin.
Petrol supply: Two carburettors.
Power: 52 hp at 7,500 rev/min.
Gearbox: Five-speed.
Weight: 474 lb (215 kg).
Speed: 109 mile/h (175 km/h).

Engine: Two-stroke three.
Petrol supply: Three carburettors.
Power: 74 hp at 6,800 rev/min.
Gearbox: Five-speed.
Weight: 423 lb (192 kg).
Speed: 126 mile/h (203 km/h).

the mini-bikes

These are the toys of the motor-cycle world. These little, amusing machines are bought in summer for the pretty toys that they are. However, they are toys that are useful and are becoming extremely popular. It is not a class of motor-cycle much respected in the U.S.A. because there, the smaller and more amusing the bike, the more pathetic it seems and one even finds miniature tricycles. American children often own one from as young as five, and their parents actually organise races for them. In this case, at least, when they fall they do not have far to go.

VAN VAN SUZUKI 125

In fact this is not a mini-motorcycle, because it is the same size as a 125, although it is very low and distinguished by its enormous low-pressure inflated tyres. Pretty and amusing to look at, the Van Van Suzuki can travel over a variety of terrains, and is especially suited to sand. Further, thanks to its big, lightly inflated tyres, it is extremely comfortable. It is also produced in 50 cc and 90 cc versions.

Technical notes

Engine: Two-stroke single.
Petrol supply: One carburettor.
Power: 12 hp at 6,000 rev/min.
Gearbox: Five-speed.
Weight: 245 lb (111 kg).
Speed: 50 mile/h (80 km/h).

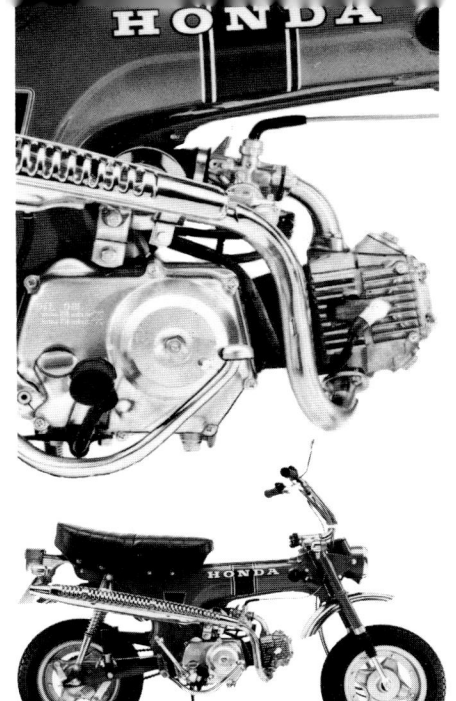

MINI ENDURO YAMAHA GT80

DAX HONDA

KAWASAKI 90MC1

This is a miniature copy of the Yamaha cross-country machine, the Enduro, complete with little telescopic forks, knobbly mini-tyres and styling similar to the Enduro. The motor, a four-speed 80 cc unit, does not lack power even when the rider weighs more than 143 lb (65 kg). The performance of the Yamaha is astonishing and one can wheelie at will.

This is the brilliant successor to the Honda Monkey Bike. The DAX has all its qualities and more as it has suspension and better roadholding, and can travel at over 35 mile/h (60 km/h). An automatic clutch assists the ease of riding. Ideal for meandering in the country lanes, or for slipping through the traffic jams.

In direct competition to the Yamaha GT80, this little Kawasaki has the advantage of more advanced technology. The engine is the same unit as used on the G7T touring model but detuned. A supple, powerful, solid 90 cc machine. Both in appearance and performance, it is a better motorcycle than the Yamaha.

Engine: Two-stroke single.
Petrol supply: One carburettor.
Power: 4·9 hp at 6,500 rev/min.
Gearbox: Four-speed.
Weight: 132 lb (60 kg).
Speed: 46 mile/h (75 km/h).

Engine: Four-stroke single.
Petrol supply: One carburettor.
Power: 5·6 hp at 8,000 rev/min.
Gearbox: Three-speed.
Weight: 143 lb (65 kg).
Speed: Approx. 43 mile/h (70 km/h).

Engine: Two-stroke single.
Petrol supply: One carburettor.
Power: 6·6 hp at 6,500 rev/min.
Gearbox: Five-speed.
Weight: 168 lb (76 kg).
Speed: 50 mile/h (80 km/h).

When talking of motorcycles, it is usually said, "Ideal in town, and intoxicating on the open road", but it is often forgotten that there is another way to ride a motorcycle. Many people, particularly in Europe, have not heard of the cross-country machine. This machine no longer restricts its rider to the title "the King of the Road", but the vast natural empire of the country-side is offered, far from the dangers of the traffic and fumes. The limits of the road no longer apply, as the cross-country motorcycle offers the same scope as a horse, without the hard work involved in maintaining that animal. And the noise? It is slight, and not disagreeable. In any case, it does not hinder a healthy outing, because indeed it produces something healthy. Starting as a game it finally becomes an exercise of skill, balance and, in fact, of sport. But what an absorbing sport—physically exhausting, and without real danger because it is impossible to go too fast on a cross-country motorcycle, and if one does fall off the consequences are never severe. It therefore offers a marvellous form of leisure. Mr. Bulto, the patron of Bultaco, has a whole squadron of Bultaco cross-country machines at his country house, so that his guests can travel around the surrounding countryside. Sometimes this motor-cycle can render splendid service. . . . In forestry areas or at shoots, for example.

These machines are especially designed and made for riding off the road and are therefore

cross country

the 125s

different from road machines. The suspension is very supple, capable of absorbing the shocks from the rough ground. The wheels, the tyres of which are knobbly for grip, are of larger diameter than those on road machines. The very rigid frame gives good handling. The engine is in 99 per cent of cases a single-cylinder two-stroke which has the following advantages. The motor is light, strong, easy to repair and narrow. Moreover, the two-stroke single gives plenty of low-down torque and power, which is vital when riding in the rough. Cross-country motorcycles are equipped with large, wide handlebars; small, narrow fuel tanks and adjustable foot-rests. All this is designed to achieve the best riding position. The exhaust pipe is raised, and so does not touch the ground at corners. The equipment already quoted is not enough to turn an ordinary machine into a cross-country model. Certain manufacturers do not seem to have understood this, and persist in producing road machines dolled up to look like cross-country models with wide handlebars and raised exhausts. The machines illustrated here are real examples, designed to go through mud, the stones of a beach, and above all, capable of climbing slopes of 40° and over. Of course, it is quite possible to also use them on the road. It is possible to go very fast through the corners, in spite of the big knobbly tyres, and a cruising speed of 60–65 mile/h (100 km/h) is possible for the most part. In town, a cross-country motor-cycle is amazing—it accelerates very quickly, and is easy to handle. For town purposes a 350 cross-country motorcycle would about equal a 125 machine.

The 125 cross-country models are all very light-weight machines, yet powerful enough to go anywhere. Nothing limits their progress, and no difficult road can stop them. They are ideal small motorcycles for beginners and are even easily managed by children.

125XL HONDA

125 YAMAHA DTF

125 KAWASAKI KS

The Honda CB125S3 tourer has a motor that is quite powerful. This motor, fitted in an adequate frame proves valuable for cross-country riding. There are certainly some minor details which are poor, but for a beginner, the 125XL Honda is ideal, and above all, not expensive.

A beautiful machine and very well equipped with both a speedometer and a rev counter. This single-cylinder two-stroke has five gears, the use of which can result in an improved fuel consumption. Like all the Japanese two-stroke motors, it has separate oiling, which is both clean and avoids the necessity for pre-mixing the fuel mixture. Weighing less than 220 lb (100 kg) and with five gears and 13 hp, the 125 Yamaha is particularly good over difficult terrain. Being in gear does not prevent the machine being kick-started.

Technically it differs from the other motorcycles as its two-stroke engine has a rotary distributor. Thus flexibility is obtained which is especially valuable in cross-country riding. On the other hand the size of the engine is larger and therefore it runs a greater risk of knocking against rocks. Aesthetically, this new cross-country 125 is unanimously accepted and its six-speed gearbox is a great asset with an engine with such a small capacity.

Technical notes

Engine: Four-stroke single.
Petrol supply: One carburettor.
Power: 13 hp at 10,000 rev/min.
Gearbox: Five-speed.
Weight: 209 lb (95 kg).
Speed: Approx. 65–68 mile/h (105–110 km/h).

Engine: Two-stroke single.
Petrol supply: One carburettor.
Power: 13 hp at 7,500 rev/min.
Gearbox: Five-speed.
Weight: 207 lb (94 kg).
Speed: 65–68 mile/h (105–110 km/h).

Engine: Two-stroke single.
Petrol supply: One carburettor.
Power: 13 hp at 6,500 rev/min.
Gearbox: Six-speed.
Weight: 247 lb (112 kg).
Speed: 62–68 mile/h (100–110 km/h).

125 SUZUKI TS

Judging by its aesthetic appearance this 125 seems to have been designed primarily for the American market. It is like the motocross machine, having an enormous exhaust under the engine. For cross-country this would be un-desirable as it reduces the clearance between the machine and ground. A wheel placed 21 in (0·53 m) to the front classes the 125 Suzuki as a general-purpose machine, and there-fore excellent for joy-riding. Its sprightly engine makes it the best current 125 machine.

Engine: Two-stroke single.
Petrol supply: One carburettor.
Power: 13 hp at 7,000 rev/min.
Gearbox: Five-speed.
Weight: 198 lb (90 kg).
Speed: 62–68 mile/h (100–110 km/h).

the 250s

The kings of the cross-country machines. The machines are not too heavy, but powerful with horsepower at low revs. They climb the toughest hills without difficulty or assistance from the feet. They can go very fast when required and do not need any special training or experience.

250 YAMAHA DT

One of the first true Japanese cross-country machines, and one that attracts even the experts in cross-country riding. It is a really good-looking machine and very well equipped. It holds the road well, and is capable of being used for moto-cross, once the engine is fitted with a kit that produces 30 hp. It is reputed to be very sturdy.

250 SUZUKI

Suzuki was the first Japanese factory to become seriously interested in motocross. In 1970 the make took the 250 cc world championship, and retained it in 1971, 1972 and 1973. This experience in motocross has been used in the making of a more sophisticated model: the TS250. This machine has inherited a strong frame, and a powerful and reliable motor. At last, the equipment is worthy of a motorway roadster, with winkers, rev counter and speedometer, and double-leading shoe front brake.

Technical notes

Engine: Two-stroke single.
Petrol supply: One carburettor.
Power: 24 hp at 7,000 rev/min.
Gearbox: Five-speed.
Weight: 265 lb (120 kg).
Speed: 75–78 mile/h (120–125 km/h).

Engine: Two-stroke single.
Petrol supply: One carburettor.
Power: 21 hp at 6,500 rev/min.
Gearbox: Five-speed.
Weight: 260 lb (118 kg).
Speed: Approx. 78 mile/h (125 km/h).

250 BULTACO MATADOR

250 OSSA ENDURO

250 HONDA XL

This machine has achieved success in various six-day international events. It is a true trials machine with its slightly detuned motocross engine and benefits from numerous ingenious technical details. The rear wheel can be removed without touching the chain. It has excellent acceleration and very good brakes.

Currently very successfully used in the endurance competition events, from which it gets the name Enduro, it is also useful for travelling more gently. Powerful, sensitive and light, it is sufficiently flexible to be ridden without difficulty by a beginner. Like its sister the Bultaco, it does not have a separate oiling system, but its good points outweigh this minor deficiency.

With this machine, Honda have constructed their first true cross-country machine, remaining true, of course, to the four-stroke motor. The motor has a single cylinder with no less than four valves in the head. The flexibility of the XL250 is astonishing, as is its quietness of operation. Even though it is a little heavy, the XL goes well off the road and is a good-looking machine.

Engine: Two-stroke single.
Petrol supply: One carburettor.
Power: 31 hp at 8,000 rev/min.
Gearbox: Five-speed.
Weight: 243 lb (110 kg).
Speed: 75 mile/h (120 km/h).

Engine: Two-stroke single.
Petrol supply: One carburettor.
Power: 28 hp at 6,800 rev/min.
Gears: Five-speed.
Weight: 205 lb (93 kg).
Speed: 81 mile/h (130 km/h).

Engine: Four-stroke single.
Petrol supply: One carburettor.
Power: 22 hp at 8,000 rev/min.
Gearbox: Five-speed.
Weight: 280 lb (127 kg).
Speed: Approx. 81 mile/h (130 km/h).

the 350s

250 KAWASAKI F11

This machine is very similar to the other Japanese models. It is even better and made especially for joy-riding, on tracks and for town use. The majority of Japanese cross-country machines are used on asphalt rather than on the mud track. Nowadays this type looks just as smart as a good 750. Those who want to ride off the roads will be pleasantly surprised by the brakes and the roadholding.

These machines are not for the amateur, because they are far too powerful. It is necessary to possess the skills of a motocross racer to do justice to the machine.

The catalogue of cross-country machines is incomplete, as not a month passes without a new machine appearing. The celebrated East German factory, M.Z., markets a replica of its Six Days Trial machine, and Jawa and Zundapp do the same. These are only to mention the most important makes, to which Hodaka should be added, a Japanese firm, almost unknown in Europe, which produces only one model, a 100 cc, having done so since 1964.

Technical notes

Engine: Two-stroke single.
Petrol supply: One carburettor.
Power: 23·5 hp at 6,000 rev/min.
Gearbox: Five-speed.
Weight: 264 lb (120 kg).
Speed: Approx. 78 mile/h (125 km/h).

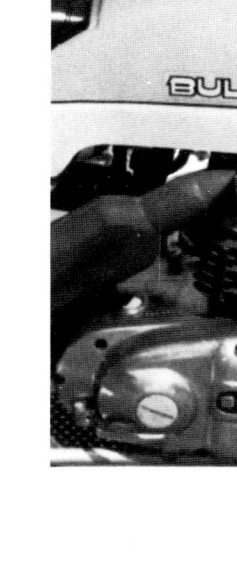

400 YAMAHA DT

Yamaha completes its range of cross-country machines with a 400 which is not much larger or heavier than a 250, but has plenty of horsepower. Its flexibility is fantastic and it produces great performances cross-country and has a top speed of over 80 mile/h (135 km/h). The machine is very pleasant to ride in town. This happy compromise between a road machine and a cross-country one makes this an ideal motorcycle. In the near future, the 400 DT will be replaced by the 500 TX, which has a non-pollutant single-cylinder four-stroke engine.

400 SUZUKI

This is again a development of the world championship 500 cc motocross winner. A lot of horsepower is contained in the matt-black motor of the 400 Suzuki and the frame is well suited to cope with its power. This machine is mainly designed for the American market, where cross-country riding is often considered to be a form of motocross.

350 BULTACO ALPINA

The 350 Bultaco Sherpa is light, supple, easy to handle, and above all, designed for competition. Bultaco have produced the 350 Alpina for the amateur, using a number of parts from the Sherpa, so the only differences are the positioning of the controls and the more comfortable seat. The engine is identical except for the gear ratios. It is a truly splendid machine for making pleasure trips over difficult terrain, in the mountains for instance.

Technical notes

Engine: Two-stroke single.
Petrol supply: One carburettor.
Power: 30 hp at 6,000 rev/min.
Gearbox: Five-speed.
Weight: 265 lb (120 kg).
Speed: Approx. 85 mile/h (135 km/h).

Engine: Two-stroke single.
Petrol supply: One carburettor.
Power: 34 hp at 6,000 rev/min.
Gearbox: Five-speed.
Weight: 297 lb (135 kg).
Speed: 85 mile/h (135 km/h).

Engine: Two-stroke single.
Petrol supply: One carburettor.
Power: 23 hp at 6,000 rev/min.
Gearbox: Five-speed.
Weight: 203 lb (92 kg).
Speed: 78 mile/h (125 km/h).

riding advice

Right from the beginning, it can be said with complete confidence that motorcycles are less dangerous than cars. Many may doubt this statement, saying that on a motorcycle the rider is only balanced on two wheels, and that in the event of a crash there is nothing to protect him. However, this argument also works the other way, because in a car accident the first obstacle is the car itself, the bodywork and the windscreen. On a motorcycle the rider is thrown off, and at the most risks breaking an arm or a leg by hitting some obstacle. However, the head is not so vulnerable as it is well protected by a helmet. The slimness, nimbleness and power of a motorcycle are its three principal safety factors. When overtaking, meeting a car head-on is never a problem, as there is enough room, and with a twist of the throttle the rider is past, in less time than it takes to explain. A wet road is no more a problem than a dry one. It is just necessary to go carefully, as in a car. In fact, one must point this out, that 80 per cent of accidents which involve both a car and a motorcycle are because of the incompetence of the car driver.

Real skill on a motorcycle is only learned at the end of many miles, and many years of riding. Spirited or sporting riding of a motorcycle is much more difficult to learn than its counterpart in a car. As a general rule a motorcycle rider cannot expect to ride well without at least two months' experience, preferably nearer two years. Young riders often seem completely at ease after only a few hundred miles' riding—too much at ease and far too sure of themselves. This confidence is frequently shattered by a crash, which is the only way to make them think. After that, they may ride intelligently, without fooling and only then will they really learn. The main rule for riding a motorcycle must never be forgotten and that is prudence.

In town. First of all, keep two fingers on the front brake lever, and a foot on the rear brake pedal. If it is necessary to brake suddenly, use the front brake. The rear is useful when braking, but care must be taken not to lock the rear wheel. When riding behind a car, keep a distance of at least five yards and keep either to the right or to the left, so that if the vehicle in front stops suddenly, avoiding action can easily be taken. If riding a very powerful machine, be careful of very violent acceleration because on this kind of machine one moment's absent-mindedness can be disastrous. One of the motorcycle's great advantages is its ability to thread its way between the cars. This requires a certain amount of attention, however. For example, when riding between two lanes of cars, it is important to watch the occupants, because they may not see a motorcyclist and could open a door negligently. It is the motorcyclist's job to look out. Moreover, beware of pedestrians, who cross between the cars without looking. In traffic jams always ride at least two yards from the parked cars at the pavement, because there are many car drivers who turn out of their parking place without looking, and they never see a motorcycle coming up. Lastly, in wet weather, do not ride on the white lines which are very slippery. If it is necessary to brake suddenly on one of these, the rider may well come off. Yellow lines are equally bad. Apart from this care, driving in town does not present any problems, and even if at the start the motorcyclist feels hemmed in by the car drivers, after a little while he will slip in and out of them like a fish going upstream.

On the open road. Here the real motorcyclists are at home, because it is here that real riding technique is needed. To begin with, the position of the rider should be studied. It must not be tiring. So, for those who want to ride really quickly, low bars must be fitted, like "clip-ons". With wide bars, above a certain speed—about 75 mile/h (120 km/h)—the wind force becomes a problem. The body should lean into the wind, the arms well stretched out, and the hands on the grips. However, the grip must not be too tight or this can cause snaking on hard acceleration on rough roads (if the rider pulls back too hard on the bars the front wheel may snake). The rider must not force the machine but he must be as one with his motorcycle. Do not ride too much to the right—not perhaps in accordance with the Highway Code—but it ensures better vision and helps avoid danger from the right. Beware of the drivers when overtaking, because it is quite certain that they will be unaware of the true speed of the motor-cyclist and will think that they have time in which to overtake, consequently pulling out just when the motorcyclist is overtaking them. Beware also of motorists coming in the other direction as they, too, have no idea of the true speed, and will overtake without thinking. How-ever, luckily, there is always enough room for a motorcycle. Anyone can ride fast in a straight line, but the corners really test a rider's skill. Be-fore going into a corner, judge it, just as one would in a car. First of all, the changing down and braking have to be synchronised. Then again, the front brake has to be used more than the back. When the speed is judged to be correct, slacken off the brakes and put on the power. This takes place quite naturally. Then a little pressure with the hand and the machine is leaned over. With very light bikes, it is enough just to lean the body. If the bend is tighter than expected do not be afraid to lean into the corner more to bring the machine round, and above all, do not be afraid and do not panic. If the corner has been taken too quickly it is still possible to brake, but only very gently, without abruptness, and more particu-larly, with the rear brake. As with a car, the corner is always taken with the power on.

the accessories

No one will disagree that motorcycles are very pleasant to ride when the weather is fine and warm. Unfortunately, however, ideal weather is not often found, and motorcyclists have to cope with sudden showers and the cold of winter. Does this mean that motorcyclists should leave their machines in the garage for half the year? Certainly not. There is adequate equipment available that permits one to ride in bad weather in reasonable comfort.

In town. There is no point in getting special equipment, unless it is very cold.

On the open road. The problem is different. Whether it is fine or wet, to go fast it is necessary to be carefully dressed, and only real motor-cycling clothing is sufficient. In fact, the classical clothing of supple material that withstands the wind, and repels water.

The boots. These are indispensable. There are motorcycle boots that are perfect, supple, easy to take off, thanks to a zip-fastener at the rear. They are made of fairly thin leather, and are not very waterproof.

The riding suit. If it is not too cold, and if it is not going to rain, the ideal suit is one made out of leather. Completely windproof, it provides maximum comfort and is light to wear. There are different kinds of suits. The racing suit is skin-tight, but not particularly hard-wearing. The road suit is thicker, lined at the knees and shoulders and allows the rider to wear a jersey underneath. A German manufacturer has produced a happy compromise between the one- and two-piece suits which consists of a pair of trousers, and a battledress top, which can be worn separately or zipped together round the waist. It is acceptable to wear no more than a pair of jeans and a leather jacket, but the latter must be up to certain standards. It must close at the neck, it must be tight at the wrists, and be sufficiently long at the back so that it does not ride up. All these leather clothes are waterproof for the length of a shower. However, if it continues. . . .

The barbour. Nothing is better in the rain than nylon or waxed cotton. The best-known suits are made in England—a lined jacket with an officer's collar, lined in velvet. The wrists have press studs, and the jacket is closed in front by a zip or by Velcro. In addition a band fixed by press studs, covers the zip. The other half of the suit, made of the same material, is big enough to go over ordinary trousers. The ankles of this over-suit are made tight by three little tabs and press studs.

These synthetic outfits have the advantage of being easy to wear and look after, but the disadvantage of being rather soft, and will billow in the wind at speed. For the man who rides every day, in all weathers, and who does not particularly care about fashion, the Trialmaster is ideal. The cut resembles the nylon equipment already described, but it is made from thick oilskin. The Trialmaster is not particularly nice to touch and has a rather distinctive smell, but it will not let a drop of water through. As it grows older, a Trialmaster develops a patina, and becomes shiny and green. A rider wearing one in this condition cannot be considered a beginner. A Trialmaster has no equal for trials or cross-country riding. Its strong texture repels thorns and scratches from branches with ease. While speaking of cross-country riding, the equipment designed especially for this must be mentioned— big waterproof leather boots and pairs of gloves reinforced on each finger by strips of rubber which protect the hand inside.

Gloves. The classical glove for the road should come high up the forearm, covering the wrist so that the wind cannot get up the sleeves. Some gloves have the first two fingers covered in chamois leather so that the goggles can be cleaned while riding. Apart from mittens made from the same material as the Trialmaster, which are not very practical, there are no completely water-proof gloves. However as a protection against the rain and cold it is possible to fit muffs to the grips of the bike. Not beautiful, but practical.

The helmet. There are two kinds of helmet, the "pudding-bowl" type, which is illegal in the U.K., and helmets with temple protection. Whichever is used, it should not be too big or too tight, and should fit comfortably. There is nothing worse than a loose helmet, bouncing about, unless it is one that is too tight.

The integral helmet is in fashion. It is full face, and gives more protection around the face in case of accident. However, if used with a visor it has some misting problems at slow speeds and in cold weather.

The goggles. As in the case of the helmet, it should be possible to forget their existence. They must not be too tight, but on the other hand, no wind should creep in, only enough air through the vents to stop the lenses from misting up. The vents are of a certain size so as to allow the air in, but not the dust. Visibility must be as great as possible.

The face mask. Again, a small piece of equipment which is very light and useful. It consists of a small piece of leather that protects the lower half of the face. When it rains, at above 60 mile/h (100 km/h) it is like being stung by needles, and the lips are especially sensitive to this. With a face mask, there is no problem because nothing can be felt, not even the cold. Thus equipped, it is possible to ride for hundreds of miles at high speed without being inconvenienced by the bad weather.

The motorcycle can also be equipped with functional accessories. For example, most machines do not have even the smallest luggage rack, although this is very useful when the rider only wants to carry a towel or a parcel. Those who do not like luggage racks can have a tank-bag, which with its plastic cover, is completely watertight. According to what use the owner wants to put it, a big road machine can be equipped in different ways. The sportsman will look for a racing riding position, and for this he will fit "clip-on" bars, a long and narrow fuel tank, a single seat, and for the ultimate, a stream-lined fairing. This last accessory is of aerodynamic shape, and can gain 3 or 4 mile/h (5 km/h) in maximum speed. Moreover, it is claimed that the fuel consumption is improved with the better air penetration. Certain types of fairing are designed to give maximum protection against the rain and cold. The only inconvenience is that the fairing can sometimes act as an amplifier, echoing the noise of the motor. The fairing can enclose the fork head. Only the speed enthusiast will go this far, other riders will probably equip their machines differently. Big handlebars ensure a relaxed position, the body upright as in an arm-chair. This type of motorcyclist does not care particularly for speed, they enjoy peaceful tour-ing and travel with baggage and spares. For them, a luggage rack is not enough, they add a big pair of panniers in leather or plastic. (The Americans and English make very good ones.) If these accessories are not sufficient, there is only one answer, the side-car. In Europe, the side-car is on its way out, but in the United States, it is enjoying a come-back. To be exact, it is being rediscovered—not as a useful machine, but because its use is very individual.

It is easy to love motorcycles, but dislike the thought of a long trip. Then there is the family man, who wants to take his machine on holiday, but has to drive the family car. Putting the machine on a train is one solution, but a few bumps and grazes on the tank on arrival must be counted on. The ideal is to possess a trailer on which one can load two or three machines.

modern design

For twenty years the design and construction of motorcycles has developed. Certainly nothing extraordinary or revolutionary has emerged, but the existing designs have been improved, to arrive at the present-day machines, which give their riders maximum security, efficiency and strength. Basically, this evolution is the result of competition, but putting this into practice has only largely been accomplished thanks to the Japanese.

Since 1955 the Japanese have understood that the motorcycle fits perfectly into the framework of a leisured society. The most advanced country in this sense, the U.S.A., was the first to be really interested in motorcycles, but there, or anywhere else, it would not have taken on in the way it has if the machines had remained at the technical level of those of the previous generation. The new motorcyclists demand performance, appearance, and above all, reliability. For them, a motorcycle should need no more maintenance than a car.

Bearing these important requirements in mind, the Japanese worked incessantly to produce entirely new models, sophisticated, and at very competitive prices. Honda was the apostle of the four-stroke motor, whereas Suzuki, Yamaha and Kawasaki are pro two-strokes. At Honda, their technical study and research centre employs no less than 800 technicians, all highly qualified. It is the same for the others, and their rivals, the important Kawasaki firm, has instructed its aeronautical section to produce motorcycles. Twenty years ago the overhead-camshaft was regarded solely for racing machines. Honda

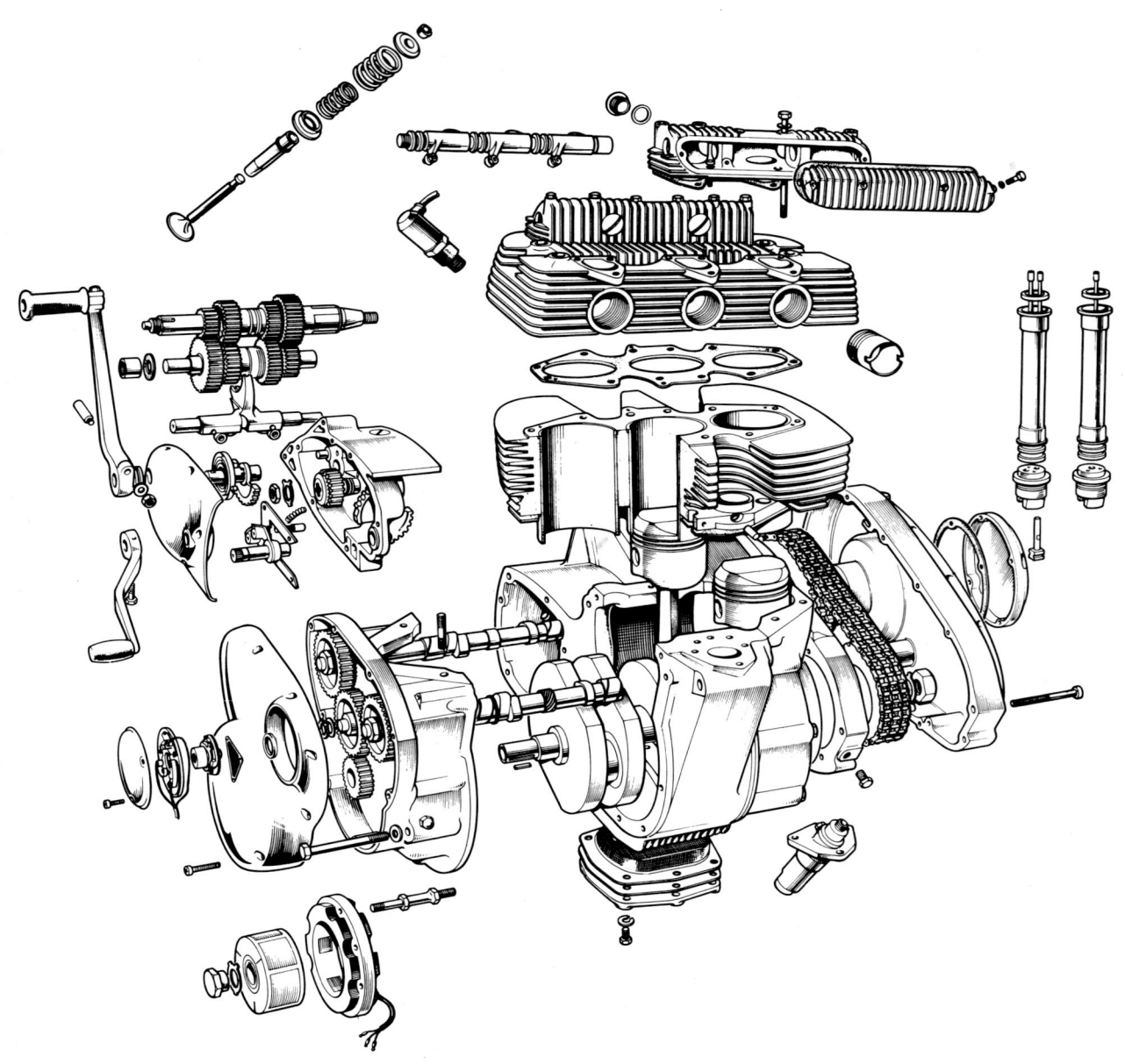

Triumph 750, three-cylinder.

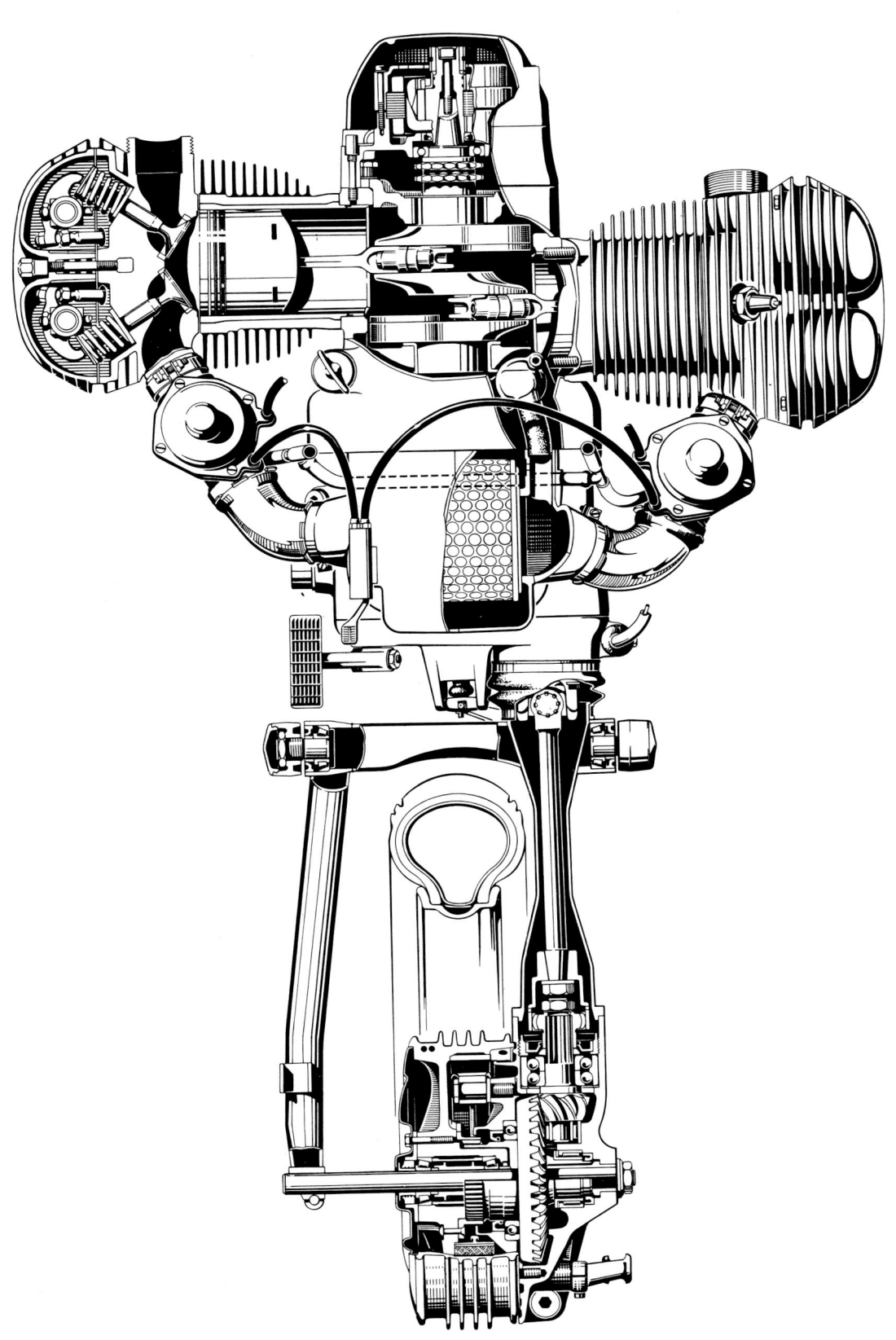

B.M.W. 750 cc.

brought "democracy" to the set-up, from 50 cc to 750. All these models, both racing and touring, have an overhead-cam operated by chain. The 450 Honda goes as far as to have two overhead-cams, and uses torsion bars to return the valves, which controls the limit of their movements. The use of single or, better, double overhead-cams has the advantage of suppressing the valves and pushrods. In an overhead valve motor, these parts, operated by an alternative movement, limit, by their inertia, the revs of the motor.

With a single overhead-cam, the safe maximum revs of a 125 cc motor is about 10,000 rev/min. It is even 8,000 on a 750 like the Honda Four. These frightening and unusual revs necessary, all the same, to obtain the specific power outputs of modern motors, are not necessarily synonymous with fragility. The care used in making the parts that go up to making the whole motor practically eliminates all risk of breakage. Moreover, the mounting of certain key pieces like the crank is effected in Japan with the same precision and tolerance as is used in the aviation industry. In fact the materials employed are of the highest quality, and it must not be forgotten that the oils used inside the motor have greatly improved. It is a long time since olive oil was recommended for the high-revving motor. The faster a motor turns the more heat it develops. In order to eliminate as much of this heat as possible, modern motors, above all the two-strokes, equip their cylinders with huge cooling fins, so big that it is sometimes necessary to interleave them with anti-vibratory patterns, so that they do not break. In the same way the cylinders and gearcases are made from light alloy of an aluminium base, metal which in particular can withstand extremes of temperature. Always, the sleeves of the cylinders are cast, and covered with a fine layer of chrome, which assists the movement of the pistons. Formerly, a two-stroke had two transfer ducts that brought the cool gas into the cylinder. The Japanese doubled this, which gave the advantage of being able to get rid of the burnt gas, and permitted better replenishment, thus increasing the power output of the motor.

Another interesting system popularised by the Japanese two-strokes is the separation of the oiling, and putting it under pressure. On a classical two-stroke, the oiling is done by having a petrol/oil mixture, which previously had been done by mixing the two together in the fuel tank. This method is inconvenient, among other things, for the necessity of mixing the petrol and oil first. In fact, according to the throttle opening, the motor has a changing need for oil. When slowing down, 1 per cent oil is adequate, whereas on full throttle, 5 per cent is needed. With the classical method, it is not possible to change the percentage, and very often, the excess at low revs causes fumes to escape and damage to the motor. The Japanese machines, with their separate oiling, do not have these problems. The fuel tank only contains petrol, and the oil is poured into its own separate tank. A pipe leads from the oil tank to a pump, and the delivery of oil through this pump is regulated by a cable joined to the throttle. So, the more the throttle is opened, the more oil is delivered by the pump, either into the carburettor, or directly into the cylinder. In addition, this same pump sends cool oil under pressure through a separate pipe to the bearings of the crankshaft, and the little ends, and by gravity oils the surfaces of the pistons and the lower ends of the connecting-rods. Using this system, the risk of seizing the pistons is considerably reduced. While on this subject it is important to note that all the new big machines, like the 750s of Triumph, B.S.A., B.M.W. and Honda, are supplied with an oiling system identical with that used on most cars. A reservoir, sometimes separate, contains approximately 5 pints of oil, and this is pumped round about once every 10 seconds by a very powerful pump. This technique is considered necessary with the mounting of the smooth-running crank and big ends. This technique, once again very similar to that of the car, has the advantage of producing a more silent motor. Silence is one of the dominant features of the modern machine, whose exhausts have been carefully studied; to begin with to lessen the noise, but now, and especially on the Japanese models, to give the best balance between inlet and exhaust. So it is important not to tamper with the exhausts because in so doing, power will be lost.

With the important gains in power from the big models, the primary transmission has been reinforced—the single chain becomes double, or even triple, row, or as on the 750 Honda, it works by two separate chains, which helps to divide the effects of torsion on the crank. Apart from the chains, for the primary transmission, a train of gears may also be used. The gearboxes have been fitted with more speeds, in the same degree as the motors have become more sophisticated, and it must be said that the number of speeds, like the number of cylinders, is a new selling point. Machines without five gears are rare nowadays. Today the clutch of a motorcycle is at least half as strong as that of a car. There are two types of clutch, each equally favoured by designers. The diaphragm clutch, as used on the Norton, Triumph, B.S.A., B.M.W., Moto Guzzi, etc., and the multiple plate, working in oil, with which the Japanese machines are equipped. Both are satisfactory in use. The diaphragm clutch is a little stiffer to start, and when changing gear, but the disc can slip when cold. In effect they are as good as each other. For the most part, secondary transmission is effected by chain. Only the big B.M.W.s, MV and Moto Guzzi use shaft drive. The advantage of a chain over shaft are minimal (decreased weight, and a very small increase in power). On the other side, a chain requires constant attention, it stretches, dirties up the rear wheel and sometimes more. On the big machines, it is often necessary to change the chain at 5,000-mile intervals.

The lack of enthusiasm which most constructors show to the shaft drive is amazing. Until fuel injection arrives, petrol is going to be fed to the motor by carburettors, which have their own reservoir, to ensure a constant supply of petrol, whatever the incline. Honda has equipped its 125, 250, 350 and 450s with carburettors in which the throttle cable does not operate a plunger, but a butterfly. When the butterfly pivots round, the air breathed in by the descent of the piston is drawn into an admission tube, where there is an area of low pressure. Nothing new about this so far. The more the butterfly pivots, that is to say, the more one accelerates, the bigger the depression, and it works now by the intermediary of little canalisations on a solid membrane, or piston, which is now lifted up, as though pushed by the depression. So, the depression only works on the elevation of the plunger, and if the throttle is turned sharply, the plunger does not lift as quickly as if it were pulled by a cable. It is necessary first that the low pressure has its effect. On carburettors with a wide inlet for the passage of the gas—this is the case with the Hondas—this system prevents flooding when accelerating hard. The carburation is much more constant, the speed of the gas column more harmonious, and the flexibility of use, as the consumption also benefits. Another little interesting detail which is found more and more often on modern machines is the flexible fixing of the carburettors on a rubber mounting. A rubber ring absorbs the vibrations of the motor, which, in shaking the carburettor, tends to upset the delicate mixing of the gas.

The rotary carburettor is a competition technique, adapted by the Japanese industry—notably Kawasaki—for the two-stroke motor. A conventional admission leads directly to the cylinder, and the skirt of the piston controls its opening and closing, which is not always very precise, especially in low gears. With the rotary valve the admission is made underneath the mass of the crank, and is controlled by a solid disc of the crank, and parallel to its bulk. An opening, or hole, is made in this disc, which shows up at each turn in its rotary movement at the admission pipe. Apart from the fact that there is now a strictly controlled admission phase, the rotary valve has the advantage of reducing the flow of cold petrol consequently producing a considerably better oiling of the lower motor. The conventional electrical equipment consists of an alternator which gives all its power from 3,000 rev/min, and a lighting coil with an automatic advance. Above 125 cc all batteries are 12 V. Electronic ignition is developing slowly, and only Kawasaki uses it, on almost all its range. This extremely complex system, although very robust —it is employed by the Spanish constructors for their cross-country bikes—has the advantage of doing without platinum points, which always have a tendency to give trouble. The power of a sparking-plug is superior to that of conventional ignition because of better combustion and increases the performance of the machine.

The frames have developed less than the mechanics. The usual frame for the medium and large machines is a duplex cradle of tubes. Two separate tubes come down from the steering-column, pass under the engine, come up behind and return to the steering-head to complete the circle. Sometimes the two upper tubes are replaced by a girder. The back fork, which pivots, is usually mounted on bronze rings, which must be greased. B.M.W. has replaced these rings by conical rollers which need no upkeep or attention. The single cradle with single down tube is used for the most part on medium and certain big models that have remained faithful, such as the Triumph, Velocette and 450 Honda, but now the simple cradle splits into two under the motor. The frames with single or duplex cradles are rivalled, above all with the small machines, by the frame with the motor suspended. This consists of a big dorsal spine—single or multi-tubed —under which the motor is hung. Norton has made an original frame for its 750 Commando. A double cradle holds the big twin-cylinder engine, which is entirely fixed to the frame by rubber mountings. At low revs, the engine can quite clearly be seen moving in the frame. This does not in any way harm the roadholding, and great comfort is gained by the elimination of vibration. The idea of comfort on a motorcycle is not a futile one. Those who have never ridden a motorcycle would be amazed at how comfortable it can be. The big, very soft double saddles, the suspension, the correct riding position give comfort worthy of any car. There is still the wind pressure which is not disagreeable until about 80 mile/h (130 km/h), and there again this can be eliminated by the use of an efficient fairing.

All motorcycle suspensions are made safe with telescopic forks in front, and one pivoted behind, and are equipped with hydraulic shock absorbers, adjustable for the weight put on them. The fork and the shock absorber have a double action; they work both in compression and extension. The braking system has developed considerably, thanks to the use of disc brakes and of double leading shoe drums (a racing technique, made popular by the Japanese). On a conventional single-shoe brake, there is always a certain lack of equilibrium. With two shoes, the forces are balanced, each shoe being controlled by a caliper. Recently the disc brake has appeared, and it is to be found on the 750 Honda. The calipers of this brake are hydraulically operated, as in a car, and the stopping power of such a brake is superior to that of a twin leading shoe drum.

In the area of equipment and finish of machines, the Japanese have once more shown the way, and others have followed. From the 250s, and even on some 125s, the instrument panel is fitted with a speedometer and rev counter. It has in addition a neutral indicator light, a full-beam light, sometimes an oil-pressure gauge, a winker light (indicators are fitted, two in front, and two behind). The electric starter, first used by Honda, is to be found on many large machines, such as Moto Guzzi, Laverda, MV, B.M.W., Harley-Davidson, and of course, on a good number of Hondas.

Another interesting Japanese invention is a fuel tap which automatically shuts off the flow of fuel when the motor stops. The principle is very simple. A membrane placed in the tap prevents the arrival of fuel when the motor is turned off. One of the sides of the membrane communicates by a small pipe with the inlet pipe of the carburettor. At the first kick, the depression, or drop in pressure, breathes air into the little pipe, and unsticks the membrane from the opening of the tap, and the fuel flows normally. Once the motor is stopped, a small, weak spring sticks the membrane back against the mouth of the tap. This system allows the rider to forget to shut off the petrol when having stopped—something which formerly had very annoying consequences with two-strokes, namely, flooding. The finish of modern machines is considerably improved: no more cables which tighten up and break, no more oil leaking from gaskets, no more little bolts falling out because of vibration. It is no longer necessary to be an expert mechanic to fully enjoy the pleasures offered by a motorcycle, and the annoyance of constant breakdowns has been alleviated. The Japanese technicians have worked on the motorcyclists' behalf, and the others have been obliged to follow.

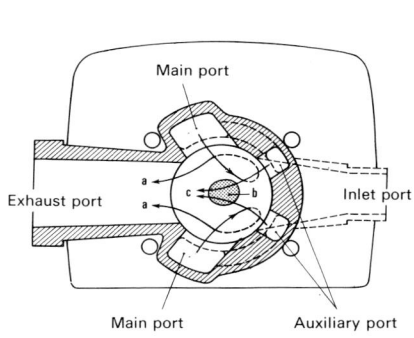

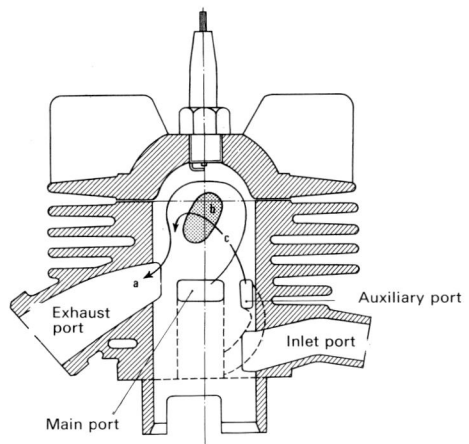

Main port

Exhaust port

Inlet port

Main port

Auxiliary port

Exhaust port

Auxiliary port

Inlet port

Main port

The five ports.

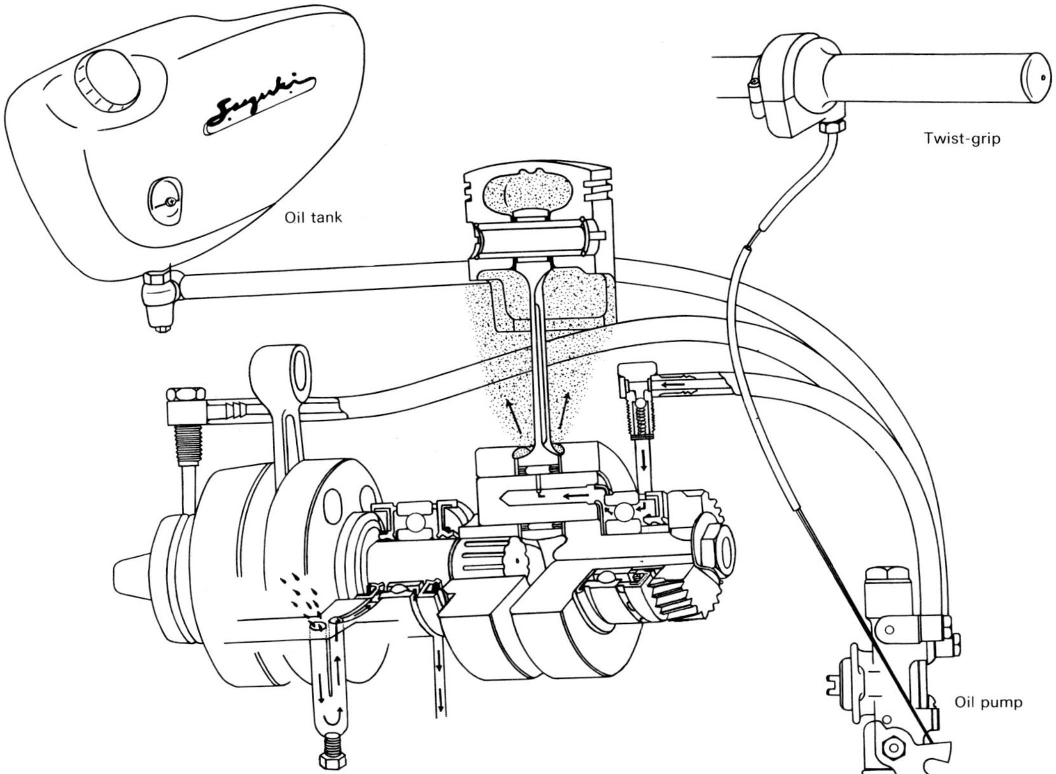

Oil tank

Twist-grip

Oil pump

The separate oiling system.

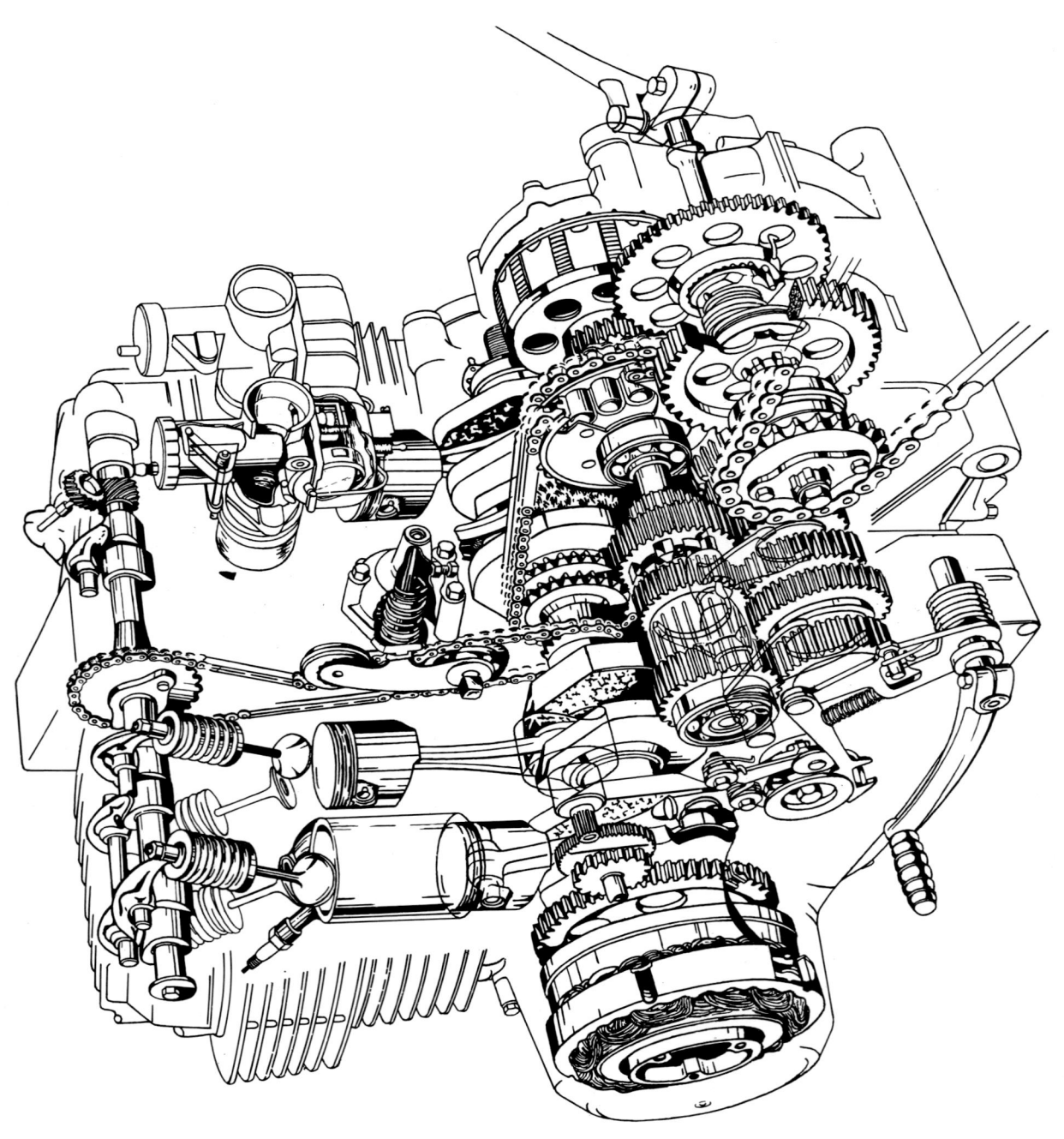

Honda 750, four-cylinder.

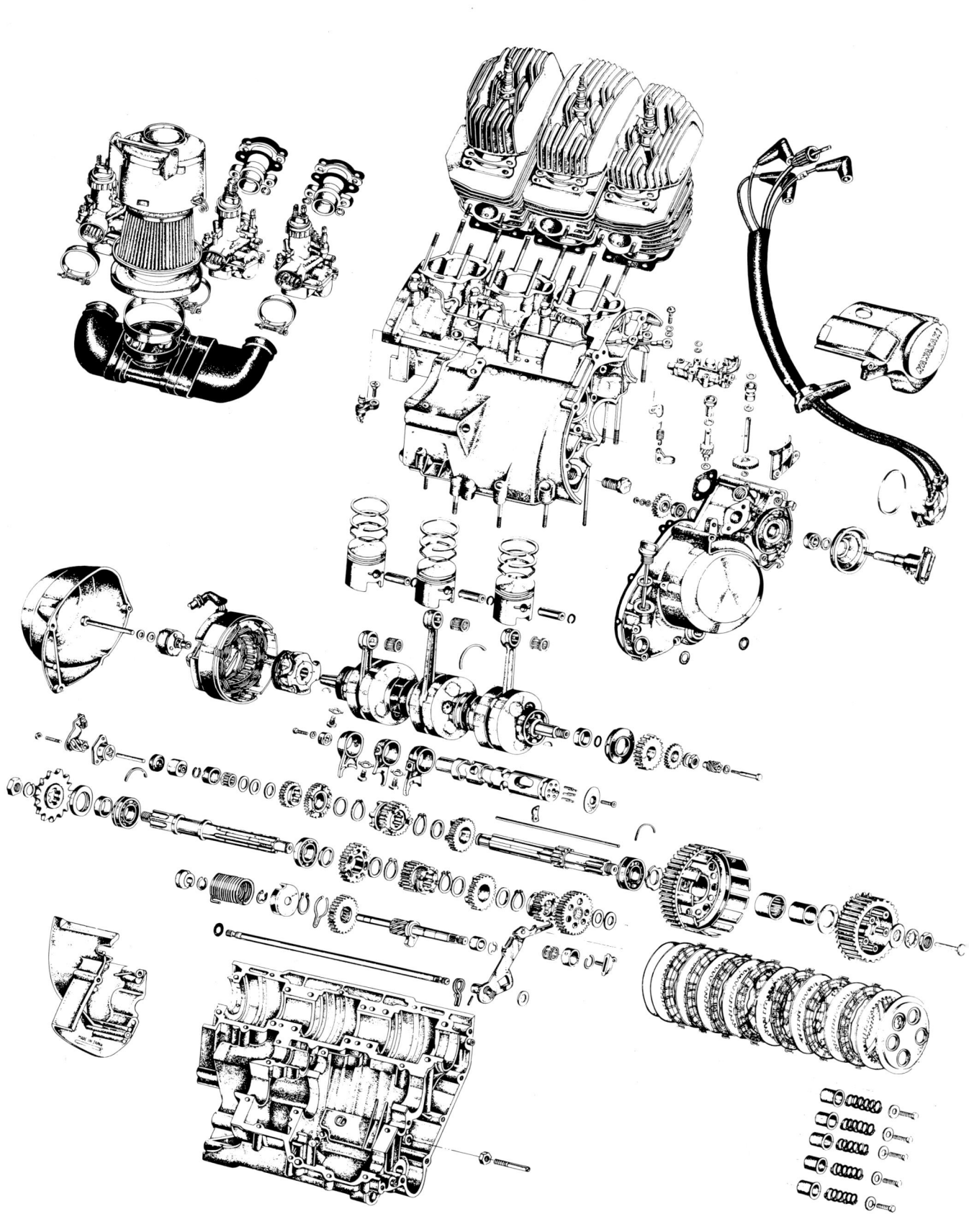

Kawasaki 500, three-cylinder.

2

the
sports

racing

It can be said that from the day there were two motorcycles of different make, there has been competition. At the beginning of the century the manufacturers tried to test the strength and performance of their machines over long distances. This was the era of the big rallies, or races, which always had their starting-point in Paris, such as Paris–Vienna, Paris–Nice, Paris–Cabourg, Paris–Madrid. Already, these races had an international flavour. In 1902 the Frenchman Bucquet won the Paris–Vienna on a Werner. The next year this same Bucquet found himself in the lead of the Paris–Madrid. This rally, which combined both cars and motorcycles, started very well, and an enormous crowd of spectators, estimated at three million, lined the route. This initial success finally developed into chaos. Some of the cars, their drivers having lost control, went into the crowd, killing many spectators. The carnage came to an end at Bordeaux when the organisers decided to halt the race. At Bordeaux, then, Bucquet was leading the motorcycle section with an overall average speed of 38 mile/h (62 km/h). In 1903 the first high-speed records were set on the Promenade des Anglais at Nice. The Frenchman, Gentry, on a Griffon, covered a mile in 1 min 16·5 s from a standing start, reaching 61·5 mile/h (99 km/h) at the end of the run.

These record attempts became duels when the records were challenged by many riders at the cycle-racing stadium at the Parc des Princes in Paris, or on the track at Canning Town. The champion at this kind of test was a Frenchman, Maurice Fournier, who rode the largest racing machine ever built. The motor of the machine made by Buchet was a giant vertical twin of 2,340 cc. In 1903 its power was close to 22 hp, and carried the rash Fournier at over 79 mile/h (128 km/h). Other monsters of the era, always French in origin, were the Fossier, the Lawson and the Clément four-cylinder. In 1904 the International Motorcyclists Federation set up the International Cup, which united five nations: Austria, Denmark, France, Germany and England. Each nation had to field three riders, equipped with racing machines made in their home country. The first real race for this cup took place in 1905 at Dourdon near Paris. The Frenchman, Demester, who started as favourite, broke down twice and left the victory to the Austrian Wondrick (Laurin-Klèment), who had covered the 168 miles (270 km) at an average speed of 54·4 mile/h (87·6 km/h). This performance becomes even more of an achievement when it is realised that the race was held on dirt roads.

Nothing much has been said of English achievements in these first years of motorcycle races. There are two reasons for this. In England, there was already a speed limit on the road, and therefore it was impossible to organise road races. Secondly, there was a law that said that motorcycles should not exceed 110 lb (50 kg). It was therefore impossible to build big motors, which alone might weigh more than 110 lb (50 kg). In the end, this last rule was modified. While they were waiting for this, English sportsmen cried out with heart and soul for a closed circuit, and got what they wanted in Brooklands. There they crowded together, and improved their designs. However, Brooklands was a speed bowl, and now they needed a real road-racing circuit.

BIRTH OF THE T.T. Finally, in 1907 the government of the Isle of Man, allowed the English motorcyclists to make use of its roads and the Tourist Trophy was born. This course became the most famous in the world. A victory in the T.T. was almost the equivalent of a world championship. On the Continent, the enthusiasm of the early years seemed to have lost its strength. Motorcycle racing stagnated and it was not until 1920 that the Grand Prix was born. First came the G.P. of France, then that of Belgium, Ireland, Italy, Holland, Germany and Spain. These races, and later the T.T., counted towards the championship of Europe. In 1949, with the addition of other G.P.s in the East European countries, the European championship changed its name, and became the championship of the world. In the beginning, this annual championship had four solo classes and a 600 cc side-car class. Later, the side-car category was limited to 500 cc and in 1962 the 50 cc category was added to the 125, 250, 350 and 500.

The regulations of these championships have been much altered since the beginning. The integral fairing, which allows even the front wheel to be covered, was banned in 1958. This type of fairing gave a better penetration of the air than those of today, and permitted incredible performances from the motorcycles of the day. The last modification to the rules concerned the number of cylinders. From 1969, 50 cc machines have been allowed only six gears and one cylinder, and from 1970 only two cylinders and six gears for the 125s and 250s. The 350 and 500 classes are still open. This ruling has been made to permit the small factories, which do not have great resources, to take part in the championships, with a good chance of being placed among the world champions.

The value of this technical limitation can be judged better in the years to come. The breakdown of points towards the title is made in the following way: The winner of a race gains 15 points, the second 12, the third 10, the fourth 8, fifth 6, sixth 5, seventh 4, eighth 3, ninth 2, tenth 1. At the end of the season the number of points obtained in the races is added up. However, it is not necessarily the one who has the most points that wins. For example, in eight races, the points from the six best results are taken. So, in 1967 at the end of the season in the 250 class there was Phil Read on a Yamaha and Mike Hailwood on a Honda, both with equal points. However, Read had four G.P. wins, and Hailwood five and so he was world champion. For the manufacturers' championship, the scoring is different: only the highest placed machine from any manufacturer counts. In this way, it is possible to have a manufacturer whose machine wins the manufacturers' championship, but which is not ridden by the rider who is world champion. In 1966 Honda won the championship of the 500 class, but the world champion was Agostini, on an MV3.

THE HISTORY OF RACING: NORTON. The technical evolution of the racing motorcycle since the beginning of the century deserves another small chapter.

In 1907 Norton won the first T.T. To be exact, in this year only, a Peugeot 727 cc engine developing 5 hp was used, in a Norton frame. This first result was the beginning of a chain of glorious victories: 34 in the T.T., 32 in the Belgian G.P.,

26 in the Ulster G.P., 20 in the Dutch G.P., 13 in the German G.P., 7 in the Italian G.P.—only to mention the most important. And, since the creation of the world championship in 1949, two titles in the 350 class, two more in the 500 and six in the side-car. During the first years of the T.T., Norton was invincible. However, in 1911 three superb American Indian machines, technically very advanced for the day with their three-speed gearboxes and secondary chain transmission managed to take the first three places. Up until 1923 the single-cylinder Nortons were equipped with side-valves. The first overhead-valve motor, a 500, developed 25 hp and the machine travelled at 95 mile/h (150 km/h). In 1930 the 500 cc single overhead-cam motor appeared. This motor was designed in 1927 by Walter Moore. In 1932 it produced 40 hp at 6,000 rev/min, in contrast to an identical 350 model, which produced 30 hp at 6,800 rev/min. These machines were capable of speeds of 112 mile/h (180 km/h) for the 500, and 100 mile/h (160 km/h) for the 350. Three years later the twin overhead-cam motor appeared, which developed 50 hp in its 500 cc form at 7,000 rev/min, and propelled the machine at 125 mile/h (200 km/h). Norton now had the motor which was to give it all its later glory.

In 1950, Cromie McCandless designed a frame which made the marque famous: the "featherbed" frame. Geoff Duke, the Norton works rider, outstripped the multi-cylinder Italian machines and indeed, in 1951 brought back the 500 cc world championship to Britain. After that it was decadence. Wishing to remain faithful to the single, Norton stopped its development programme. The four-cylinder Italian machines had progressed so far that Norton preferred to retire rather than construct a completely new machine. Meanwhile, many projects were being studied. There was a four-cylinder, twin-cam, desmodromic valve motor, a machine with a horizontal motor as in the Moto Guzzi, and a curious single-cylinder motor in which the valves were replaced by a rotary cylinder. Norton was also to produce the Manx, for sale to the private rider, a machine that was a slightly detuned replica of the official racing model. This very strong machine was improved over the years by brilliant engineers like Francis Beart, Steve Lancefield and Ray Petty, who achieved power outputs equal, if not superior, to the factory motors. It was with one of these machines that Mike Hailwood won the T.T. in 1961 beating the MV4 of Gary Hocking. Even today a good Manx will produce 52 hp, and travel at over 130 mile/h (210 km/h).

Since 1972 Norton has been reintroduced to racing thanks to its sponsor John Player. The

machines contesting in the Formula 750 championships and Daytona races, were 750 Commandos. In 1973 Peter Williams, engineer, tuner and Norton rider, constructed a very handsome and effective monocoque frame. In order to lower the machine's centre of gravity, the petrol tank is divided in two and placed on both sides of the cylinders. As the level of the liquid in the tanks is lower than that of the float chambers of the carburettors. Norton uses a pumping system which is operated by oscillating arms, as used by Guzzi in 1957. On the whole, however, the John Player Nortons are technically very advanced. With a very competitive engine Norton is seriously trying to restore its fortunes.

RUDGE. Rudge is another English make that distinguished itself in the thirties. This make had three competition models, a 250, a 350 and a 500, all of which won the T.T. at least once. The motor was a single cylinder with four valves. Sunbeam also made themselves famous in the Isle of Man in the twenties using a single-cylinder motor, with twin exhaust ports, operated by valves.

Velocette is one of the earliest makes of English motorcycle, and the first to produce real racing machines for the private rider. This was the KTT, a 350 cc machine. This machine ridden by Alec Bennett, brought home its first T.T. victories in 1926 and 1927, the motor, a single-cylinder, single overhead-cam, developed 25 hp, and propelled the KTT at 87 mile/h (140 km/h). Ten years later, the motor of the KTT had not changed in form, but its power had been raised to 35 hp. In 1936–39 it scooped almost all the first places in the 350 cc category. After the announcement of the world championship, the engineers at Velocette made a great effort and produced the twin overhead-cam KTT which developed 35 hp, using commercial fuel. It must be mentioned that before the world championship, petrol was unrestricted, and by clever mixing, it was possible to obtain very high octane fuels. This 350 cc twin overhead-cam KTT won two world titles, and that was the end of the racing Velocettes. Like the Norton, the reconversion to multi-cylinders was necessary. Just before the Second World War Velocette built a 500 made from two 250 cc twin overhead-cam motors, supercharged. A secondary transmission by cam and shaft was to be tried on this machine, which made a brief appearance at the T.T. in 1939.

A.J.S. The last great English make, the A.J.S. (the initials of the inventor, A. J. Stevens), won

its first T.T. in 1914. In 1921 a 350 cc, called the "Big Port" because of its large inlet port called the tune in this category. It achieved three consecutive victories in the T.T. in its class, and even one in the 500 class. In 1927 the pushrods of the A.J.S. single were replaced by a single cam operated by a chain. This technique was to characterise all A.J.S. racing motors in the future, whether 250, 350 or 500. In 1939 A.J.S. produced a supercharged 500 cc V-four producing 80 hp, but the post-war rules put this monster into the museum. Among the English constructors only A.J.S. seems to have understood that the reign of the single-cylinder machines had come to an end, in the face of the Italian multis. In 1947 A.J.S. built a 500 cc Porcupine a superb twin overhead-cam—gear driven—the motor horizontal in the frame, producing 45 hp, and it was with this machine that Leslie Graham, father of works Suzuki rider Stuart Graham, led the Gilera four of Pagani, and brought back the 1949 world championship. In 1950 and 1951 it needed the enormous talent of Duke and the speed of his Norton to withstand for the last time the assault of the powerful Italian fours. A.J.S., for its part, continued to improve the Porcupine, and when the make withdrew in 1954 the twin overhead-cam motor was developing 54 hp at 8,500 rev/min.

In 1948 at the same time as it produced the Porcupine, A.J.S. produced singles, with a single chain-driven overhead-cam. These machines were intended for the private riders, and were called the 7R for the 350 and the G50 for the 500 version. One 7R participated officially in competition after it had been fitted with a three-valve head—one for inlet, and two for exhaust. This machine, which developed 37 hp at 7,600 rev/min won the Junior T.T. of 1954. The G50 followed the same path as the Manx Norton. It was in every way the machine of the private rider. However, although they were very strong, these motors were not everlasting. Exchange parts are rare since Colin Seeley reconstructed a whole series in 1966. Today, the power of a G50 is similar to that of a Manx, about 50 hp. In reality, then, only the Manx and the G50 represent English design in the G.P. field.

For many years the 500 cc races were enlivened by the appearance of these old singles. Because there is a factory machine, the unapproachable MV—and then behind, very far away, the real struggle with the pack of single-cylinder riders—whose performances are well worth while. The future seems to be quite a compromise for these old ghosts of a golden era. Already some Italian makes such as Linto and Paton are interesting themselves in the vice-championship, and in 1969 a Linto ridden by the Swiss, Marsovszky finished behind the MV3 of Agostini and in front of the Norton of the Englishman, Nash.

B.M.W. To return to the history of the makes of racing motorcycles, the Germans must be discussed. B.M.W. (Bayerische Motoren Werke) made their first racing machine in 1925. It was only a souped-up touring machine. The motor was, of course, a flat-twin, and the secondary transmission was by shaft. This first motor, a 500 cc side-valve, developed 20 hp at 4,800 rev/min. In 1930 the valves were put on the head, a compressor was used, and the power went up to 35 hp. This machine made an attack on the speed records, but with a 750 cc engine producing 75 hp with a compressor. Ernest Henne, in 1932, reached 152 mile/h (244 km/h). In 1935 B.M.W. built its first 500 cc engines with a single overhead-cam, always fed by a Zoller compressor. This engine was considered at the time to be the fastest in the world, reaching speeds of 137 mile/h (220 km/h). In 1937 a new attempt on the record with the 500, and this time completely faired, it went at 174 mile/h (280 km/h). In 1939 Georg Meier took part in the T.T. and won the 500. After the war B.M.W. abandoned compressors, and built the Rennsport—still a flat-twin single overhead-cam which was shaft driven. The first Rennsport models achieved 50 hp at 8,500 rev/min and reached 60 hp at 9,500 rev/min in 1954. Again, the B.M.W. beat all its rivals in pure speed, but its handling was not exemplary, which explains the absence of good results on the race-track. Later, this fabulous engine was no longer used on solos, but equipped the B.M.W. side-cars which gained an impressive number of titles.

D.K.W. To begin with, the D.K.W. (Dampf Kraft Wagen) was constructed at Zschopau near Dresden in East Germany. After the Second World War the D.K.W. factory set up in West Germany. Since its beginnings, D.K.W. has made two-stroke engines. The first racing machine, a 175 water-cooled model, appeared in 1926. In 1931, the racing engineer, Zoller, designed a curious motor inspired by the Italian make, Garelli. This 250 cc motor had three pistons, of which two worked in parallel in the motor one behind the other, joined by a forked connector-rod on the same throw of the crankshaft. The third piston was placed horizontally, and operated the compressor. The motor was water-cooled. In 1938 the compressor piston was placed vertically, in line with the two others. This slightly unorthodox 250 won the T.T. in 1938. In 1939, compression by piston was changed to compressor by a fan. After the war, when compression was not allowed, D.K.W. changed to

suit the current environment of 1952, with a 350 three. This air-cooled motor had two vertical cylinders facing the front and one horizontal. It developed 35 hp at 10,000 rev/min. In 1955 the power output passed 42 hp and the maximum speed was over 130 mile/h (210 km/h). With such performances D.K.W. was in a position to win the world championship, but in 1956, the racing division had to shut its doors.

N.S.U. (from the name of the town, Neckarsulm) is one of the most ancient motorcycle firms in the world, whose sporting activities started in 1910, but it is true to say that the first competitive machine was the single-cylinder single overhead-cam 500 which won the Italian Grand Prix in 1930. Its motor resembled closely that of the Norton of the same era. In 1939 N.S.U. made a 350 and a 500 twin overhead-cam in which each cam was operated separately by a shaft with conical return. It was supercharged by a compressor. This type of engine was used after the war to set outright speed records at Bonneville. In 1956 a 350 and a 500, both streamlined, respectively, travelled at the fantastic speeds of 188 mile/h (304 km/h) and 210 mile/h (338 km/h), the motors of these machines developing 73 and 110 hp. N.S.U. was not only interested in speed records and challenged also in the world championships in 125 and 250. In the 125 class, N.S.U. entered a small single four-stroke with twin overhead-cam, which developed 15·5 hp at 10,000 rev/min, the Rennfox, which had a maximum speed of 99 mile/h (160 km/h). In the hands of Werner Hass, this 125 took the championship in 1953. The 250, called the Rennmax, was in some ways a copy, without a compressor, of the 350 and 500 already described. It developed, in the 1952 version, 27 hp at 9,000 rev/min. The following year, with 30 hp at 10,000 rev/min, it won the world championship, and retained the title for 1954. At the end of the 1954 season, the 250 N.S.U. was capable of 137 mile/h (220 km/h) thanks to the power of 39 hp at 11,500 rev/min. This power was equal, if not superior, to that produced by the best 350s of that era. N.S.U. had proven their superiority and decided to retire to attack the records already mentioned, but in 1955, N.S.U. were still spoken of in Grands Prix.

The twin-cylinder twin overhead-cams were put in the museum and it was a single-cylinder single overhead-cam directly developed from the 250 Max touring made that took part in the championship. To start with, the motor developed 20 hp; once worked on at the factory, it gave 29 hp at 9,500 rev/min, and which, with a good fairing, could attain 124 mile/h (200 km/h). At the controls of this machine, the Sportsmax,

The German Lunemann takes off on the little bridge at Ballaugh in the Tourist Trophy. ▶

only a modest machine—Herman Müller was crowned world champion, the constructors' title returning to MV Agusta.

M.Z. After the removal of D.K.W. to West Germany, the Zschopau factory was used for the construction of other machines with two-stroke motors, for M.Z. (Motorraderwerke Zschopau). The first racing M.Z., a 125 single-cylinder, appeared in 1950. The following year Daniel Zimmermann adapted the 125 to take a carburettor with rotary valve. This system was not new, it's true, but the results prove that innovations in the racing department of M.Z., directed by Walter Kaaden, apply also to its factory models. Up to 1957 M.Z.'s participation in Grands Prix was very spasmodic. Then the 125 developed 16 hp at 8,300 rev/min. By joining together two of these 125s Kaaden made the 250, with some 30 hp.

In 1958 these ratings went up to 20 and 36 hp, and M.Z. gaining their first great victories. From 1962 M.Z. were prepared to carry off the world championship in 125 and 250 as they were superior to the Italian four-strokes. However, they were not prepared for the arrival of the Japanese. In 1963 the cylinders and covers of the M.Z. engines were wholly cooled by water. On the two-stroke overheating caused a loss of power and the cooling by water permitted a constant and relatively low temperature. In 1969 the M.Z. 125 and 250 developed 30 and 50 hp and reached 124 mile/h (200 km/h) for the 125 and 143 mile/h (230 km/h) for the 250. These performances put M.Z. at the head in the battle of the twin cylinders. Logically the efforts of Walter Kaaden would be crowned with success, all he needed was a good rider.

JAWA AND CZ are two Czech factories whose racing services have produced a multitude of models which are technically very original. In 1955 Jawa built a 500 twin featuring twin overhead camshafts. The operation of these was achieved using two cams with conical return. The first, vertically mounted behind the cylinders, transmitted the movement to the other. This being horizontally mounted and connected to the two overhead camshafts. The first 500 Jawa gave 45 hp at 8,000 rev/min. This engine structure was adapted for the 250 and 350 cc engines. In 1963 the 350 developed 52 hp at 11,400 rev/min, thanks to a head with four valves per cylinder. Then Jawa abandoned the four-stroke engine for a two-stroke one. In 1965, a 250 twin two-stroke fed by two rotary valves, produced 43 hp at 12,000 rev/min. In 1967 Jawa produced a 125 V-twin, the cylinders facing the road. This engine produced 30 hp at 14,000 rev/min. For Jawa,

the 125 twin served only as a basis of study for a four-cylinder of 350 cc which appeared in 1968. The four cylinders were placed in a V, two horizontal and two leaning towards the front. Each pair of cylinders had its own separate crank which afterwards was joined to the other by pinions. The four cylinders were water-cooled and fed by four rotary valves. The gearbox contained seven gears and the power approached 70 hp at 13,000 rev/min. This machine proceeds today in its delicate balance.

The first CZ racing motorcycles appeared at the same time as the Jawa, in 1955. Consequently for CZ, the important machines were four-stroke 125, 250 and 350 singles with double overhead-camshafts. As with the Jawas the overhead-cams were directed by two cams with conical return. The first examples of these engines developed 14·5 hp at 11,000 rev/min for the 125, 24 hp at 8,500 rev/min for the 250 and 30 hp at 8,500 rev/min for the 350. In 1964 CZ decided to change its 125 and produce a twin, still with double overhead-cams. This modification brought an increase in power of almost 10 hp per gear to the single and the top speed of the twin 125 approached 118 mile/h (190 km/h). The latest production of CZ, the four-cylinder 350 double overhead-cam, appeared for the first time at the Czechoslovak Grand Prix in 1969. In order to reduce the frontal area of the machine, CZ has put the four cylinders facing the road, the overhead-cams being controlled by a train of gears. The 1969 prototype was equipped with four valves to each cylinder and claimed a power of 52 hp at 13,000 rev/min and a gearbox with eight gears.

Since they were set up in 1949 the world championships have been largely dominated on the whole by Italian racing machines. In the 125 class from 1949 to 1969 the Italians won eleven times. In the 250 during the same period, they won ten times. In the 350 they had eleven victories and in the 500, a record, with seventeen titles. This crop of titles was no accident, the Italian engineers were really superior and only the Japanese managed to topple them in the sixties. Yet, if the championships had been established after the First World War, the Italian domination would have been seriously threatened by the British racing machines. In carrying off the French Grand Prix for 350 cc in 1922, Garelli started the long list of Italian victories on foreign race tracks. The engine of this machine was a two-stroke with two pistons driven by a single crank. The two pistons had a common combustion chamber, but two separate cylinders. In 1921, this engine was equipped with separate greasing which shot oil in to the carburettor according to the speed it

◀ *Neck and neck. Ivy followed by Read on the 125 Yamaha fours. (pp. 90–1)*

rotated. This technique is today applied to all Japanese two-strokes. In 1927 Garelli ceased to compete.

BIANCHI knew its hours of glory and achieved a maximum of victories in the 350 class, between the year 1925 and 1930, the engine, a single with double overhead-cam, developed 25 hp in 1927. The first Bianchi rider of this time was Tazio Nuvolari, the future famous racing-car driver. In 1930, Bianchi built a 500 identical to the 350, a double overhead-cam driven by a vertical shaft. This 500 was to be ridden by Alberto Ascari among others. Ascari was to be found again at the handlebars of a Bianchi four-cylinder double overhead-cam with forced feed. It was in 1939 that this machine developed 80 hp for a speed of 136–143 mile/h (220–230 km/h). Well after the war, in 1960, Bianchi made 250 cc and 350 cc twins with twin overhead-cams. The 350 was more competitive and produced 50 hp at 11,000 rev/min. It was with this machine that Tino Brambilla, the future Ferrari official, kept the lead from the MV4, during several circuits of the Italian Grand Prix in 1960. Giuseppe Pattoni, a Milan craftsman, built in 1963 a 250 twin whose engine design was very similar to that of the Bianchi. This new racer, the Paton, changed two years later into a 500. The twin overhead-cam of the Paton was driven by a cascade of pinions placed between the twin cylinders. The Paton which is a machine for the competition rider developed in 1969 55 hp at 10,000 rev/min.

DUCATI. The first Ducati competition machines appeared fairly recently, in 1955; they were small motorcycles, 100 cc and 125 cc, with a single overhead-cam which became a year later a twin overhead-cam. In 1956, the 125 developed 16 hp at 11,500 rev/min for a top speed of 106 mile/h (170 km/h). Still in 1956 the engineer Taglioni put desmodromic valves on the Ducatis. The intention was to suppress the springs of the valves. The recall of the valves was assured by a cam which controlled a fork which lifted up the valve. The opening was controlled by two axles worked by a cam with a conical recall. The advantages of the desmodromic valve are among others to suppress valve bounce. The first 125 desmodromic valve provided 17 hp at 12,500 rev/min. In 1958, this engine gained another 2 hp and drove the machine at 112 mile/h (180 km/h). For Ducati the 125 title seemed to be certain, but a series of minor incidents thwarted the excellent efforts of this small firm. In 1959 Ducati built a 125 desmodromic twin valve producing 22·5 hp at 14,000 rev/min. Unfortunately it was not often seen racing. Mike Hailwood, very much im-

pressed by the performance of the 125 single, ordered a 250 twin made up by combining two 125s from the Ducati factory. This 250, made to measure, developed 43 hp at 11,600 rev/min in 1960. In 1961, Hailwood, approached by Honda, deserted his Ducati.

MORINI. The first Morini racing machine, a 125 single two-stroke won the Italian championship in 1948. The next year the two-stroke engine was replaced by a four-stroke with single overhead-cam, so improving the power from 8 to 12 hp. Some time after the 125 was transformed into 175 with double overhead-cam driven by a chain. The 175 Bialbero soon became a 250, still with a double overhead-cam. In 1958 the chain which drew the camshafts was replaced by a train of pinions; the Rebello 250 already had its definitive shape which was to be reviewed and corrected as the years went on. The Rebello of 1958 developed 32 hp at 10,500 rev/min, in 1966 35 hp at 11,000 rev/min and in 1963, 37 hp for a maximum speed of 143 mile/h (230 km/h). It was with this last version that Tarquinio Provini was only beaten by two points in the world championship by Redman's Honda 4. It must also be said that the Morini held the road extremely well and that Provini had talent to spare.

BENELLI. Benelli made his first campaign in competition with a 175 cc single with single overhead-cam in 1927. Three years later the single overhead-cam disappeared to give way to a double overhead-cam controlled by a number of pinions.

In 1935 Benelli abandoned the 175 cc to build a 500 cc double overhead-cam single developing 50 hp, then a 250 of the same mechanical structure and providing 25 hp at 8,000 rev/min; this power was obtained with normal carburation. It is with this last machine forcibly fed that Ted Mellors wrought such havoc in the Isle of Man just before the war. In 1940 Benelli built his first 250 cc four. This water-cooled engine with double overhead-cams was fed by a compressor, and because of this it could not compete in the world championship. Benelli also turned on a new account to the double overhead-cam single and in 1950 when it developed 27 hp at 9,000 rev/min, the Benelli 250 single won the championship. The following year, when he was more or less in the lead in the championship, the official Benelli driver, Dario Ambrosini, was killed in the French Grand Prix. For the Pessaro factory this was a hard blow from which it recovered in 1960 to make the 250 double overhead-cam air-cooled four. This first version developed 40 hp at 13,000 rev/min.

Wizard with machinery, talented driver, Helmut Fath with Wolfgang Kalauch as passenger.

►

JARNO SAARINEN

5·73 BOHEM

Yamaha 500.

However, it was only in 1964 that the four-cylinder Benelli regularly competed in Grands Prix. It was still ridden by Provini who won the Spanish Grand Prix, but was injured in the T.T. In 1969 after the withdrawal of the Japanese factories, Benelli was a scarecrow figure in the 250 category. The title would not be less warmly disputed until the last Grand Prix by the Italian fours, one private 250 Yamaha and one 250 Ossa. The last word rightly was with Benelli. This last model, which was never seen again in competition because of new regulations, produced 50 hp at 16,000 rev/min and had an eight-speed gearbox and was credited with a top speed of about 143 mile/h (230 km/h). In the future, Benelli challenged the 350 and 500 categories, always with four-cylinder twin overhead-cam engines, driven by a train of pinions. One version with an engine of four valves to the cylinder was tried on the 250 but it was said to be not much faster than the two-valve version.

AERMACCHI. Aermacchi/Harley-Davidson is a relatively new firm whose first racing machines appeared in 1960, with Harley-Davidson providing the financial backing. The Aermacchi racing machines were largely derived from road machines. They had a horizontal cylinder style engine and this technical simplicity has enabled them to make a competition model for the customer in 250 and 350 cc classes. For the works machines the power had, in 1969, been brought up to 32 hp at 10,000 rev/min for the 250, and 42 hp at 9,000 rev/min for the 350. A 350 overbored to 382 cc was lined up in the 500 cc races. Its extreme lightness 242 lb (110 kg) allied to real power (43 hp at 8,300 rev/min) made it a rival of the English singles. The engineer Tino Tonti who designed the Bianchis had the idea of coupling together two Aermacchis to make a new 500, the Linto. The result was astonishing; the Linto developing 65 hp at 10,000 rev/min and was capable of going at more than 155 mile/h (250 km/h). It lacked just a little strength or it would have been the best of the 500s for competition customers. In 1970 Aermacchi showed his first two-stroke engines: first a 125, then, a year later Aermacchi made twin-cylinder two-stroke racing machines to compete with the Yamahas, which closely resembled their Japanese rivals. It was only in 1972 that these machines, ridden by Pasolini in 250 and 350 classes proved to be competitive. Their power is respectively 50 hp at 11,400 rev/min for the 250, and 60 hp at 10,800 rev/min for the 350. Since 1972, Aermacchi have used the name Harley-Davidson. The 250 twin-cylinder two-stroke engine got better and better and enabled Villa to carry off the title in both 1974 and 1975. The engines were then developing 64 hp.

MONDIAL. Since 1948 Mondial has specialised in small-capacity machines like the 125. The first racing Mondial, a single with a double overhead-cam carried off the Italian Grand Prix in 1949; for a trial run this was a master stroke. This exploit was not an isolated one. For the first year of the world championship Mondial gained the title for the 125 and repeated it in 1950 and 1951. This triple champion is in fact little different from the 1949 model. It only underwent changes of an aerodynamic order as the fairings became more and more enveloping: the engine remained the same and developed 12 hp at 9,000 rev/min. After some years in eclipse due to the superiority of the MV, the 125 Mondial regained its title in 1957 thanks to Tarquinio Provini and a more powerful engine by 6 hp; the gearbox also contained seven gears. The same year, a 250 souped-up from a 125, a twin overhead-cam single, gained the world championship in the same category. Afterwards, Mondial built a new 125, still a double overhead-cam single but with desmodromic valves. This engine claimed a power of 20 hp. Unfortunately it was not tested because in 1958 Mondial retired from racing. Among the unfinished prototypes there was also a 250 double overhead-cam twin built by joining together two 125 world championship engines. More recently, Mondial produced, with the co-operation of the Villa brothers, a 125 two-stroke single and a twin two-stroke, both with horizontal cylinders and fed by rotative distributors. However, these very fast machines lacked precision. On their own the Villa brothers produced Villa motorcycles destined to be sold on the private racing market. The 125, a two-stroke single cooled by water and fed by a rotary valve was credited, in 1969, with a power verging on 30 hp at 11,400 rev/min, otherwise the Villa brothers worked on a 350 four-cylinder two-stroke with a rotative distributor.

GILERA. The history of racing Gilera motorcycles falls into two epochs: that of the singles of 1927 to 1937, then that of the fours of 1935 to 1957. The first epoch was not very glorious and the singles, at first inverted then with a single overhead-cam, only distinguished themselves in feats of endurance. The second on the contrary had six world championships to its credit. The very first 500 cc four-cylinder Gilera was in fact built in 1927. The first example which did not take part in any race developed 26 hp at 6,000 rev/min. In 1935 the exceedingly powerful water-cooled Rondine was born. This twin overhead-cam four driven, between the two pairs of cylinders, by a crowd of pinions, developed, thanks to its compressor, 80 hp at 9,000 rev/min. This machine attacked the pure speed records and was capable of reaching 155 mile/h (250 km/h). Equipped with a fairing, the Rondine, which resembled an aeroplane rather than a motorcycle, attained in 1937 170 mile/h (274 km/h) over the flying kilometre. In 1939, the Gilera four, with fuel injection developed 85 hp and won the European championship. After the war an engine with conventional carburation had to be built. The water-cooling was abandoned, the four cylinders facing the road were less inclined towards the front than on the Rondine being fed by two carburettors. Otherwise the two overhead-cams were still driven by a cascade of pinions in a slanting shape. Power claimed: 50 hp at 8,500 rev/min; speed 124 mile/h (200 km/h). In 1950, Umberto Masetti took the world championship for riders with a Gilera four. The following year Duke, riding a Norton, needed all his talent to oppose, for the last time, the powerful Gileras who, with 55 hp at 10,000 rev/min, won the championship for constructors in 1952, the four cylinders were now being fed by four carburettors. To hold all the trump cards Gilera engaged Geoff Duke in 1953 whose first task was to modify the frame of the 500 four which from this time was equipped with five-speed gearbox. Naturally, Gilera won the title. In 1954 the power was brought up to 65 hp at 10,400 rev/min for a speed of 149 mile/h (240 km/h). Duke was unbeatable and proved it again the following season. In 1956, Gilera did not participate in all the Grands Prix and was forced to relinquish the title. 1957 was the last racing year for the Italian fours; like Guzzi and Mondial the Gilera factory announced its retirement from competition. As a final flourish Gilera carried off the 500 cc title for the last time and also the 350 title. The 350 cc four developed 49 hp at 11,000 rev/min. These enchanting fours made a brief appearance in 1963–64 under the banner of the "Scuderia" Duke. They were also ridden by the Englishmen Hartle and Minter and by the Argentinian Caldarella who outstripped the MV4 of Mike Hailwood in the United States Grand Prix and in another twenty or so races.

GUZZI. The racing service at Guzzi's has achieved many wonders. There are so many different models that for the clarity of the text the history of the singles, and then that of the multis must be related. The very first 500 single appeared in 1921. Already the engine was horizontal. This distinction was to characterise the whole Guzzi singles production. In 1923 they had the first racing victory for the 500 single (inverted) with two valves on the head. The following year this engine (88 × 82 mm) was equipped with an overhead-cam (transmission by conical returning axle) which directed four valves. This machine developed 22 hp at 5,500 rev/min and won the European championship. Afterwards, in 1925, the 500 machine (four valves) was further improved to give a power of 32 hp at 6,000 rev/min. This 500 was the prototype for the construction in 1925 of the first 250 which had only two overhead valves. The career of this machine was dazzling, winning among others, three world titles.

In 1935, Guzzi and Stanley Woods realised an ambition in carrying off the T.T. with the 250 and 500 (the 500 had two cylinders). The victorious 250 developed 22 hp at 7,500 rev/min and was fed by a mixture of petrol, benzanol and alcohol. It required that to achieve speeds of 106 mile/h (170 km/h) in 1935. In 1937, the 250 cc Guzzi was souped-up and developed 38 hp at 7,800 rev/min with a speed of 124 mile/h (200 km/h) without a fairing; and partly streamlined it even reached 132 mile/h (213 km/h). After the war and for the world championships Guzzi created the Gambalunghino and gained the constructors Championship in 1949, 1951 and 1952. The last title was gained with a machine which developed 27 hp at 8,500 rev/min with four valves. In over-boring a Gambalunghino, Guzzi realised in 1953 a 320 cc which was soon replaced by a true 350 cc developing 33·5 hp at 7,500 rev/min. In its first year of existence this 350 claimed the title. For 1954, the 350 single gained an order of valves with twin overhead-cam. The same principle of distribution was to be applied to the 250 which gained a little power from it, but not enough for the world championship. The 350 continued its brilliant career, with the constructors championship in 1954, 1955 and 1956. In 1957 the Australian, Keith Campbell was world champion. Afterwards, Guzzi retired from competition.

From 1953 to 1957, the 350 cc Guzzi engine had gained exactly 5 hp, but the top speed developed from 124 mile/h (200 km/h) in 1953 to 143 mile/h (230 km/h) in 1957. It was not the five little horsepower that permitted this important gain in speed, but a profound study of the body, of aerodynamics (Guzzi had a wind-tunnel) and a search for lightness. To lessen the midship frame Guzzi put the petrol tank on the engine, and the carburettor was now placed higher than the tank and fed by an electric pump. At the beginning an ingenious system was used with a swinging arm to put this pump into action. By using very light metals Guzzi accomplished a miracle which was expressed by a total weight of 216 lb (98 kg) for the 350 cc. The first multi-

At over 125 mile/h (200 km/h) Findlay, viewed from above.

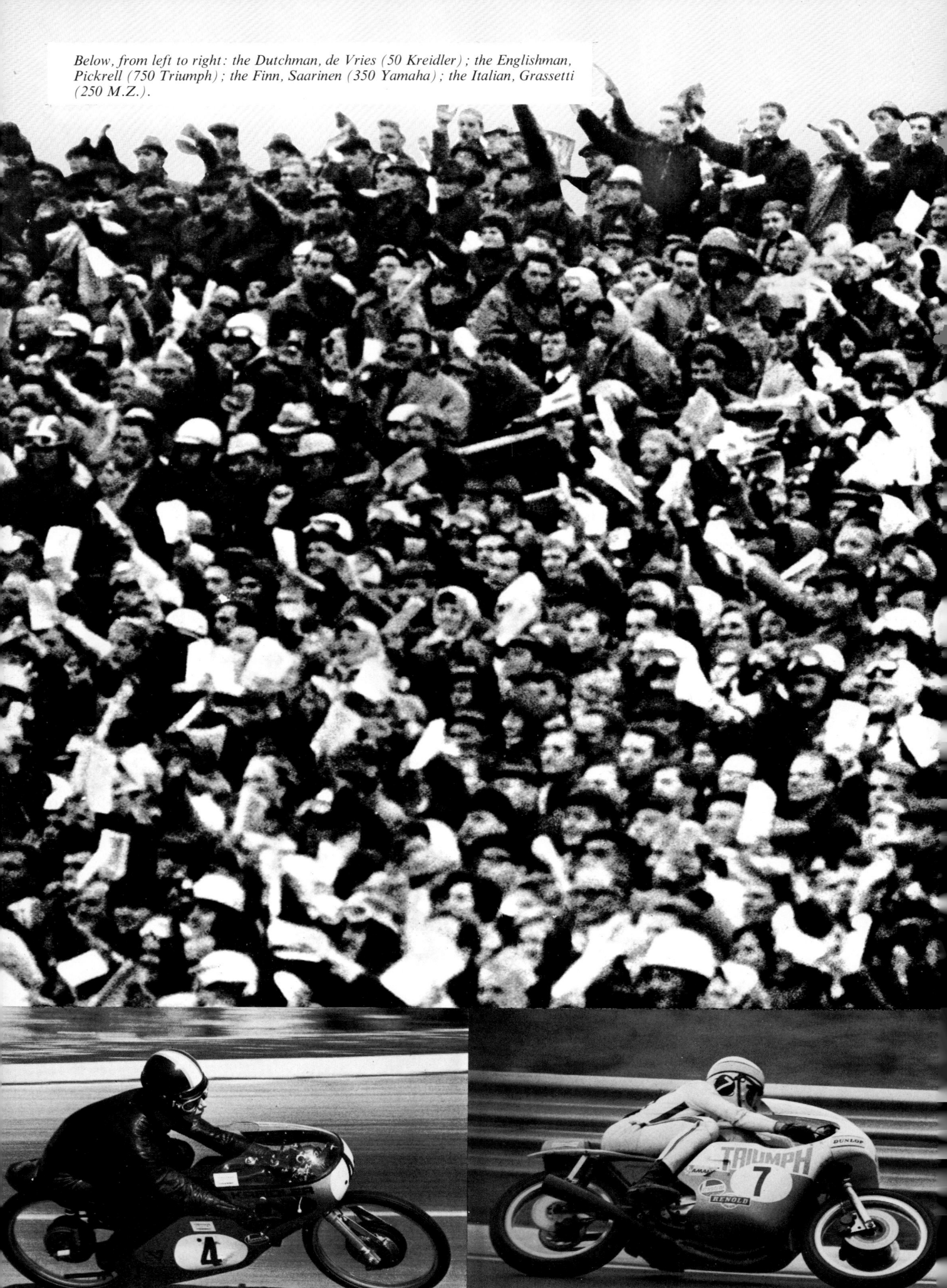

Below, from left to right: the Dutchman, de Vries (50 Kreidler); the Englishman, Pickrell (750 Triumph); the Finn, Saarinen (350 Yamaha); the Italian, Grassetti (250 M.Z.).

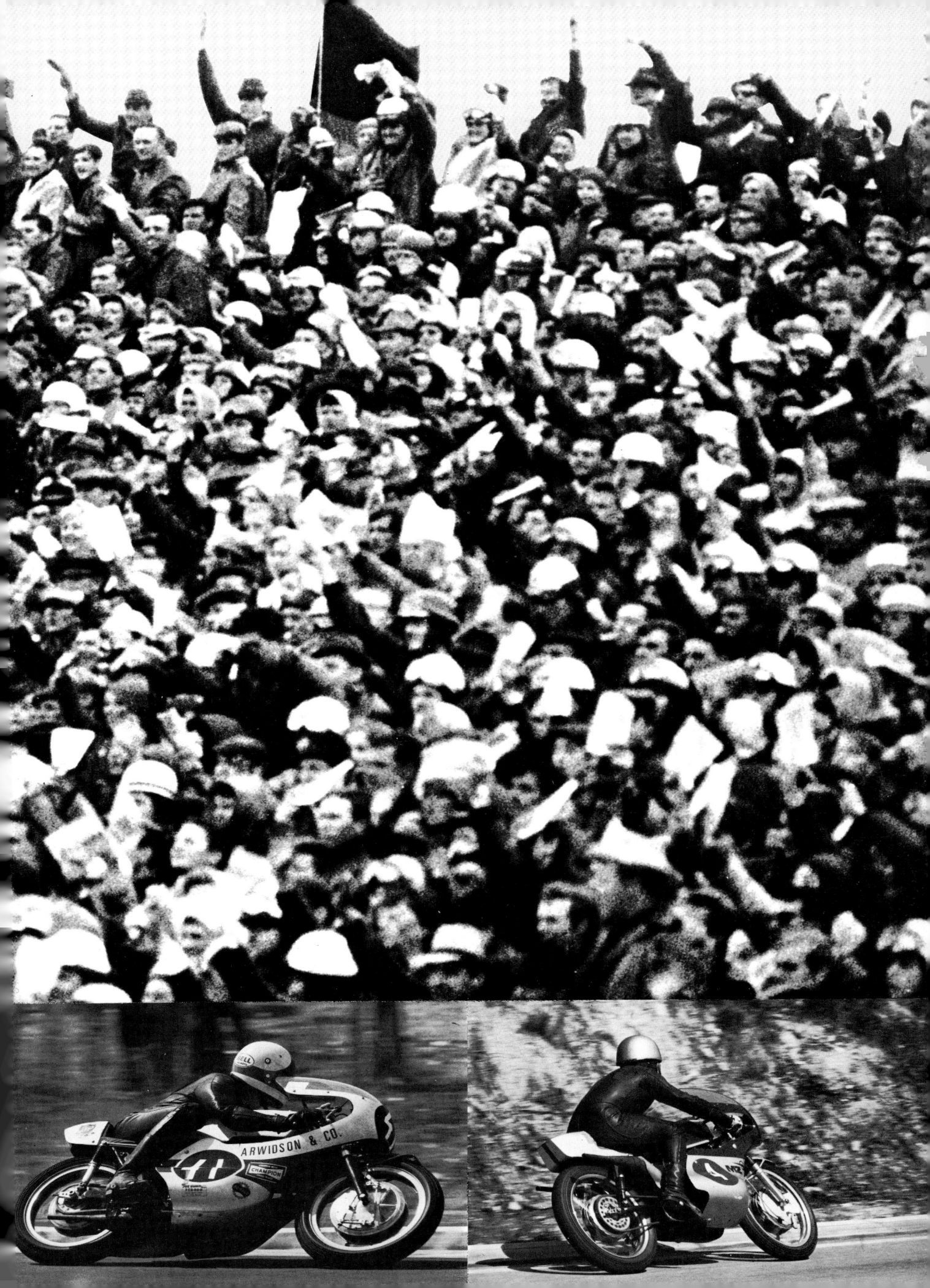

cylinder Guzzi was made in 1930, an experimental four-cylinder water-cooled 500, but in fact the first racing multi-cylinder was made in 1933. Guzzi sought to replace his four-valve single and joined together two 250 cc world championship engines. Generally when two engines are coupled they are put side by side, but this was not the case with Guzzi. The two 250 single overhead-cam engines formed a V wide open at 120°. The engine developed 44 hp at 7,000 rev/min in 1933 (ordinary petrol). In 1935, this Guzzi won the 500 cc T.T.; not since 1911 had the English seen a foreign 500 beat their machines. After the war the Guzzi twin won several Grands Prix but never the championship. In 1951 its power exceeded the 46 hp at 8,000 rev/min, using commercial petrol. During the epoch of the compressor engines (1939–40) Guzzi made a 500 cc three-cylinder with twin overhead-cams. The three cylinders facing the road were tilted towards the front at 45°. Like most of its contemporaries, the Guzzi, souped-up, developed 80 hp. Another model, which had little success, was the 250 twin with double overhead-cams fed by two carburettors. It did gain some records in the Grands Prix of 1947 and 1948.

In 1951, Guzzi made a very unorthodox 500 four. The cylinders were fitted with a double overhead-cam, which was not extraordinary, but they were placed one behind the other, in line, along the frame and were water-cooled. This engine, very much in the automobile style, had shaft transmission and the carburettor was fed by indirect transmission. It developed 53 hp at 9,000 rev/min for a speed of 143 mile/h (230 km/h). Its performance continued to improve until 1954, the year when Guzzi unveiled its even more extraordinary engine, an eight-cylinder 500. This engine was composed of two groups of four cylinders in an open V of 90°. Each range of cylinders possessed two overhead-cams controlled by a cascade of pinions and each cylinder was fed by a carburettor. The gearbox held six gears. The first eight-cylinder version developed 65 hp at 12,000 rev/min, the second, in 1957, approached 80 hp and the speed slightly exceeded 174 mile/h (280 km/h) with an integral fairing. Like the 500 fours, the true potential of the eight was never achieved and, like many other Guzzi racing machines, was the work of the engineer Giulio Carcano. The year 1969 marked the return to competition of the Guzzis in the sense of speed records. It does not seem that Guzzi intended to challenge the world speed champions, but rather the 24-hour races of endurance using machines derived from the series of 750 Guzzi V7.

MV. The last great Italian mark and only one that did not announce its retirement in 1957. MV, when it was only its own concern, had gathered world champion titles since 1952, and in 1969 it had reached its thirtieth (seven in 125, five in 250, six in 350 and twelve in 500).

The factories which competed for the world championships swallowed up fortunes in their racing careers, but on the other hand the publicity so gained helped to sell their current machines. For MV it was not the same, because the current production was almost negligible and the publicity was reflected in the manufacture of MV helicopters—and also made famous the name of their creator, the Count Agusta. The first MV racing machines (Meccanica Verghera) in 1948 were the 125 two-strokes which had already won the small national races in Italy. In 1950 the first four-stroke was made, a 125 single with a twin overhead-cam driven by a cascade of pinions. This engine developed 12 hp at 10,000 rev/min. In 1952 three more hp were produced at 10,800 rev/min and MV won its first title. After being eclipsed by the superior N.S.U. for a year MV came back in strength in 1954 and announced 18 hp at 11,000 rev/min and more than 110 mile/h (180 km/h) for the 125. This was the beginning of a whole series of victories. In 1956 the 125 with an integral fairing gained another 2 hp and 12 mile/h (20 km/h). After 1957 MV had no competitors worthy of mention until 1961, the date of the arrival of the Hondas. To build the 250, MV has not made any great problems for itself. It was enough to reconstruct the same engine as the 125 but with a greater capacity in the case of the 203 cc which gained its first title in the 250 class in 1955. This "little" 250 developed 26 hp at 11,000 rev/min. The following year the capacity of the engine was augmented to 249 cc for a power of 30 hp. With the withdrawal of the Italian competition in 1957, MV remained alone and had no difficulty in gaining the victories. For this, the single would have sufficed, but MV produced in 1959 a 250 based on the coupling of two 125 cc. This machine reached 137 mile/h (220 km/h) thanks to a power of 37 hp at 12,500 rev/min. It gained the title in 1959 and 1960.

Ten years earlier, MV had produced the 500 four. In its first version, this engine, a conventional double overhead-cam four with its cylinders facing to the road, developed 50 hp at 9,000 rev/min. The transmission was by shaft drive. In 1952 the shaft transmission was replaced by a chain and the power increased to 10 hp. The MV did not lack power, but the frame left much to be desired. Happily the ex-official rider of A.J.S., Leslie Graham, modified it considerably. Unfortunately however he was killed in 1953 during the 500 race at the T.T. The same year MV produced the 350 four, in some way a scaled-down model of the 500. In 1956, MV engaged John Surtees who continued Graham's work. His first win in 1956 was easy as Gilera, the great rival of MV, did not compete in all the championship races. After the last brilliant flash of the Gileras in 1957, MV remained alone on the track, it seemed that these powerful fours (more than 70 hp) were invincible. The same thing applied to the 350, but there the domination of the MV came to an end with the arrival of the Japanese in 1963. The 500 was unchallenged until 1966. Mike Hailwood had taken the role of John Surtees who had moved on to cars. In 1966 Hailwood was invited by Honda to ride the 500 Japanese machine which he rode to victory, and the constructor's championship. The championship of the riders returned again to MV, thanks to Giacomo Agostini who rode a completely new MV, a three-cylinder. The first three-cylinder with twin overhead-cam was not more powerful than the old four-cylinder, but a perfect frame allowed it to make full use of all its horsepower. Again in 1967, MV dominated Honda which gave up competition at the end of the season. In 1968–69 Agostini had no real rivals and carried off all the Grand Prix events in which he participated. The 1969 version of the 500 MV three with four valves per cylinder developed 80 hp at 13,000 rev/min and had a speed of 168 mile/h (270 km/h). The 350 was yet another miniature copy of the 500, it developed 60 hp at 13,500 rev/min and could reach 155 mile/h (250 km/h). MV had won world championship titles since 1952. In 1972 it had achieved its thirty-sixth (seven in 125, five in 250, nine in 350 and fifteen in 500). In 1972 the domination of the MV was not so all-embracing as in previous years, and if the 500 remained queen of the category, the 350 three was itself outclassed until MV brought out its 350 four, which developed 70 hp at 14,800 rev/min. In this category the four-stroke seemed to be more and more threatened. It needed all Agostini's talent for MV to retain its title in the 1973 350 class. The following year, MV did not take part in this category, in order to devote itself to the 500 four with which it again secured the crown. Its power then exceeded 100 hp. In 1975, confronted with Yamaha, and especially Suzuki, the MV lacked performance and was cursed with disastrous roadholding ability.

HONDA. The first Japanese make to be interested in the world championships was Honda. Already in 1959 the 125 cc Honda machines were at the T.T., where they were placed sixth, seventh and eighth. All the competing machines were present at the finish except one (an American) which had fallen. Technically, the 125 seemed very sophisticated compared with the rest of the competitors. They had two cylinders, a twin overhead-cam, four valves per cylinder, twin ignition, but only achieved 18·5 hp at 14,000 rev/min (as a reminder, the MV single of the time produced more than 20). In 1959, in Japan only, there appeared a 250 double overhead-cam four with, as on the 125, a shaft drive on the right side of the engine and four valves per cylinder. The power was announced as 35 hp at 14,000 rev/min. In 1960, Honda completely rebuilt its racing machines. The 125 had still two cylinders and the 250, four, but the control of the twin overhead-cam was made by a central gear train. These new Hondas, which made a brief appearance in Europe, were geared respectively to 20 hp at 13,500 rev/min and 40 hp at 13,000 rev/min. In 1961, the Hondas were powerful enough to gain the championship in the 125 and 250 classes (21 hp for the 125 and 42 hp for the 250), and for even more impact the Japanese firm gave the competition over to the best riders of the time: McIntyre, Hailwood, Taveri, Hartle and Phillis. For the first time in 1961, Honda won the 125 and 250 championships, and by 1967 these two titles had been followed by sixteen others. The year 1962 saw the creation of the 50 cc category: Honda was interested in it and produced a twin overhead-cam single with four valves geared to 10 hp at 14,000 rev/min for a speed of 87 miles/h (140 km/h). However, opposed to the two-stroke Suzuki, this machine was not competitive. Throughout 1962, Honda set its heart upon the 350 category. To obtain this capacity the competition service bored out a 250 to 285 cc. It won the title ridden by a newcomer to Honda, Jim Redman. In 1963, Honda was beaten by Suzuki in the 50 and 125 classes but Redman regained the 250 and 350 titles. These last 340 cc machines were geared to 50 hp at 12,500 rev/min for a maximum speed of 143 mile/h (230 km/h).

To compete against the two-strokes of small capacity, Honda produced in 1964 a 125 twin overhead-cam four with four valves per cylinder and eight speeds. This 125 cc, estimated to have a speed in excess of 124 mile/h (200 km/h), was geared to 25 hp at 16,000 rev/min. The 250 four was held at bay by the 250 Yamaha twin. In order to regain the 50 cc title, Honda produced a mechanical jewel, a 50 cc twin with twin overhead-cams and four valves per cylinder and a gearbox with ten gears. This little engine turned with the frightening speed of 20,000 rev/min to produce 15 hp and drove the machine at 103 mile/h (165 km/h). In 1965 the 50 cc won, but the 125 and 250 were beaten by the two-stroke twins.

The Honda team: above, 50 cc twin,
250 cc six-cylinder; below, 125 cc five-cylinder,
500 cc four-cylinder.

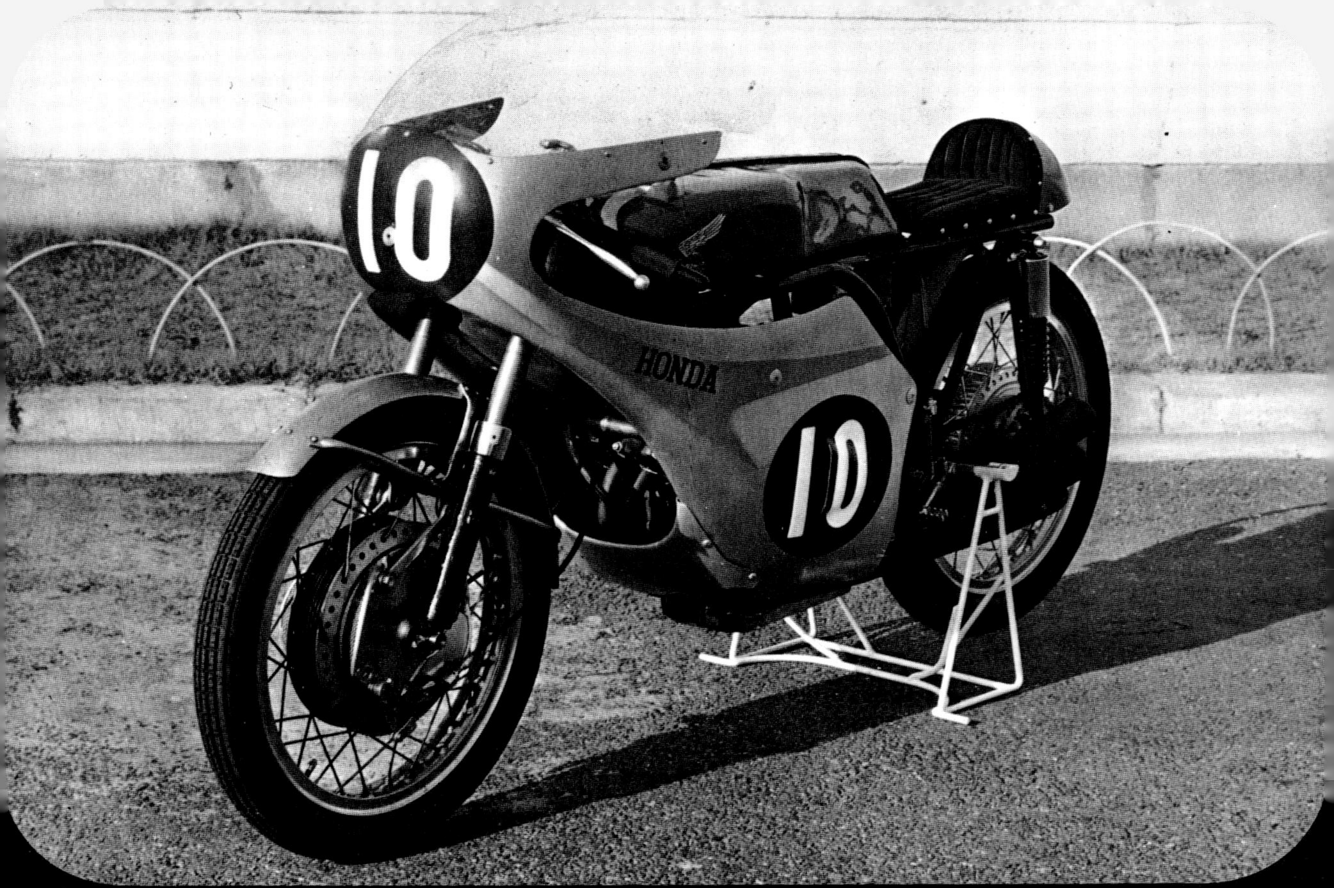
10
HONDA
10

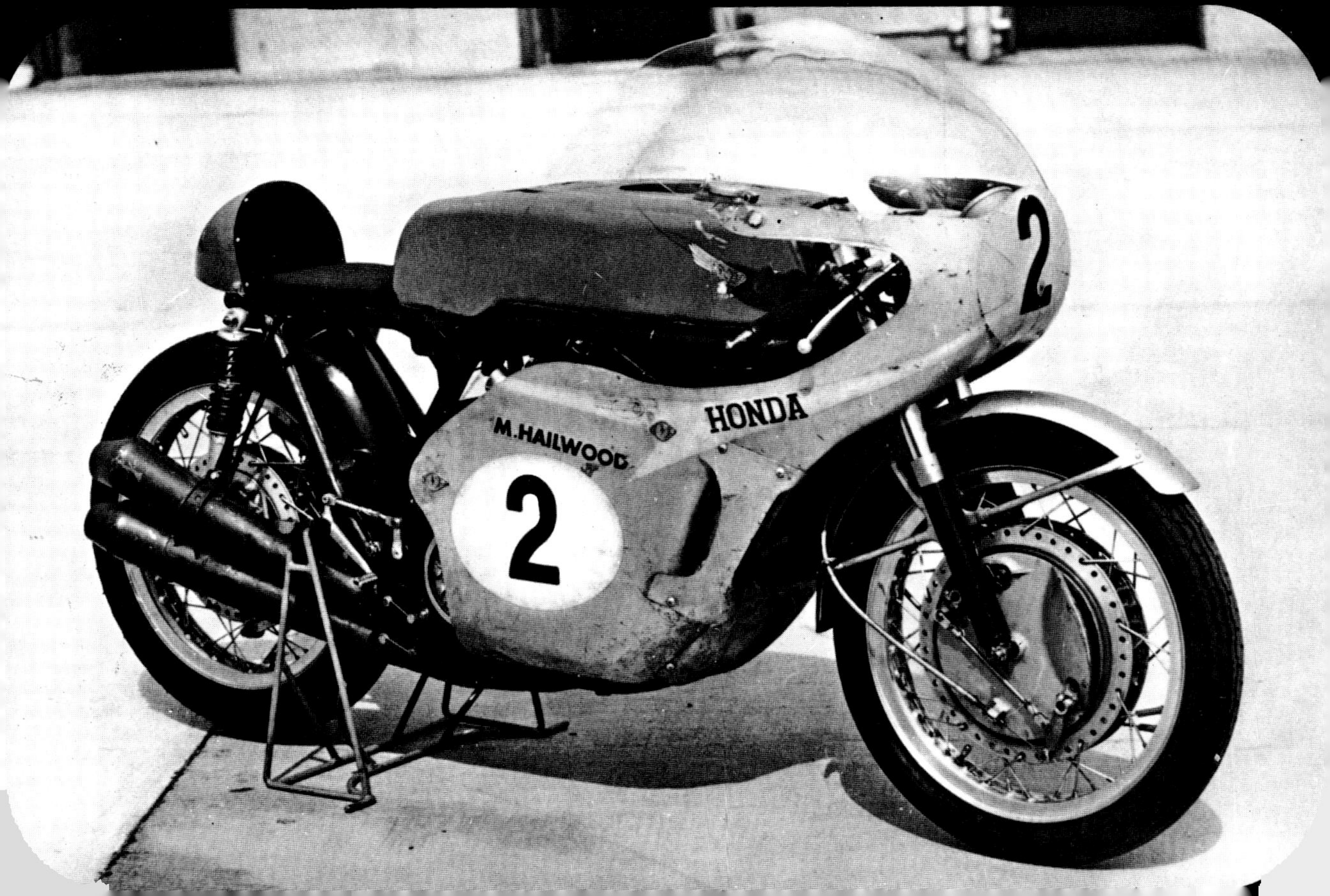
2
HONDA
M. HAILWOOD
2

Above: 50 cc Suzuki twin, 250 M.Z. twin.
Below: 250 Ossa single, 250 Yamaha four

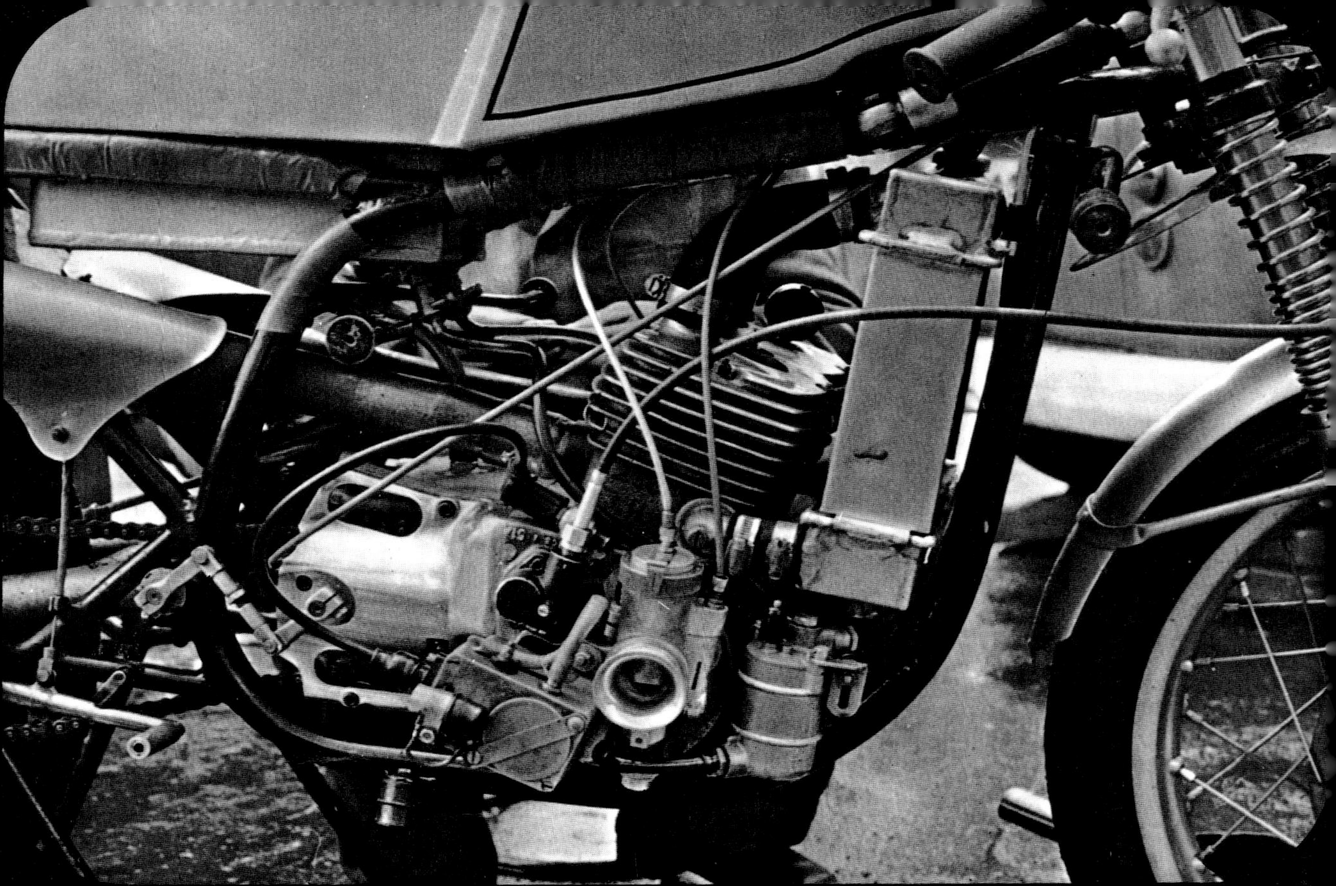

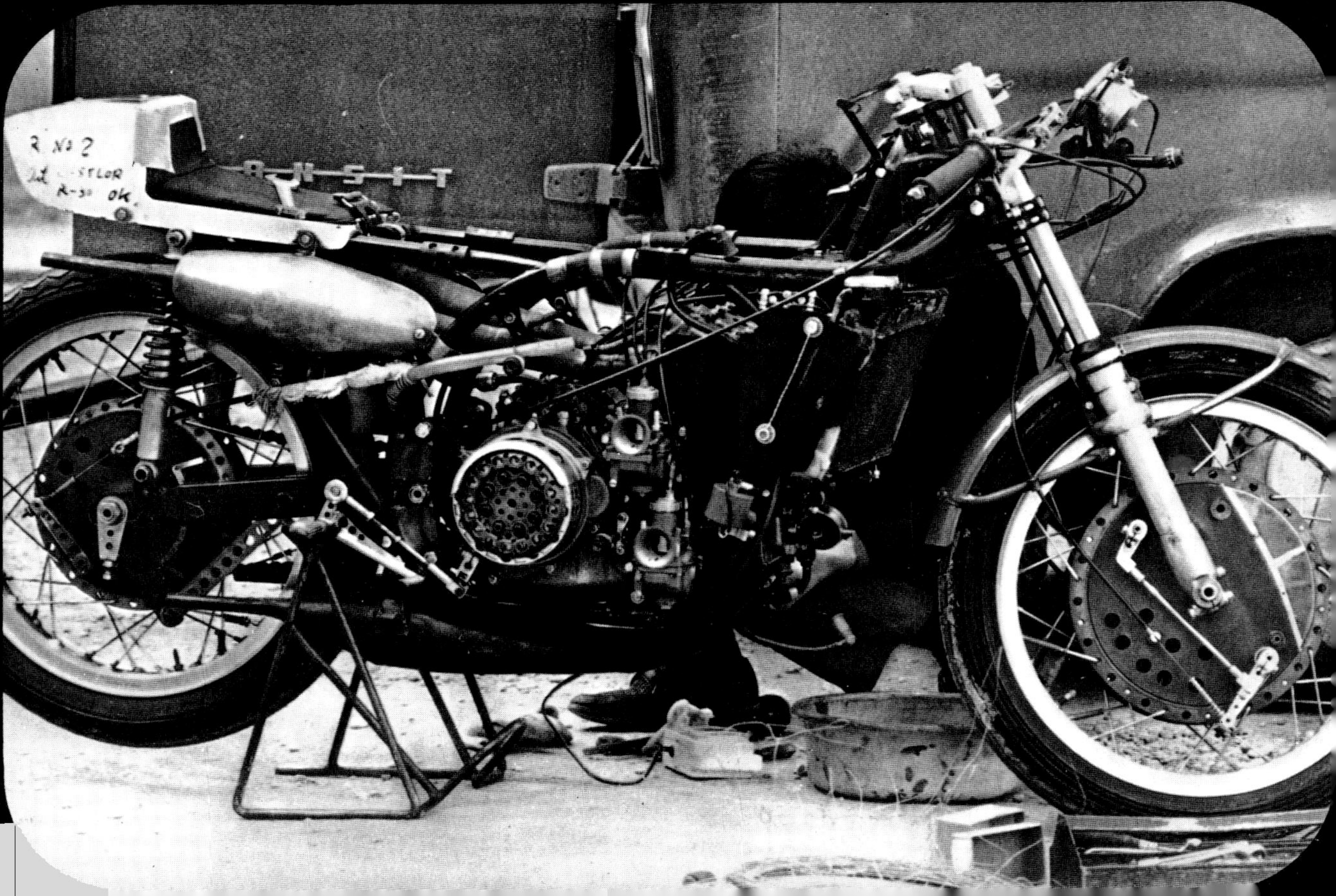
R No 2
OK

The unconquerable 500 MV, four- and three-cylinder.

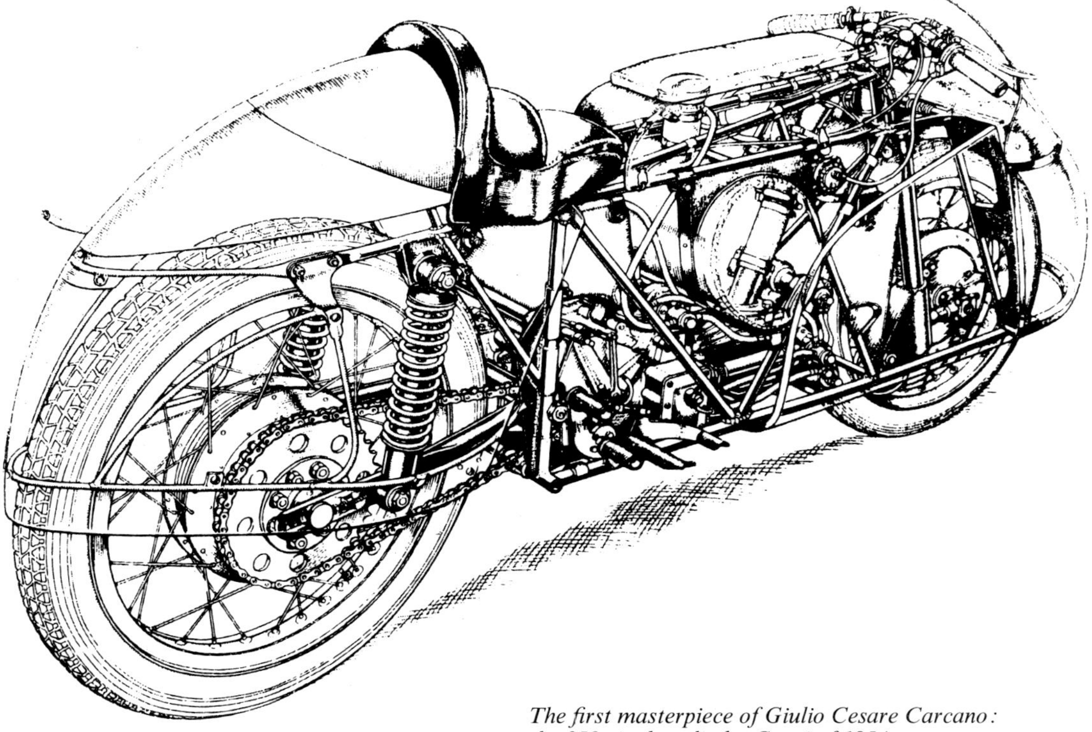

The first masterpiece of Giulio Cesare Carcano:
the 350 single-cylinder Guzzi of 1954.

The second masterpiece of Carcano, the 500 cc eight-cylinder
Guzzi of 1957.

The year 1966 marked the zenith of the Honda's reign at the Grands Prix. The works drivers were: Ralph Bryans and Luigi Taveri for the 50 cc and 125 cc, and Mike Hailwood was responsible for the 250, 350 and 500. The 50 cc twin was geared to 16 hp at 22,000 rev/min for 110 mile/h (180 km/h). The 125, completely new, had five cylinders, still the twin overhead-cam and four valves per cylinder; it was geared to 30 hp at 18,000 rev/min and exceeded 124 mile/h (200 km/h). The 250 was also new and it was a six-cylinder twin overhead-cam, four valves per cylinder, six speeds, geared to 54 hp at 17,000 rev/min and timed in the T.T. at 143 mile/h (230 km/h). The 350 remained with four cylinders, but it was geared to 60 hp. Finally, the enormous 500 four-double overhead-cam with four valves per cylinder claimed a power of 85 hp at 12,000 rev/min and a peak speed of 168 mile/h (270 km/h). The frame of this bike never equalled the power of the engine and Mike Hailwood had to fight hard to bring back the title to Honda. In 1966 then, Honda was world champion for constructors in the 50, 125, 250, 350 and 500 classes. From now on Honda had nothing to prove and retired from competition at the end of the 1967 season after gaining the 250 and 350 titles. For this last, the machine used was a 250 six-cylinder bored out to 292 cc, which gave it a power of 64 hp at 17,000 rev/min. Just like Guzzi, Honda interested itself in competition from the angle of endurance tests which the 750 four, contested, using machines directly derived from mass-produced ones.

SUZUKI. The second Japanese factory to follow Honda in Europe was Suzuki, which appeared at the T.T. of 1960 with the 125 twin. Just as the Honda was the desperate defender of the four-strokes, so the Suzuki was that of the two-strokes. The first competition models of the Suzuki were the 50 cc, which won the championship of this new cubic capacity in 1962. The engine, an air-cooled single and supplied by one rotary valve, was geared to 10 hp at 11,000 rev/min. It required very little improvement and this little single easily overcame the attacks of the 50 cc Honda in 1965. At Honda's announcement of the production of a 50 cc twin, Suzuki also constructed a two-stroke twin supplied by two rotary valves and water-cooled. This engine, which had a gearbox with twelve gears, was geared to 16 hp at 18,000 rev/min and was propelled at 105 mile/h (170 km/h).

In 1966, using this machine, the German Anscheidt won the riders' world championship, the constructors' title going to the twin Honda. Like Honda, Suzuki announced its retirement at

the end of 1967. During that last year of "official" racing the twin 50 Suzuki was geared to 18 hp at 18,000 rev/min and on the Spa circuit had a top speed of almost 118 mile/h (190 km/h). The gearbox enclosed a record number of fourteen gears. In 1968 Anscheidt, who had kept a 50 twin for his own use, won the championship. The first 125 racing Suzukis in 1960 had two cylinders (air-cooled) supplied by two rotary valves. Under the direction of the engineer-racer Ernest Degner (ex-official of M.Z.) this machine achieved speeds fast enough in 1962 to worry the Hondas and finally beat them in 1963. Then the twin Suzuki was geared to 22 hp at 11,000 rev/min and the top speed verged on 118 mile/h (190 km/h). To give competition to the 125 Honda four which was champion in 1964, Suzuki built a completely new twin two-stroke water-cooled engine and equipped it with a gearbox of nine gears. The RT64A of 1965 was geared to 30 hp at 14,000 rev/min and regained the 125 cc title. The year 1966 saw a new domination by Honda then it was the turn of the Yamahas in 1967 and 1968. Suzuki tried its hand at a 250 with two air-cooled cylinders supplied by two rotary valves. In 1961, this machine was geared to 37 hp at 11,000 rev/min to reach 42 hp with the same performance the following year.

In 1963, Suzuki launched into the construction of a 250, four-cylinder two-stroke once more. The four cylinders were placed in a square and each required a feed by rotary valve. The cylinder block was water-cooled and the gearbox had six gears. This very powerful 250 (55 hp at 12,000 rev/min) was unfortunately beset with many mechanical faults and Suzuki did not pursue the project. In 1969 two 125 ex-factory Suzukis, bought by private riders, finished in second and third place in the world championship in their category, and the following year, the German, Dieter Braun, still on an ex-factory 125 cc was crowned world champion. From now onwards Suzuki was mainly interested in the American races, such as the Daytona 200, and for this the factory built racers, of 500 cc derived from the standard model, then the 750 cc was used. The racing version of the standard 750 G.T. was tuned to about 120 hp and was capable of achieving 174 mile/h (280 km/h). Then tyre problems arose. In 1974, Suzuki made a re-appearance in the world championship 500 class with a four-cylinder, two-stroke water-cooled engine. This engine developed more than 100 hp and was the most powerful of that year. It kept its advantage in the following year, but is still proving too fragile.

YAMAHA is certainly, along with M.Z., the

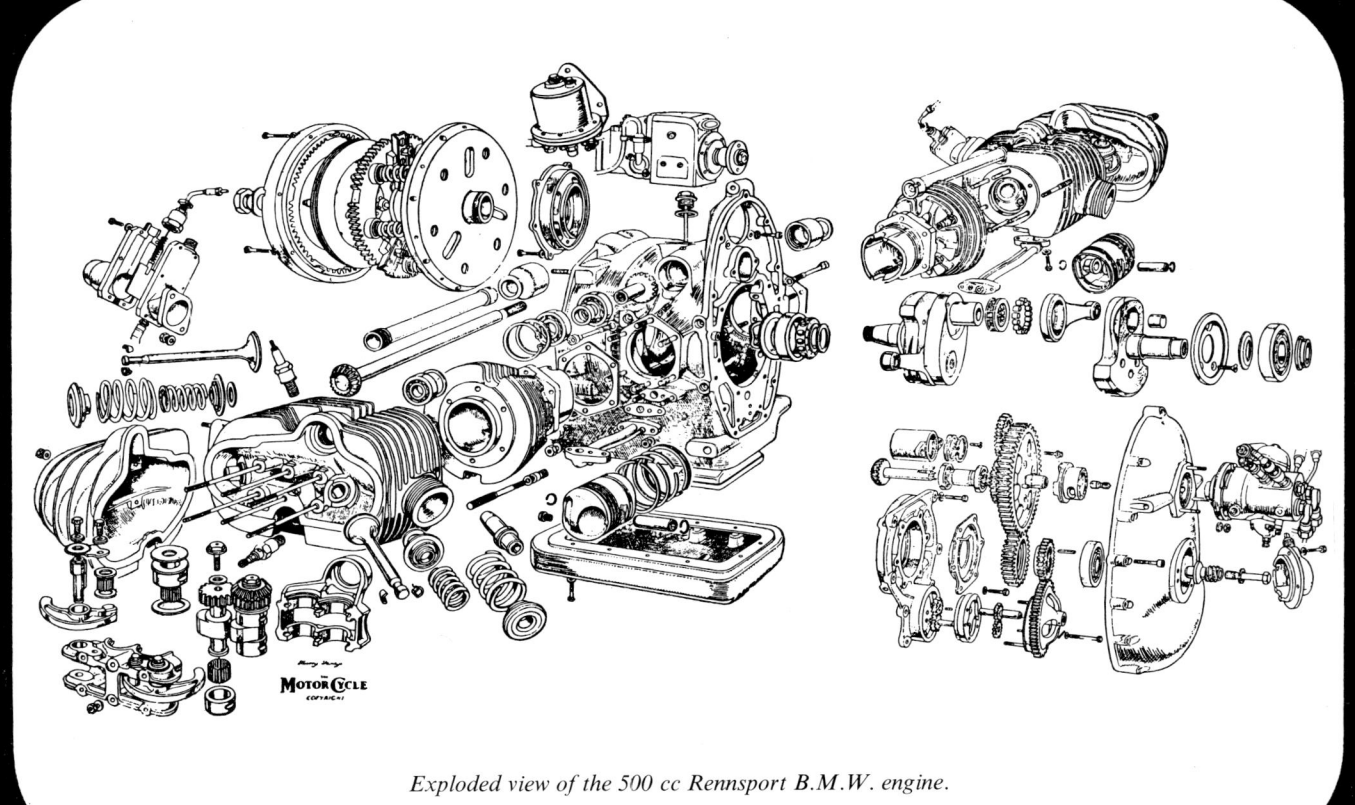

Exploded view of the 500 cc Rennsport B.M.W. engine.

make which has most improved the two-stroke competition engine. Yamaha did not choose the T.T. to make its entry into Europe, but the French Grand Prix in 1961.

During this Grand Prix, the Yamahas 125 and 250, both air-cooled twins and supplied by two rotary valves finished in eighth position. After a year of intensive work, Yamaha returned to Europe in 1963. In its essentials the 250 bike had not changed, it was still simple and conventional, but packed tight with horsepower (47 hp at 13,000 rev/min) which gave it a peak performance of 143 mile/h (230 km/h). With the RD56 (the name of this new 250) the Japanese rider, Fumio Ito, won the Belgian Grand Prix, beating the Honda four with a new record. In 1964 Yamaha engaged Phil Read and Mike Duff. The former gained five victories in Grands Prix and the 250 title. The RD56 gained the title again in 1965, but the arrival of the six-cylinder Honda forced the Yamaha racing service to make a new 250. This was a four-cylinder two-stroke placed two by two forming a V of 90° opening towards the front. The four cylinders were water-cooled

and supplied by four rotary valves; the gearbox had eight gears and the first version of this machine was geared to 58 hp at 14,000 rev/min for a maximum speed of 149 mile/h (240 km/h). In 1967 Yamaha engaged Bill Ivy as well as Read, but neither of them were able to beat the Honda six, or rather Hailwood.

The last racing year for Yamaha was 1968. The 250 four was announced at a power approaching 70 hp at 14,400 rev/min, and its top speed was now more than 155 mile/h (250 km/h). As with the Honda 500, this enormous power was not fully employed because of a "frame" failure. The evolution of the 125 Yamaha followed exactly the same pattern as that of the 250. Before 1965, the two-stroke 125 twin was air-cooled. In 1965 a water-cooling system appeared on this 125 which developed 30 hp at 14,000 rev/min and had nine gears. The top speed registered at the T.T. was more than 125 mile/h (200 km/h). Not satisfied with these performances, Yamaha, in 1966, built an exact replica of the 250 four but at 125 cc. This machine gained the world championship in 1967 and 1968. To gain the latter title

The 500 cc Gilera four-cylinder of 1954.

The Norton double overhead-cam, with "Featherbed" frame of 1950–51.

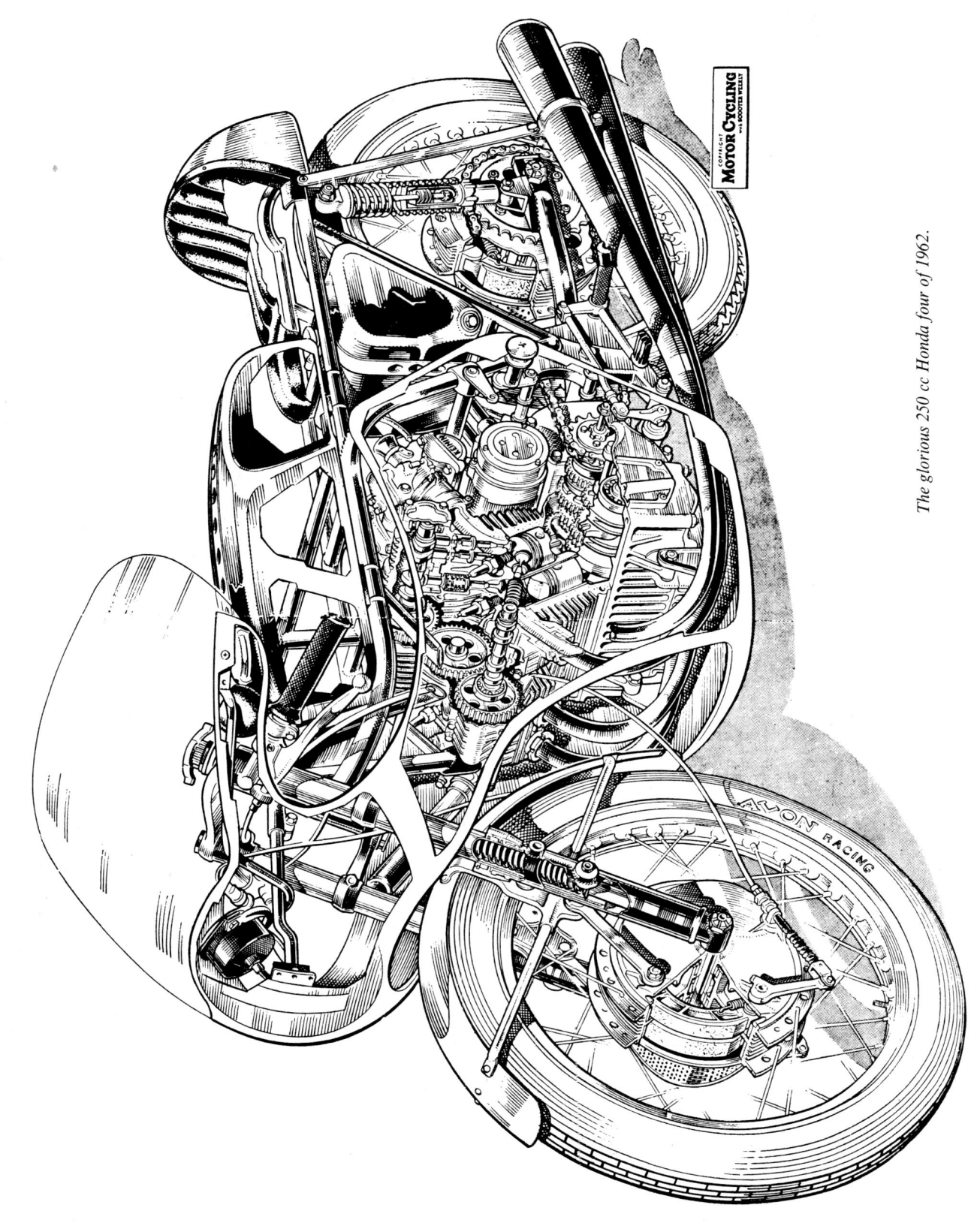

The glorious 250 cc Honda four of 1962.

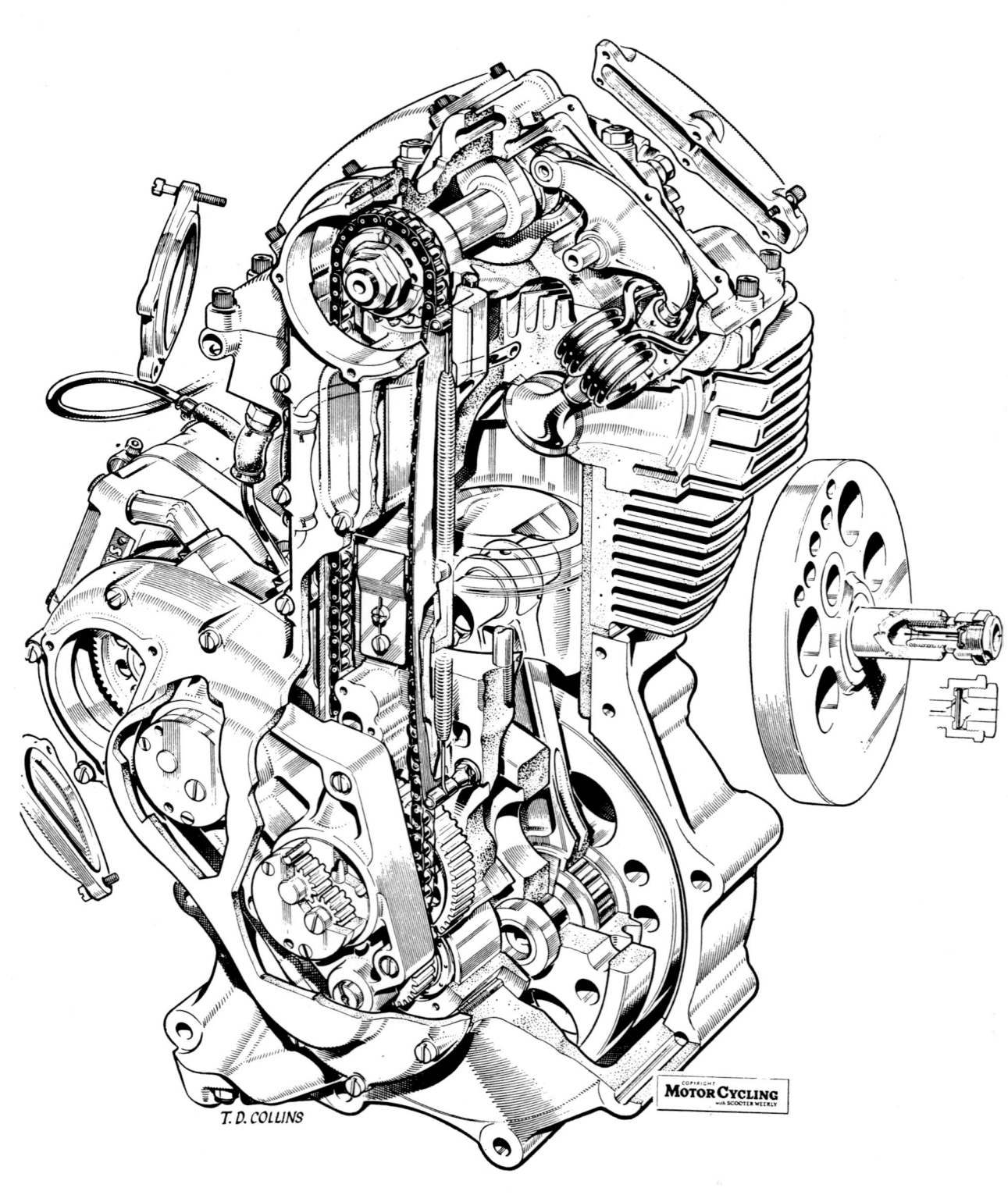

T. D. COLLINS

*The single overhead-cam engine of the A.J.S. "7R", the G50
is an identical design.*

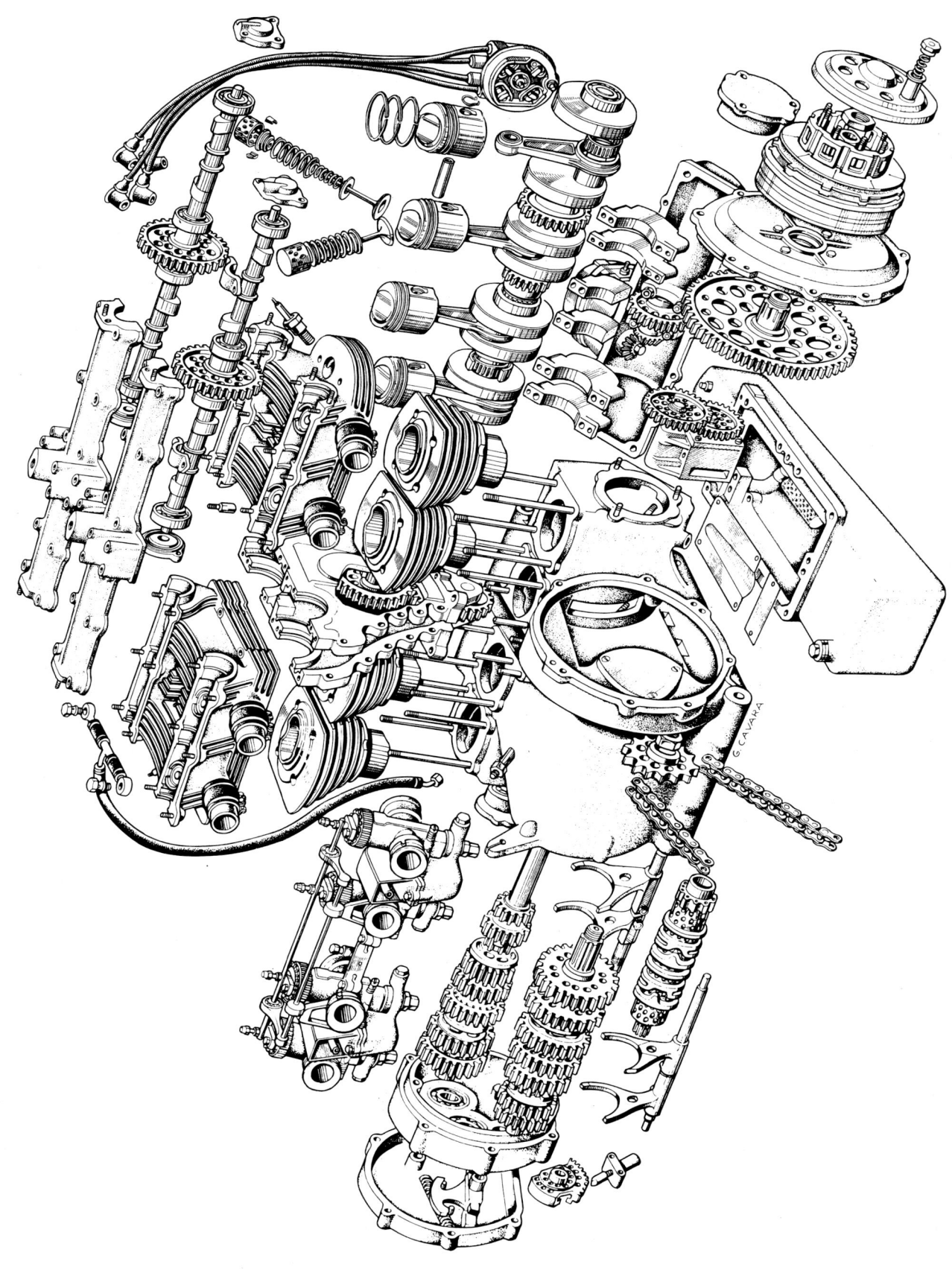

The four-cylinder 250 cc Benelli of 1965.

(*Drawings reproduced with the kind authorisation of Edisport, Milan.*)

The champions of the "teacup"-sized motorcycles (50 cc): the German Anscheidt (Suzuki); the Spaniard Nieto (Kreidler).

this little machine developed 40 hp at 18,000 rev/min and was capable of nearly 133 mile/h (215 km/h). With these fours Yamaha obtained the highest specific powers that had ever been registered in their respective cubic capacity. With new rules limiting the number of cylinders, it is unlikely that any machine will rob them of this record.

Yamaha has not completely abandoned racing. Along with the factory programme Yamaha has put on the market some machines for the private entrant (all two-stroke twins with two carburettors) which have had great success. It should be added that they are mechanically extraordinary. The 125 developed 24 hp at 11,000 rev/min, the 250 44 hp at 10,000 rev/min and the 350, 54 hp at 9,500 rev/min. Their top speeds were respectively 110 mile/h (180 km/h), 130 mile/h (210 km/h) and 139 mile/h (225 km/h). In 1970 the rule to limit the number of cylinders in the 250 category to two was put into effect. It was a windfall for Yamaha which renewed its victories in 1971 and 1972. In the second year Yamaha, semi-officially, had put water-cooled engines in its 125, 250 and 350 machines. Apart from the cooling system, they were identical to the competition and it was with one of these machines that Jarno Saarinen of Finland was world champion in the 250 class, and seriously threatened the MV of Agostini in the 350. The water-cooled Yamahas developed about 55 hp and 65 hp, respectively. In 1973 Yamaha officially entered competition again, with a 250 twin, which developed more than 55 hp with a weight less than 220 lb (100 kg), and a 500 cc two-stroke water-cooled four, twice as powerful as the 250 and able to beat the MV. These machines were ridden by Hideo Kanaya and Jarno Saarinen who dominated the world championships in these two categories . . . till the tragic accident at Monza. For 1974, Yamaha recruited Giacomo Agostini, who easily carried off the 350 title, but was beaten in the 500 class by Read on an MV. The new 500 Yamaha four was not completely in tune.

KAWASAKI was the last Japanese make to take an interest in racing and even then not a very serious one. In 1965, in the Japanese Grand Prix, a long string of Kawasakis presented themselves on the starting grid. There were four or five 125 cc two-stroke fours. Perhaps they did not achieve the expected results—in any case they were seen no more. For this Japanese Grand Prix there were not only the 125 fours but also water-cooled twins fitted with two rotary valves. One of these machines was entrusted to the Englishman, Dave Simmonds, who in some way, was the only

Kawasaki representative in the Grands Prix. As long as Suzuki and Yamaha ran officially the Kawasaki had no chance of winning. At last, in 1969, Dave Simmonds won the championship hands down, with eight Grands Prix. His machine had not altered since 1966, but still developed 30 hp at 14,000 rev/min and could reach 118 mile/h (190 km/h). Kawasaki, like Yamaha, was concerned with selling the racer. Its latest production in this line was a 500 cc version of the fantastic three-cylinder road machine. A power rating of 75 hp at 9,000 rev/min was announced for this racer, giving a top speed of more than 150 mile/h (240 km/h). Remember that at the beginning the Kawasaki three developed 60 hp. At the time of the emergence of the 750 Tourer a racing version appeared which contested the Daytona 200 in 1972. This machine, like the 750 Suzuki, developed 100 hp. In 1975, Kawasaki adopted a water-cooling system for its three-cylinder 500 cc and 750 cc machines, but the 500 cc still lacks power. The year 1975 also saw the appearance of a 250 cc with two water-cooled cylinders aligned one behind the other producing more than 60 hp.

To end this condensed history of the makes of racing motorcycles the Spanish machines must be briefly mentioned.

BULTACO made itself known by the world records gained in 1960 with a 175 cc single. The two-stroke engine was supplied by a conventional carburettor. In keeping this style of engine, Bultaco made no attempt to rival the Japanese multis. Moreover, the Spanish factory tended to aim more at private riders who wanted a simple machine with very little upkeep. The Bultaco "competition client" (private entrant) models created a furore in 125 and 250 classes, in 1967. They were water-cooled singles supplied by a carburettor. In order to continually improve its "client" models, Bultaco officially raced some factory machines. In 1969, the 125 "factory" model developed 30 hp at 12,000 rev/min, the 250 30 hp at 9,800 rev/min and the 350 45 hp.

DERBI is the 50 cc Spanish special. Already in 1965 this make competed in the world championship, but it had little hope of success against the combined Japanese factories. However, as these factories retired from racing, Derbi came nearer to gaining the victories. In 1969, Derbi had only two worthwhile adversaries left—the Kreidler and the Jamathi. The former had known its hours of glory in 1963–64, when Kreidler disputed the title with Suzuki. The 1969 models were recruited by Kreidler in Holland. The

Jamathi is a much more recent production. It is the work of three Dutch workmen, who made their machine in imitation of an ex-factory Suzuki. In 1968 the Jamathi, ridden by Lodewijkx won the Dutch Grand Prix. In 1969, the Jamathi had a power of 14 hp at 14,000 rev/min, its engine being water-cooled. The 1969 season, which saw the application of the new formula (one cylinder and six speeds) for the 50 cc class, was strongly contested. The first Grands Prix were largely dominated by the Kreidler. Halfway through the season the new Derbi appeared developing 15·5 hp at 14,500 rev/min. The engines had the peculiarity of possessing water-cooling for the cylinder, the block . . . and the crankcases of the engine.

Right up to the last Grand Prix, Jamathi, Kreidler and Derbi devoted themselves to a merciless fight. Derbi finally emerged the winner and for the first time in the history of the sport a Spanish machine ridden by a Spaniard (Angel Nieto) won the world championship. In other fields, Derbi was still trying to perfect a two-stroke twin with two rotary valves. The two water-cooled cylinders were sharply angled towards the road. This machine developed 32 hp at 14,000 rev/min in 1970. The following year it won the world championship again and repeated it in 1972, again ridden by the famous Angel Nieto. In its last version, the Derbi developed 40 hp at 15,000 rev/min, almost as much as the extraordinary 125 Yamaha four in 1968. The 50 cc Derbi single was very similar to the 50 cc Suzuki twin which developed 18 hp at 18,000 rev/min. Francisco Tombias, the inventor of the Derbis, also produced a 250 very similar to the 125 and developing 61 hp at 12,500 rev/min.

OSSA. The 250 Ossa was a phenomenal machine: it had an air-cooled cylinder, a rotary valve and a six-speed gearbox. Consequently it was extremely simple mechanically, but nevertheless it still held the lead over the Italian double over-head-cam four and the Japanese twins. During the 1969 season, the Ossa, ridden by Santiago Herrero won three Grands Prix and led the championship class until the last race when a fall by Herrero ruined all the hopes for the tiny Spanish stable. Could an équipe, only composed of one machine, one rider, one mechanic and an engineer who had built the engine, really be called a stable? The head of this mini-stable was Eduardo Giro, the engineer who created Ossa. In 1963, when he had not yet completed his studies, Giro amused himself by drawing a racing motorcycle. Feature by feature this design was that of the 1969 engine, but at the time Giro had no possibility of constructing it. When it is

considered that this two-stroke single developed 42 hp at 10,000 rev/min with a speed approaching 137 mile/h (220 km/h) and that it had been thought of in 1963, it can be appreciated what a tremendous achievement it was.

THE CHASSIS. The technical evolution of racing machines was mainly centred on engine development and to a lesser extent the construction of the other parts.

At the beginning of the century, the frames of motorcycles were very much like those of bicycles, consisting of three tubes soldered into a triangle. Then, to house the steadily enlarging engines, these tubes were cut, separated and bolted down onto the front and back of the engine, and so the frame with single bearer plates was born. Until about 1930 most racing machines had a frame with single broken-bearer plates. Certain makes, such as Ducati, remained faithful to this kind of frame. The frame with simple bearer plates split into two tubes under the engine appeared in 1931 with the Norton machines and at the same time N.S.U., Velocette, Benelli and Bianchi adapted it. The frame with double bearer plates split under the engine was not used much; among the adepts were Jawa and CZ in 1960. For thirty years, the frame of the great majority of racing machines has been the double bearer plate. This is in fact two single bearer plates, unsplit, placed side by side, and joined together by a certain number of cross pins. Sometimes the upper part of this frame is made of two parallel tubes, sometimes of one big tube, and sometimes of a trellis, as on the Guzzi. The most important makes which used a double bearer plate were: A.J.S. with the Porcupine, B.M.W. from the time it entered racing; D.K.W. from 1930; CZ, M.Z., N.S.U. in 1951; Norton, which in 1951, produced the celebrated "Featherbed"; Benelli since 1951; Bianchi since 1955; Gilera in 1939; MV since its début; Mondial in 1948; Morini on the Rebello in 1960; Kawasaki, Paton, Bultaco, Derbi, Yamaha, certain Suzuki models (125 and 250) and Honda (250 of 1962 and 500).

On the majority of its models, Honda used the frame with "suspended" engine. This was a double bearer plate the two tubes of which "descending" were cut a little below the steering column to rejoin just at the back of the engine block. So, the engine was suspended at the level of the cylinder by the two stumps of the tube and fixed on to the back of the two tubes going up again off the frame. This design of frame was employed by Suzuki for the 50 cc. The technique of the suspended engine was rediscovered for the Aermacchi, but there, the upper part of the frame was formed by a big beam bent down towards the back. This beam could be replaced by a trellis of little tubes, as on the Linto and Kreidler. N.S.U. has equipped its Rennfox, Rennmax and Sportmax with a frame, with a suspended engine held in a sheet-iron shell, commonly called a T-frame as the design looks like the letter T. The low engine was fixed to the lower part of the T. At last Ossa made an innovation in constructing a box frame which looked vaguely like a horizontal Y. The leg of this letter formed the superior part of the frame which contained the petrol tank and which was fixed to the steering column. One of the arms served to fix the engine at the back and the other to fix the dampers and also to serve as the saddle. This frame in soldered aluminium plate did not weigh more than 15 lb (7 kg). The first racing machines did not have suspensions, fore or aft. The Indian of 1911 was equipped with a substitute suspension in front made of a system of small rods and flat springs (remember that in 1906, the four-cylinder touring F.N. was equipped with a fork like a parallelogram).

It is in fact practically impossible to know exactly when such and such a system was invented or applied for the first time as the technical evolution of the motorcycle was due to the work of men who did not always patent their inventions. The first victorious Norton in the T.T. in 1907 had a parallelogram-style fork with springs outside the parallelogram. Soon the coil of springs was put inside the parallelogram, and this was the front suspension used up to the Second World War. Then the first front telescopic forks appeared (B.M.W. already had one in 1935). The telescopic was challenged by the balance fork (N.S.U., Guzzi and the first Hondas) and by the oscillating Earles type (B.M.W., MV, M.Z.). Today, all the forks of racing machines are telescopic. Up to 1938 racing motorcycles had no rear suspension. In 1935, a 500 Guzzi, furnished with an odd rear suspension, won the T.T.; this suspension, called "elastic" had a damping device working horizontally, parallel to the arm of the back fork. Apart from this system the first rear suspensions were suspended on the hub. After the war, oscillating rear suspensions were general on all the modern machines and furthermore the dampening devices were adjustable. At the beginning of the century, racing machines had no brakes at all because they were used purely to set up speed records on the circuits. Afterwards, for road races, they were equipped with brake shoes. As on contemporary bicycles, the back brakes pressed on the rim of the belt of the secondary transmission. Since 1920, the drum brake at the front has appeared, with the rear brake having a larger diameter than the front brake. Since this time the brake drum has

developed a great deal but it preserves the same mechanism. The very first was a single shoe which progressed to two single shoes on each drum. The diameter of these brakes grew from 4 in (100 mm) to 9 in (250 mm). The disc brake worked hydraulically was used in racing for a little while but most riders seem to prefer the old drum. In 1965, Honda equipped its fabulous 50 cc twin with a brake shoe, the jaws of which worked on the rim of the front wheel just like a bicycle.

If one were to describe in a few words the prototype of a modern racing motorcycle chassis it would be this:

"Frame with double bearer plate, front telescopic suspensions, oscillating rear suspensions, adjustable damping devices, front brakes with four leading shoes (two double shoes) and back brakes with double leading shoes."

Tyres have also developed a good deal. Before the advent of the "triangulars", in 1963, the tyres had a rounded shape and on bends the contact with the track was relatively slight. The triangular which was invented by Dunlop has, as its name suggests, a triangular appearance. Going straight, the motorcyclist rides on the point of the triangle and on the bends on one of the sides of the triangle, so allowing a large amount of rubber to come into contact with the road. The hysteresis of rubber has allowed enormous progress to be made: it is enough to see the angles which present-day riders can take to realise this. On a 500 like the MV3, a back tyre lasts the length of one race and one practice, that is about 310 miles (500 km). In 1974, the cantilever frame with a single shock-absorber under the fuel tank made its appearance. This system allows greater clearance for the rear wheel. The same result can be obtained by severe bending of the rear shock absorber, as on the 500 Suzuki.

THE SIDE-CARS. Although they have taken part in the world championships since their creation in 1949, the side-cars have always been and always will be on the fringe of the championships. Not that the spectators hold aloof from this sport, on the contrary, but the manufacturers do not see a means of gaining useful publicity in the three-wheelers. The use of the side-car is as old as that of the motorcycle, but the side-car races only made their début in the 1920s. At this time the side-car factory which developed the famous Jaguar car was founded in this country. The first racing side-cars were precisely the same as standard ones with perhaps the engine slightly tuned. The side-car, rightly called, was attached to the machine by swivel joints, so the car and the motorcycle did not form a rigid combination. If this system presented an advantage in comfort when touring, on the race-track steering such a machine was an acrobatic feat. The slightest bend taken a little fast made the side-wheel want to lift and all the weight of the passenger was needed, to readjust the trapeze-like structure on a light centre-board, to keep it on the ground. The driver struggled with a fork, often too long, which twisted like a single steel wire.

It was only after the Second World War that the racing side-car was seriously developed. This development was largely due to two men—the Swiss Haldemann and the Englishman Oliver. The first made the rigid side-car ensemble, the second produced the first "outfits" and in consequence started a whole new form of riding. The outfit is the name given to modern side-cars—ones that are no longer a motorcycle plus a side-car but entirely homogeneous. In comparison with a conventional machine, the wheels are of smaller diameter, the fork is shortened, the frame is lengthened, so that the driver does not sit but drives with his knees on side "gutters" and the passenger no longer gets out over the wheel of the side-car but in front on a level with the tarmac. To lower the ensemble even more, the petrol tank is put in the side-car. The technique of riding a side-car so built is exactly the same as a monocoque. It consists in making the three wheels of the combination slide with the same coefficient adherence, whence comes the usefulness of the passenger who judiciously weights the wheel most affected by centrifugal force.

With his revolutionary combination driven by a 500 cc Manx Norton engine, Eric Oliver seized the first three world championship titles. The Oliver technique was taught to and soon equipped most of the racing side-cars. By contrast, the Norton engine began to run out of steam and relief was given by the B.M.W. Rennsport engine, the same which equipped the B.M.W. private entrant solo model in 1953. A good Rennsport develops 60 hp at 9,500 rev/min and has a lot of torque at low revs which is indispensable for side-car racing. Thus began the long, long reign of the B.M.W. engine in the side-car class. From 1954 B.M.W. never once lost the constructors' title up to 1972, winning a total of nineteen world championships. In nineteen years the Rennsport engine changed little. The dimensions of its cylinders for long distance races became square, then super-square, the supply of petrol was produced by carburettors, and then by indirect injection, but the power never improved greatly. Today, the best Rennsport engines develop 65 hp at 10,000 rev/min and are capable of speeds of more than 130 mile/h (210 km/h). For a good ten years, the B.M.W. firm has made no more racing engines, and for

ten years the Rennsports have been sold on the black market at the price of gold, so highly are they prized. The first engine to seriously challenge the Rennsport was the Gilera four of Frigerio which was followed by that of Milani. These engines had enough power to beat the Rennsports, but the chassis of the Italian machines were rather old-fashioned.

In 1964, Florian Camathias of Switzerland fitted a Gilera four to his outfit. He enormously improved in other ways the technique of the outfit and created the super-outfit. More than ever, pilots and passengers were on the level of the ground, as the complete height of Camathias's side-car was no more than 28 in (70 cm), and the mudguard was fixed by a F.I.M. rule at 4 in (10 cm). Ex-B.M.W. driver and world champion for this make in 1960, Helmut Fath, marked a new stage in the history of the side-car. In 1961 Fath was badly hurt and during his long convalescence he drew the plans for a 500 cc four-cylinder engine. In 1965 the U.R.S. (named after Ursenbach, the village where Fath lived), had its first race but getting into top form was difficult. The four-cylinder double overhead-cam motor driven by a central gear train was air-cooled, and faced the road. Soon Fath equipped his engine with an indirect injection with four mixers and then with eight mixers (two to each cylinder). In this last version (1968) the U.R.S. developed more than 70 hp at 13,500 rev/min and it was with this engine that Fath won his second world championship driver's title, that of the constructors' going to B.M.W. The U.R.S. engine was also used in the solo races but it lacked a good frame and was not competitive.

If the champions of the solo machine are the English or the Italians, in the side-car they are almost exclusively German. Only the Swiss Scheidegger succeeded in 1965 and 1966 in challenging the superiority of the Germans of whom the greatest was Max Deubel (four times champion) and the last side-car driver to drive sitting down. Today, on the driving-list the side-car category is dominated by the German, Klaus Enders. The year 1975 marked the end of B.M.W's reign. Rolf Steinhausen won the championship driving a König. This two-stroke four-cylinder water-cooled engine has a power of 90 hp. As regards the chassis, the side-car outfit is inexorably developing the techniques of automobile engineering.

THE GRAND PRIX CIRCUITS. Each year, a dozen circuits scattered all over Europe receive the competitors for the world championships. In certain countries, these circuits change almost every year, thus in West Germany Nürburgring

The phenomenal Giacomo Agostini.

and Hockenheim are used alternate years and in Spain, Montjuich and Jarama. The new Madrid circuit of Jarama was originally constructed for car racing. Protection rails circle the winding track which lacks very sharp curves. The surface of the track is very good, although the wide, white painted strips, which form the boundaries of the two sides of the track are extremely slippery. The circuit is suitable for machines of no more than 250 cc. The riders of large machines rightly find that Jarama is totally lacking in steep bends which can be taken fast. At its first Grand Prix in 1969, Jarama suffered a grave blow partly due to the bad weather but also to a lack of publicity, which resulted in only 3,000 or 4,000 spectators being present to watch the races.

MONTJUICH, situated in Barcelona in the magnificent Montjuich park, is the second great Spanish circuit. This is not an artificial circuit, but a road circuit as it is usually used as a normal road. Montjuich is very beautiful with long curves, little corners, esses and everything that is required. The surface, recently renewed, is perfect. As at Jarama, numerous safety rails border the corners. This safety system is not entirely for the good of the motorcycles and often dangerous, so the organisers ought to put straw bales in front of these rails. The safety problems for a motorcycle rider are very different from those which racing drivers recognise. When a motorcyclist falls off, he usually slides and if he does not come up against an obstacle he does not risk being badly hurt. Therefore the ideal would be to make a clearance area in sand or soil on each major bend. However, as such modifications would be very costly, only protection rails are put up. The racing-car driver prefers this system as he knows that if he leaves the track his car will hit the safety rails, bounce back onto the track, and although it will be partly destroyed, he will be protected as he is strapped into the seat. However, in the same circumstances, the motorcycle riders and their machines will be crushed against the protection rails. The motorcycle rider is aware of this and the risks that he runs, and it is perhaps because of this fact that it is rare for a rider to exceed his ability. Motorcycle racing is the sport of clear-headed men. During the Spanish Grand Prix some 20,000 people crowd the edges of the circuit. One of the most spectacular spots is the large bend after the stands. There, the riders of the 500s take off into the air over a hump at almost 125 mile/h (200 km/h). The races finish very near to Barcelona, at about 2 p.m., and as soon as the Grand Prix finishes, the spectators rush to the Arena on the Plaza d'Espagna to watch a bull-fight.

HOCKENHEIM, which is situated very near the Karlsruhe–Mannheim autoroute, is a very fast circuit, but not dangerous as all the bends are ideally constructed. This circuit is distinguished by two very different sections. The first one, near to the start, is a series of little bends. The rider, therefore, has the problem of finding the correct gearing which will permit the maximum speed on the straights and also the correct speed on coming out of the turns. For the spectator Hockenheim is marvellous. There are stands, capable of holding more than 100,000 spectators, overlooking the whole series of bends and the start. When the spectacle is over, the tens of thousands of spectators quickly disperse, as if by magic, and the empty tiers, strewn with litter, breathe out a sadness which is not encountered elsewhere.

NURBURGRING. In the neighbourhood of Koblenz, the Nürburgring is characterised by twists and turns and richly adorned with bends Prix was run on the south loop of the Nürburgring with a lap distance of 4·7 miles (7·7 km). In 1970 the north loop of 14·1 miles (22·8 km) was used for the first time. To describe the Nürburgring circuit is to describe hell for a motorcycle racer or racing-car driver. The track which is narrow and very bumpy, is bordered all the way by trees or ravines. It digs deep into the woods, rushes down steep slopes, climbs up steep hills, plunges into depressions, spins off to the right or left, turns back on itself, returns to a giddy descent, jumps the humps, and covers more than 170 bends in a distance of 14·1 miles (22·8 km).

To know this circuit well and to memorise every bend, it is necessary to do at least 100 laps. However, the Nürburgring is a circuit which is highly regarded by both riders and spectators who come in great numbers to be present at this race, which in some ways has the attraction of motocross with all the machines jumping and bouncing from the dips to the humps.

CLERMONT. Without any argument this is the most beautiful circuit in France situated as it is in the mountains of the Auvergne near to Clermont-Ferrand. Its mountain track and many bends make it frequently compared with the Nürburgring. However, here the surface is completely even. The Auvergne circuit is a road circuit and perfectly maintained. It is considered to be relatively difficult, but it is enormously popular with the riders and it was the favourite of Mike Hailwood.

The second French circuit, the Bugatti at Le

Mans, does not bear comparison with Clermont-Ferrand. It is very similar to Jarama. The riders do not like it much and the spectators do not like it at all, as the stands are such a distance from the track that it is difficult even to read the numbers of the machines.

ISLE OF MAN. This circuit used for the Tourist Trophy is unique. Its history is quite simply that of the motorcycle. It honours the makes, crowns the champions, but also kills and will kill again. . . . It is a sacred monster, an unimaginable spectacle which every motorcyclist should see. The Isle of Man has a certain degree of autonomy from Britain allowing it, among other things, to ignore the obligatory speed limits. This particular, most attractive circumstance was used in 1907 for the creation of a road circuit 15·8 miles (25·4 km) long which was traversed ten times. In the first races, only strictly mass-produced machines were allowed to participate. They were divided into two categories: singles and twins, with no limit on cubic capacity. In 1911, the competitors in the T.T. for the first time used the "Mountain" circuit covering a distance of 37·7 miles (60·7 km). The start was in Douglas, the capital of the island. The road track ran straight through the suburbs and then sharply, at Quarter Bridge, it turned to the right to plunge to the bottom of a very wide valley and cross two villages, Union Mills and Crosby.

On this section all kinds of twists and turns are met together with long straights where maximum speeds (almost 155 mile/h (250 km/h) for the fastest machines) are registered. At Ballacraine, the circuit swerves again to the right and follows for several miles the bottom of a very enclosed valley, where the sun never penetrates, that runs parallel to the coast. There are many small bends down in the valley. Afterwards the track crosses a succession of hills and goes through three villages: Kirkmichael, Ballaugh and Sulby to reach the watering-place of Ramsey. This 15·6 mile (25 km) section is particularly difficult because of the problem of the twisting bends. The circuit goes straight through the centre of Ramsey before reaching the mountains. The road climbs for 7 miles (12 km) to reach 1,640 ft (500 m), just at the foot of Snaefell, the highest mountain in the island. After this the circuit descends again into Douglas.

In 1911 this circuit was made of beaten earth, a fact which did not deter the champions of the period from taking the bends at more than 50 mile/h (80 km/h). That same year the junior categories (350 cc) and senior (500 cc) were established. In 1914 already 160 competitors were enrolled. In 1922, the 250 cc were added to the 350 cc and 500 cc, the 125 cc only appeared in 1951, the 50 cc class competed from 1962 to 1968, the organisers cancelling it because of the lack of riders. The sixtieth year of the T.T. saw the appearance of a race for mass-produced machines which were grouped under 250, 500 and 750. Side-cars first made an appearance in 1923 then disappeared three years later. A new attempt made in 1933 had further set-backs. In 1954 another circuit opened for the side-cars and at last the main circuit received them in 1960. All these races were run over three or six laps of the circuit which represented 113 to 226 miles (182 to 364 km). Due to the length of the races it is not possible to run all the categories in the same day and at least three days are necessary, allowing two races per day and time for the riders to rest.

The Tourist Trophy lasts a week and there is another week of practice. In order not to hinder the traffic during the day (remember that the T.T. is a road race) the trials take place very early in the morning (about 4 a.m.) and late in the evening, about 7 p.m. These dawn trials have something unreal about them as it is hardly light when the first riders, warmly clad, hurl themselves on to the track, rousing the villages with their exhausts. In the evening, in the setting sun, thousands of mosquitoes are crushed on the goggles of the riders who wipe them quickly with a little wet sponge fixed to the screen of the fairing. There are many reasons for these long practice sessions. In the first place it is necessary to go over and over the course to memorise the difficulties of the circuit and then, taking into account the state of the circuit which has an appalling surface, the riders have to regulate their suspension very carefully. A machine prepared for the T.T. is wholly individual. There even are specialist "preparers" such as Francis Beart who only sends his machines to the T.T.

On the eve of the race the machines are examined by a technical board of inspectors and sealed under a huge tent from which they are not allowed to emerge until they present themselves at the start. Each year a growing number of riders take part in the T.T. In 1969 there were more than 500, 120 of whom were in the senior category. It is not possible to allow all these riders to leave at the same time—the departures are timed in two's every 10 s. The riders who have made the best time in practice leave first. It is therefore a contest against the clock, and two riders have been known to finish with a tenth of a second between them although they had never caught sight of each other on the track.

Tremendous efforts are made to ensure that the race gets the widest possible coverage. Numerous recording points transmit the positions of the

Four famous ex-champions: left, Santiago Herrero and Bill Ivy (bottom), right, Jarno Saarinen and Renzo Pasolini (bottom).

135

riders to the control tower which immediately passes on the information to the radio commentator on the island. Thus the spectators, scattered around the 37·7 miles (60·7 km) of the circuit can follow the race minute by minute. On the evening of the race the *T.T. Special Examiner* comes out which describes the events of the day. In several places the T.T. circuit is very spectacular: there is Bray Hill basin down which the 500 cc riders hurl themselves at more than 124 mile/h (200 km/h). At the bottom the suspension is crushed down as far as it will go and sometimes even the bottom of the gearcase touches the track. On emerging from the Bray Hill basin, there is the jump (always taken at more than 124 mile/h (200 km/h)). There the machines take off with the front wheel at 20 in (0·5 m) from the ground. The bridge at Ballaugh is celebrated for its hump. This is crossed at 37 mile/h (60 km/h) and the machines and side-cars take off and fall back heavily two or three yards further on, sometimes with the front wheel crossed. At Bungalow there is a fairly fast bend which would normally be no problem except for the fact that there are railway lines which cut right across it.

In general a Grand Prix course does not exceed 124 miles (200 km). So for the T.T. there are enormous petrol tanks which are still insufficient for the riders of the 250, 350 and 500s which lap the circuit six times. On a well-organised stand the refuelling stop should not take more than 40 s. The Isle of Man is the most dangerous circuit in the world, the track is lined with ravines, cliffs, forests, stands of timber, or even houses, low walls, pylons, and yet there is not a single bale of straw. Rare indeed are the years when a fatal accident is not recorded. It must not be ignored that the 500 competitors taking part cover, counting practice and race, a total of 124,000 miles (200,000 km) and that 80 per cent of these are Englishmen who are not accustomed to road circuits. In a T.T. race the rider has two objectives: first to win, then to exceed the "ton", that is to say the 100 mile/h (161 km/h) barrier for the lap. Until 1969, only twenty riders had succeeded in doing this, the first was Bob McIntyre who in 1957 exceeded the "ton" on a 500 Gilera four. Then a 250, a 350, and even a 125 Yamaha four ridden by the late Bill Ivy achieved this extraordinary performance. At the present time the absolute lap record has been held since 1967 by Mike Hailwood (500 Honda four) who recorded the breathtaking speed of 106 mile/h (175 km/h). Mike Hailwood also holds the record for the number of T.T. victories with twelve trophies.

The Tourist Trophy is primarily a race, of course, but it also has a unique atmosphere.

Several days prior to the first practice dozens of ships arrive from England and Ireland and unload tens of thousands of motorcycle fanatics. Most of them disembark with their machines and in no time change the peaceful little island into a motorcyclist's paradise. During the T.T. the whole of the Isle of Man lives the life of the motorcycle. The motor accessory shop changes into the motorcycle accessory shop, the bookshops only display books about motorcycles. The photographer replaces family portraits with photos of the competitors. In the roads of Douglas thousands of motorcycle riders come and go, draw up and roar away with a frightful amount of noise. There are also splendid sports machines to be seen, brilliant vintage models and . . . some mythomaniacs who are taken for competitors. When night comes the excitement redoubles. The dance of the motorcycles grows faster, beer flows in torrents, fish and chip stalls are besieged. The exhausts of the tourists' machines deafen the ears, and one could go mad . . . all these bikes pulsing with life . . . it is marvellous. However, at midnight, at one stroke, everything stops, the law is respected. The Sunday preceding the races is an extraordinary spectacle well called "Mad Sunday". This is when the motorcyclists who have come as spectators ride the T.T. course. The authorities cannot forbid this and content themselves with providing a safety service identical to that on racing days and in the hospitals they prepare beds to receive some of the "Mad Sunday" crowd. The days when there is no racing are spent exploring the island or in attending different displays of motorcycle riding, such as trials, gymkhanas, motocross, drags. . . . Distractions are not lacking on the Isle of Man, and it can easily be understood why the T.T. is a Grand Prix quite on its own.

ASSEN. From 1927 to 1955, the Dutch Grand Prix was called the Assen Tourist Trophy on account of its 10 mile (16 km) long track. In 1955 the Drenthe circuit was built still near to the town of Assen in the north of Holland. This very even circuit is the most beautiful in Europe. Surface, the setting out of the bends, safety—everything is perfect. The spectators are admitted to practically the whole circuit and make use of little tiers which overlook a great number of the bends. The races here are always very thrilling because the competitors are selected very carefully. The spectacular side is provided by the sharp bends which can force the riders on to the covers, very often after Assen they are obliged to change their boots which have worn out by constantly raking the earth on the bends. Every year a crowd estimated at 140,000 spectators attends this Grand Prix which always takes place on a Saturday. During Friday night thousands of spectators arrive at Assen without any accommodation (Assen has very few hotels). They amuse themselves in the town filling the cafes and overflowing into the roads, so that from midnight on it is impossible to walk on the pavements. The whole town sings and drinks until dawn. Not everyone finds amusement in the town, and many prefer to go straight to the circuit to be sure of a good position next day. They sleep under the stars on the earth terraces, taking everything the weather offers.

SPA. Spa, in Belgium, is notable as an extremely fast, and therefore dangerous, circuit. Most of the bends can be taken at more than 124 mile/h (200 km/h) and only a hairpin bend restricts the speed occasionally. Spa is above all the circuit which really fits the riders' skill on the big bends. On the small bends a great number of riders are necessarily equal and a second-class rider can go through them as quickly as a champion, at the most the experienced rider will only gain a few yards in braking.

However, on the large bends the difference is obvious, the champion negotiates it with 18 to 25 mile/h (30 to 40 km/h) advantage over the second-class rider, which results in a gain of some 100 yd on coming out of the bend. To take a big bend quickly requires certain gifts on the part of the rider and an unshakeable confidence in his machine and himself.

Today, the Australian Jack Findlay is certainly the greatest specialist on ultra-rapid circuits. At Spa, his favourite circuit, he can take the great Burnenville bend at more than 136 mile/h (220 km/h). At this speed the bike sideslips the two wheels and as in a car he controls this skid by steering against it lightly. . . . There are not many places for spectators at Spa, but those that exist are fantastic, particularly that at Eau Rouge from which one overlooks the hairpin at La Source, the starting-grid, and the superb S bend at Eau Rouge.

SACHSENRING. The Sachsenring is situated near Dresden, East Germany, and it earns its name because it goes through the town of Sachsenring. Once again it is a road circuit and what a road . . . it is well worn, very slippery . . . but on the other hand, marvellously laid out, comprising take-offs, large bends and little twists.

The East German Grand Prix draws 200,000 spectators. This extraordinary number is obtained by massive publicity and in offering to the public a unique enjoyment. This enormous crowd, coming from every corner of East Ger-

many, walks along the 5·3 miles (8·6 km) of the track the night prior to the race. Thus it is able to visit all sideshows and drink stalls spread around the circuit. At dawn a vast cleaning service carefully washes the surface of the track, and between each race a carpet is laid over certain parts of the track to permit the spectators to pass from one side to the other without dirtying it. Opposite the stands by the starting-grid ingenious spectators have put up a large pole, with a chair and umbrella fixed at the top to ensure they have the best vantage-point on the circuit.

BRNO. The Czechoslovak Grand Prix is run on the Brno circuit in Moravia. Although it is smaller, the circuit can be compared to that on the Isle of Man. As on the Isle of Man, the track is not marvellous, particularly in the wet when it becomes extremely slippery. As with the T.T., it passes through three villages, scales a small mountain, winds into the hollow of a valley and is a very beautiful circuit. At Brno the audience is half the size of that at Sachsenring. Most camp in the mountain forest, where they light innumerable wood fires and sing round them throughout the night. This community atmosphere is one of the characteristic qualities of the Czechoslovak Grand Prix.

THE G.P. CIRCUITS. After the Czechoslovak Grand Prix the Continental Circus turns up in Sweden on the Anderstorp circuit which resembles, on a smaller scale, that of Assen. The straight line of this circuit is also the landing-strip of a little aerodrome. Anderstorp is one of the most modern circuits in Europe. Then they proceed into Finland, to Imatra, which is a very bumpy road circuit which promoted Hailwood to say that Imatra was the fastest motocross circuit in the world. The week before the races the whole village has a carnival, making this a very picturesque Grand Prix.

In Northern Ireland, near to Belfast, the Ulster Grand Prix takes place on the Dundrod circuit which has developed a good deal since its inauguration in 1925. Originally Dundrod had a straight of 4 miles (7 km) where a record number of blown-up engines were recorded. The circuit today is popular with both riders and spectators. It is situated in the mountains but does not however contain great irregularities. The only drawback this Grand Prix has, is that it is cold and it almost always rains during the races!

MONZA. Some miles from Milan the Monza autodrome serves as the setting for the Italian Grand Prix. After Spa this is the fastest circuit. There are only five bends, one of which is para-

Symphony for the maestro, Mike Hailwood.

bolic, the most spectacular of all the bends is the "Curva Grande". Unfortunately, no spectator is admitted to it, the public only having the use of three stands. In 1969 and 1972 the Italian Grand Prix had an escapade on the Imola circuit which demands more skill than that of Monza.

Newly promoted to Grand Prix, the Yugoslav circuit at Opatija (near Rijeka) would be perfect if it did not include two very tight hairpins and a great number of white lines painted on the track. The north part of the circuit is made up on one side with a very high percentage of little twists and of a descent with steep bends. The south part which runs along the Adriatic is a succession of twists, fairly fast, and ends in a long bend which ends exactly on the finishing line. The beauty of the situation in which the Yugoslav Grand Prix takes place adds a holiday flavour to this Grand Prix, which for this reason ought to have a great success in the future. Of all the circuits mentioned only six are artificial: Jarama, Hockenheim, Nürburgring, Assen, Bugatti, Monza. All the others are road circuits.

THE CONTINENTAL CIRCUS

"Continental Circus" is a magic expression, full of mystery and adventure, which designates the company of Grand Prix riders and the wanderings that they make each year in attending race after race with their caravan. It is difficult to define the origins of the Continental Circus. It began with the creation of the Continental Grand Prix in 1925. Then, as now, from the start of the season, the British riders left *en masse* to put on their show and gain victories on all the circuits—like a circus of some kind. Today, the Continental Circus is always composed of a great majority of British who are for the most part private riders. The works riders follow the Continental Circus, but they do not live like the private riders, their official conditions constrain them to live a more exalted way of life. However, for practical reasons certain riders, such as Mike Hailwood, prefer to live in caravans in the riders' park.

In the Continental Circus all the riders are professionals and live entirely on the small racing prizes they obtain. Only the works riders can earn a good living, the others have quite a job to make ends meet and are glad to go short and economise on hotel expenses with the aid of their caravans. Sometimes they fail and have to give up the Continental Circus and return home. Many British Commonwealth citizens take part in the Continental Circus arriving from New Zealand, South Africa, Rhodesia . . . and above all from Australia. All arrive in Europe without a penny to their name, but full of ideas for their future. The harsh realities of the race do not frighten them and their unshakeable faith in the motorcycle helps them in difficult moments, and there are many. . . . The great reward of their efforts is to sign a works' contract. While waiting for this, they start off again every spring on the Continental Circus. The winter is spent in Britain preparing their machines. In February they arrive in southern Spain, at Alicante, to take part in the first international race. From there they go to Italy: Rimini, Riccione, Imola . . . to the start of the Grands Prix. The great caravan of the Continental Circus arrives there on the Thursday for practice and leaves on the Monday or Tuesday to go to the Bugatti circuit in France. Then there is a long journey to Opatija for the Yugoslav Grand Prix which takes place one week after the French Grand Prix. After Yugoslavia, the Continental Circus returns to England for the Tourist Trophy. From the Isle of Man they go to Holland (Dutch T.T.). The following week they are in Belgium, then in East Germany, then in Czechoslovakia, and then there is an interval of two weeks before the next Grand Prix in Sweden. The riders take advantage of this to return to Britain or Italy to strip down and rebuild their machines. From Finland they go to Northern Ireland and from there to Monza for the Italian Grand Prix. The last Grand Prix takes place in Spain at the end of September.

During the whole of this season the Continental Circus riders will have covered 31,000 miles (50,000 km) at the wheel of their van and 6,200 miles (10,000 km) on the circuits. For the bachelors to be away for eight months of the year is no problem, but the married riders and fathers of families cannot separate themselves for so long from their responsibilities. Therefore wives and children also form part of the Continental Circus. Unless there are enormous financial means at home, the nomadic life of the Continental Circus is the best way of gaining a place on the list of the famous motorcycle riders. A great number of the best riders in the world have come from this hard school. Before the world championships were instituted, the supreme aim of a rider was to win the Tourist Trophy. The first great motorcyclists were winners of the T.T. Among the most celebrated was Alec Bennett who won five T.T. races including the Senior T.T. in 1927 with the first overhead-camshaft Norton. At the finish of this race he was warmly congratulated by the celebrated writer George Bernard Shaw who was a great motorcycle enthusiast.

STANLEY WOODS. At the same time the Irishman Stanley Woods began his brilliant career as a motorcyclist which was sealed by ten victories in the T.T. firstly with Norton, then with Guzzi. The great rival, but nevertheless the friend, of Stanley Woods was Jimmy Guthrie, he gained six victories in the T.T. riding A.J.S. and Norton machines. Other outstanding stars of this period were: Harry Danieli; Jimmy Simpson, the first rider to exceed a 60 mile/h (96·6 km/h) average in the T.T. in 1924 on a 350 A.J.S.; Graham Walker and Wal Handley, who won two races in the same week, the 175 and the 350, in 1925. Percy Hunt repeated this achievement in 1931 in winning the Junior and the Senior T.T. Freddie Frith, youngest of the group even won the first 350 cc world championship with a Velocette. From 1920 to 1940, the supremacy of the English riders was incontestable. The first "foreigners" to win the T.T. during this period was the Italian Teni Omobono who in 1937 won the 250 race on a Guzzi. The following year, the German Ewald Kluge, the works rider of D.K.W., won the 250. One year later another German Georg Meier brought, for the first and last time, a 500 B.M.W. to victory in the T.T. In the small and medium classes (125 and 250) the first years of the world championships were dominated by the Italian engineers and riders such as Bruno Ruffo, Nello Pagani (the father of Alberto Pagani, semi-works rider for Linto) and Dario Ambrosini. This supremacy was contested in 1953–54 by the German make N.S.U. and its rider Werner Haas. The reign of the N.S.U.-Haas combination was brief but spectacular. The 125 and 250 N.S.U. were certainly very good machines, but Werner Haas was perhaps the best rider that Germany has ever had ... he was killed in 1956 in an aeroplane crash. During the same period, in the 350 and 500 classes, British riders called the tune with Fergus Anderson, Bill Lomas and, above all, Geoff Duke.

GEOFF DUKE. This great champion began with Norton and won four titles for them, two of which, in the 500 cc class, he achieved against the powerful Gilera four. He made up for the lack of power by his skill in riding and the road-holding of the Nortons which were equipped with the "Featherbed" frame. This excellent frame forced him into a very smooth, unobtrusive style on the machine, his knees pressed against the petrol tank. This devilishly efficacious style became a legend. When he moved on to Gilera Geoff Duke gained another three world titles in the 500 cc class.

Before Duke rode Gileras, their top rider was Umberto Masetti, followed by Bandirola and Pagani. It was against this renowned team that Duke fought with his Norton. From 1956 to 1960 the majority of the 125 and 250 victories came to the Italian MV works rider, Carlo Ubbiali, who counted at the end of his career nine world

championships (six in the 125 and three in the 250 class). This record has only been beaten by Giacomo Agostini and equalled by Mike Hailwood. From 1956 to 1960 John Surtees called the tune on his MV4 in the championships. Paradoxically Surtees's seven titles have no great value when it is realised that MV then had no competitor which could worry them. Carlo Ubbiali had the same advantage from 1957 to 1960, which allowed him to snatch five titles without much difficulty. Later, similar circumstances served Mike Hailwood who, on the 500 MV4 easily gained four titles. Jim Redman did the same in the 350 class but on Hondas, and lastly Giacomo Agostini, who after the retirement of the Hondas, rode alone in front and won all the 350 and 500 titles. This is not to say categorically that these riders were not true champions, the superiority and talents of all these riders cannot be doubted. John Surtees has always been recognised as one of the five best English motorcycle riders, and moreover Surtees has undeniable talents as a tuner of engines. MV owe him a great deal. After 1960 in four categories out of five, the world championship was the affair of the Japanese. On the other hand the riders were for the most part Europeans or English-speakers. Among the most famous Japanese riders are Fumio Ito (Yamaha, winner of the Belgian Grand Prix in 1963), Kunimitsu Takahashi (Honda) particularly at his ease in the rain, and Yoshimi Katayama (Suzuki) who narrowly missed the world championship in the 50 cc class.

ERNST DEGNER. In its first year in 1962 the 50 cc championship was won by the German, Ernst Degner. Before being with Suzuki, Degner raced for M.Z. and was closely involved in the tuning of the engines as he was also an engineer. It is perhaps for this reason that M.Z. and the first Suzukis seem to be related. ... In testing a 250 four, Degner was gravely injured in 1964 and although he raced again afterwards it was without success.

Hugh Anderson, a New Zealander, succeeded Degner in the 50 cc championship. Although of medium height, and very thin he seemed huge on his minuscule 50 cc Suzuki. To turn he brought his leg completely out of the fairing with his knee on a level with the track; the Hugh Anderson riding position became a legend. Between 1963 and 1965, Anderson was crowned world champion four times (two 50 cc titles and two 125 cc titles). He retired from racing in 1967 to devote himself to motocross. The Irishman Ralph Bryans was of a very similar build to Anderson, but he had the ability to hide himself completely

The great Phil Read, here seen on the 125 Yamaha four. ▶

behind the fairing of his 50 cc Honda. Bryans (50 cc champion in 1965) soon became used to riding the powerful 250 and 300 cc six-cylinder Hondas on which he came second to Mike Hailwood. There are riders who are "made" for one class, such as the German Hans-Georg Anscheidt in the 50 cc. He began as a works rider for Kreidler, then becoming tired of always being a vice-champion, he went to Suzuki and won his first title in 1966 and retired in 1968 with three championships to his credit. Anscheidt was a very careful rider and an excellent technician. These two qualities made the Japanese call him "Golden Boy". Today Anscheidt races a little in Formula 3.

ANGEL NIETO. Of all the 50 cc riders who have been World Champions, the little Spaniard Angel Nieto is the youngest. In 1969, when he was only twenty-two, he won the title on his Derbi against all odds. The average age of motorcycle champions is about twenty-six years because in general there ought to be a good ten years' practice to reach the top level. The high-spirited Nieto has passed all the preliminaries and seems to be well on his way to a very successful future. In contrast to Nieto, Luigi Taveri of Switzerland had to wait until he was thirty-two to gain his first championship in 1962 on a 125 cc Honda. His lengthy experience earned him the title of "the rider who never falls". He recaptured the title in 1964 and 1966, and when he retired from racing he was almost forty.

BILL IVY. The lamented Bill Ivy had the ideal proportions for a 50 cc rider, that is to say about 5·2 ft, 110 lb (1·60 m, 50 kg). However, the 50 cc class did not interest him for long because he preferred a 500 with plenty of horsepower. Until 1966 Bill Ivy raced in the 500 cc class on a G50 Matchless and he was crowned king of Brands Hatch: a distinction given to the fastest rider on the circuit. Then "Little Bill" signed a contract with Yamaha to ride the 125 and 250. In 1967 he gained the 125 cc title. After Yamaha withdrew, at the end of 1968, Ivy concentrated on cars, although he did not forsake motorcycles entirely. In 1969 his début in Formula 2 was an eye-opener and when he was not racing on four wheels he was racing a 350 Jawa four (factory model). It was on this machine that Bill Ivy was killed at Sachsenring. Ivy was very popular and had an extraordinary personality, on the track he gave the whole of himself, in a harsh but very spectacular style. Fate decreed that he was not killed through any mistake of his own but through a mechanical failure.

The 1969 world champion in the 125 cc class was Dave Simmonds. He was a semi-works rider for Kawasaki, that is to say that Kawasaki provided him with all the means to race but let him straighten out all the mechanics himself. Dave Simmonds was both an excellent mechanic and an excellent rider in spite of a broken elbow that occurred in a fall in 1967 and prevented him from stretching out his arm completely. He was killed in a caravan explosion in France in 1972.

JIM REDMAN. The Rhodesian Honda works rider ruled the 250 class in 1962 and 1963 and the 350 cc class from 1962 to 1965. He was the perfect professional rider. The victory only interested him from the point of view of how much money it brought him. He took no unnecessary risks and his motto was "win at the lowest speed possible". It was an excellent formula but not so easy to apply as Redman well knew. The first rider to compete on Honda was Tom Phillis. He won Honda its first title in the 125 in 1961, but he was killed the year after during the Junior Tourist Trophy. Phillis's best friend was Gary Hocking who, riding an MV4, won the 350 and 500 world championships in 1961. This great rider, very much affected by the death of Phillis, retired from motorcycle racing to try cars which cost him his life. As well as Tom Phillis and Gary Hocking, 1962 was a fatal year for Bob McIntyre, the Stirling Moss of motorcycles. McIntyre never won a championship although he had the potential, riding for Gilera and then Honda. His greatest exploit was to be the first to lap the Isle of Man circuit at an average of more than 100 mile/h (161 km/h).

Kel Carruthers the 250 world champion in 1969 is the best example of the success which a private rider can achieve. Carruthers emigrated from Australia in 1966, accompanied by his wife and his two children. In Australia Kel had reached the peak of success having won everything on his 250 ex-factory Honda four. In Europe, it was a different story as places are scarce, but Carruthers had at his disposal a 125 Honda production racer, a 250 Aermacchi and a 500 Norton. In 1968 Carruthers, who had made himself noticed the year before, was given a 350 cc Aermacchi factory engine. With this machine he finished third in the championship, behind Pasolini (Benelli 4) and Agostini (MV3). At the beginning of 1969, Kel Carruthers was appointed Aermacchi works rider and rode a 125, a 350, and a 383 cc. In the Tourist Trophy, the Benelli factory wanted him to ride the 250 four, he was best in practice . . . and signed a contract. Not all "private" riders have had such a meteoric rise to fame.

JACK FINDLAY, another Australian, arrived in Europe about 1958 and experienced all the disappointments imaginable. No money, no connections, mechanical failures, both minor and serious falls, a friend who was killed, loneliness, swindling managers . . . he really had to be dedicated not to give up in the face of such an avalanche of difficulties. Findlay kept his courage up well and today is considered to be one of the best riders on large-capacity machines.

Although he is already one of the old brigade, the Swiss/Hungarian Gulia Marsovszky is always a formidable enemy especially when the track is wet. Like Findlay, Marsovszky is a motorcycle enthusiast who in his career had many reasons for giving it up. The recent discoveries were: Kent Andersson, Rodney Gould, Santiago Herrero and Renzo Pasolini. The latter was first rider for Aermacchi and before riding for this firm he was the Benelli works rider. His weak point was long bends, his strong point little twists and turns. He died after a fall during the Italian Grand Prix in 1973.

In contrast the Spaniard Santiago Herrero (Ossa) had a partiality for very fast circuits like Spa, and also rode extremely fast on little winding circuits. In one and a half seasons of Grands Prix, Herrero pulled himself up into the top flight and even led, until the race before the last, the 250 world championships of 1969. The 1970 T.T. proved fatal for him. The Englishman, Rodney Gould, had already made his name in 1968 on a Yamaha special, the engine of which was placed in a Bultaco chassis.

In 1969 he rode the very fast 250 and 350 Yamaha production racers. Only too often hindered by technical failures, Rodney Gould showed a very promising and impressive skill in riding. Like Gould, the Swede Kent Andersson, was discovered in 1968 riding a 250 cc Yamaha production racer; his performances were all the more noticeable because he was clad in a superb white suit with red bands. In 1969, still riding a 250 Yamaha, Andersson won two Grands Prix and finished second in two others, which brought him into second place, behind Carruthers in the final classification. Andersson could go further, above all in the wet.

Since 1969, there have been new stars like the Swede Jansson who performs daring feats in the 125 class on his Maico and the German Dieter Braun, 125 world champion in 1970 on a Suzuki. The Englishman Barry Sheene who was discovered in 1971 and who in his first G.P. season finished vice-champion of the world in 125 class and lastly the Finnish rider Jarno Saarinen who was undeniably in the class of the great like Read, Ivy and perhaps even Agostini

and Hailwood. Saarinen was world 250 cc champion in 1972, also the first motorcyclist to regularly beat Agostini in the 350 class. In 1973 he won the Daytona 200 during his first visit. One month later at Imola, Italy, he excelled and at the first Grand Prix at the Paul Richard circuit, he beat Agostini at the 500 class. This very promising beginning of the season forecast a double title for Saarinen. Unfortunately, the very person who was considered to become Hailwood's successor was killed at Monza in the same accident as Pasolini.

PHIL READ is a rider about whom much has already been said but he will be spoken of again and again in the future. Read's first great victory was back in 1961, when he won the Junior Tourist Trophy on a Norton. In 1963 he signed with Yamaha and won the 250 cc title the following year; a title which he regained in 1965. The technical excellence of the Yamaha four, and the end of the supremacy of Hailwood were to bring him to the fore in 1968 when he gained a double victory in 125 and 250 classes.

This year Yamaha no longer had to fear the competition of the Hondas who had withdrawn from competition the year before. So, before the season had begun, Yamaha had vaguely given instructions that the 125 title should be won again by Phil Read, and the 250 title by his colleague Bill Ivy. However, seeing these two titles within striking distance, Read took no notice of the orders and consequently incurred violent criticism. Apart from that, Phil Read is a very great rider, certainly the best today, and if Read finds himself entrusted with a competition machine in whatever category the holders of the titles may have fear of being dethroned.

GIACOMO AGOSTINI is the new Italian idol in motorcycle sport. He succeeds Ubbiali, Masetti and Tarquinio Provini. The latter won the 125 and 250 world championships in 1957 and 1958 riding Mondials.

Provini turned up again on the Morini which seriously worried the Honda four ridden by Redman, later he rode the Benelli four. A bad fall in the Tourist Trophy forced him to retire from competition in 1965. Provini had a very effective style of riding but one that was very difficult to imitate. In order not to lose speed, Provini did not lift even his head above the screen of the fairing; he hid completely behind the shell.

Agostini had a more conventional style but a very effective one. Formerly, before joining MV, Agostini rode Morinis and with this machine he beat the Benelli four ridden by Provini on the Imola circuit. Agostini was then twenty-two

years old. The Count Agusta noticed the young prodigy and signed him for MV for the following season to second Mike Hailwood in the world championships. In fact Count Agusta correctly believed that Agostini would improve his riding by contact with Hailwood and that perhaps . . . one day an Italian rider on an Italian machine would be unbeatable. In 1966 Hailwood left MV for Honda, and finished the season equal in points to Agostini. However, the latter had an additional Grand Prix victory and thus gained his first title. He repeated this achievement the next year, although it is true that Hailwood was hindered by a fragile engine and a poor frame. The greatest compliment that could be paid to Agostini was pronounced by Hailwood when he said publicly that Agostini was the only rider he seriously feared. After the retirement of Honda and Hailwood, Agostini was unbeatable in the 350 and the 500 classes, so he was content to break lap records for the glory and also for the money, because with each record broken the Count Agusta gave a reward to his rider. Certainly Agostini profited by the slack period in Grand Prix racing to win his titles (thirteen by 1973), but during this time he continually improved. He is an extremely conscientious rider and capable of achieving great things when necessary. Today he is the best and is the only rider who has thirteen titles and more than 100 Grand Prix victories.

MIKE HAILWOOD is the greatest motorcycle rider of all time. Certainly it is difficult to assert this without comparing him to Guthrie, Duke, Surtees and others, but if one considers that the list of a rider's honours is the criterion all the same of his superiority over the others then, truly, Hailwood is the greatest. Before describing his dazzling career, it must be noted that Hailwood's exceedingly rich father encouraged and helped his son at the beginning, but already Hailwood had phenomenal gifts as a rider.

Hailwood competed for the first time at seventeen years of age. The following year at the 1958 Tourist Trophy, he finished third in the 125, seventh in the 250, twelfth in the 350 and thirteenth in the 500. When twenty-one years old Hailwood won his first world title on a 250 Honda four. The same year (1961) he won the Tourist Trophy in the 125 (Honda), 250 (Honda) and 500 (Norton). In the 350 the engine of his A.J.S. exploded when he was in the lead in the last but one lap. This triple victory in the Tourist Trophy was unique in the annals of motorcycle sport. In 1962 he signed with MV and for four years running won the 500 cc title. In 1966, he went to Honda and won two titles, the 250 and 350. The following year he won both titles again and for the second time had three victories in the Tourist Trophy. With the retirement of Honda at the end of 1967 Hailwood decided to leave motorcycle racing to try car racing where he has also had success.

From 1961 to 1967, Hailwood won at least one world championship every year. He has collected nine titles in all and had twelve victories in the Tourist Trophy. Hailwood, nicknamed "Mike the Bike", is not only the best rider but also has a very strong personality. He has a tremendous physique and plenty of charm, although he accepts defeat very badly, particularly when it is due to some mechanical failure. This strong personality has the peculiar power of paralysing his adversaries who lose much of their ability when faced with the master Hailwood. Knowing this, Hailwood makes use of a particular technique. During the first laps of a race, he allows himself to be preceded for some yards by his most dangerous opponents, like a cat plays with a mouse. The mouse, frightened by Hailwood the cat, seeing himself already lost, makes mistakes . . . and suddenly in one lap Hailwood gains 100 to 200 yd and is never overtaken again.

◀ *Klaus Enders and Wolfgang Kalauch.*

The Finnish style—Jarno Saarinen followed by Teuvo Lansivuori.

motocross

By definition, motocross is a cross-country speed trial. A motocross circuit may be laid out in a disused quarry, in the hollow of a valley, or on the side of a hill . . . in fact anywhere where the ground is naturally uneven. On average a motocross circuit is about a mile long. Over this distance the rider meets the maximum of difficulties, such as dizzy descents at 70°, abrupt climbs, slippery twists, enormous holes, huge humps, straight stretches full of deep potholes . . . and sometimes to intensify the excitement organisers even make artificial springboards.

The nature of the surface also forms a problem on the circuit. For example, in racing, a sandy surface is much more painful than one of clay. The traps of the surface are one thing, certainly, but the physical resistance of the riders is an even more important thing. Motocross is a very exacting sport and is probably the hardest sport ever invented. The rider has to hold the two handlebars for 45 min with a pulse beating at more than 100, sometimes even 200 . . . hold on when at each second the body receives violent shocks in the arms, the legs, the back . . . everywhere. Then there is the dust which gets into eyes (in spite of goggles), mouth and nose. Once this dust gets wet it turns into mud and causes acute discomfort.

Sometimes a pebble, dislodged by a wheel, hits the rider full in the face and stuns him, sometimes he knocks his hand against a tree-trunk or a fence, sometimes his foot meets a stone or a root. In a word, motocross is no sinecure, and those who take it up are true sportsmen and fanatics. However, motocross is not a very dangerous sport. There are certainly more falls than in circuit riding, but these are at far lower speeds, 62 mile/h (100 km/h) is a maximum. Moreover the earth deadens the falls so that they rarely result in more than a sprain. A "bad fall" is rarely fatal. For the world championships the motocross trials are restricted by a rule which allows two trials of 45 min each. The first of each trial gains a point, the second two points, the third three points, etc. The winner of the Grand Prix is the one who has gained the least points. For example, a rider who finishes first in both of the trials gains two points. As for road racing, the winner of a Grand Prix chalks up fifteen points in the Championship, the second twelve, the third ten. The distribution of points for the make of the machine is done in the same way as for road racing. There are two motocross championships: the 250 cc and the 500 cc.

The history of motocross began in 1924, after a trial in England. To make their trial different the organisers of the Scott Trial decided to time certain inter-zones which led to "non-stop" zones. Other organisers put forward an idea of suppressing the "non-stop" and of leaving only the inter-zones which would all be timed, thus transforming the trial into a speed race over a cross-country course. For this first test in 1924, forty competitors finished out of eighty starters. Afterwards, to simplify the controls, the distances were reduced and the difficulties were concentrated in one place.

Until the Second World War, motocross was only practised in England. After the war, it reached the Continent and in 1947 the first international meeting was organised which brought together Belgians, French, Dutch and English. Each nation was represented by five riders on 500 cc, but only the three "cross men" who were best placed gained points and contributed to the win of their team. This trial of teams was called the Motocross des Nations. Since 1947 and until 1972, twenty-six Motocross des Nations have been run and fifteen have been won by English teams. Much later, in 1961, the Trophée des Nations was created and restricted to riders of 250 cc machines, the rules being the same as those of the Motocross des Nations. Up to 1969 Sweden has won five trophies.

In the 500 cc class, a European championship was established in 1952 and this became the world championship five years later. That same year, 1957, the 250 cc machines, at the height of their popularity, fought for the European Cup which became the world championship in 1962.

Bryan Wade hits the springboard. ▶

153

*In colour: (pp. 158–9)
the Frenchman, Christian Rayer, tackles the trees.*

The side-cars: as brutal as the solos.

▼

Physically, motocross is the most testing sport

The champion, the Belgian Joël Robert (250 Suzuki). (p. 162)

Today the two classes compete in twelve Grands Prix spread throughout Europe, some thirty motocrossmen racing on each class. It often happens that a 500 cc Grand Prix takes place on the same day as a 250 cc Grand Prix is scheduled in another country. This forces the motocrossmen to specialise in one class.

A motocross trial can be organised with the minimum expense (no track to build) which explains the numbers of tracks that have sprung up in many countries (more than 300 in France). Each meeting draws from 3,000 to 100,000 spectators according to the country, and always at least 15,000 when it is a Grand Prix. This popularity makes it possible for the organisers to pay the riders well who for this reason do not live in the same manner as circuit riders. There is no Continental Circus in motocross.

The first motocross machines were those of large cubic capacity, 500 cc and sometimes more. At the time, before the war, they were more like road motorcycles than real cross-country machines. They had no rear suspensions as yet. These did not really develop until after the creation of the first international races. The 500 cc of the years between 1950 and 1955 weighed a good 375 lb (170 kg) and produced some 40 hp! There were F.N. (Belgian), Matchless, B.S.A., Norton machines . . . all four-stroke inverted singles. In 1956, the Englishman Leslie Archer won the European championship on a Norton, with a single overhead-camshaft, derived from a racing engine.

In its first year the world championship came to a Swede: Bill Nilsson who rode an A.J.S. Crescent. The engine was a 350 cc A.J.S. 7R racing engine, bored out, and the chassis came from a Crescent, under the mark Husqvarna. In 1958 F.N. won their last victory and withdrew from competition. In 1959, a Swedish machine, the Monark inverted single, won the championship. Up to 1963, Swedish machines and riders gained four titles of which three went to Husqvarna (inverted single) and one to Lito. This last machine is an achievement in craftsmanship due to Sten Lundin who was world champion in 1959 on a Monark, which was then immediately withdrawn from competition. Lundin, engineer at Monark, then built an engine, the Lito, which was very similar to a Monark. With this machine he became champion in 1961.

The Englishman, Jeff Smith, put an end to the Swedish reign in 1964. His machine was a 420 cc B.S.A. The following year, when Smith regained his title, the B.S.A. had a capacity of 440 cc and reached 480 cc in 1969. This climb towards the maximum authorised capacity was paralleled by a considerable reduction in the total weight of

the machine. Between the B.S.A. of John Draper which won the European championship in 1955 and that of John Banks, vice-champion in 1969, there was a good 132 lb (60 kg) of difference. This reduction in weight was obtained by liberally using ultra-light metals, such as titanium, for the frame and the engine. Today a works B.S.A. 500 does not weigh more than 220 lb (100 kg) and produces some 40 hp. Unlike racing machines, motocross machines do not need a lot of power. For a 500 40 hp is the maximum required while a 250 only requires 30 hp. More horsepower would be a handicap as the machine would be too difficult to handle. Jawa and CZ have built 480 cc models which produce some 50 hp, but they were found to be unrideable and they had to be detuned. For a 250 the problem is a little different. Greater power would not be harmful, but to get it, torque in low gear is lost and this is catastrophic in motocross. A less powerful and more supple engine is preferable to an over-powerful, tuned one. To go back to the 500 cc B.S.A. which does not lack flexibility, it remains the last four-stroke engine to defend itself honourably in the world championships. In the opinion of all, the B.S.A. is the motocross machine that is the most intelligently conceived and as a result, the most perfect.

After 1965, apart from B.S.A. all the 500 cc are two-strokes and do not exceed 400 cc for the power reasons which have been mentioned. The creation of the first 360 cc two-stroke single heralded the start of the 1960s. At the time the German mark Maïco temporarily retired from competition, having produced a 250 cc two-stroke. The works riders for Maïco, Walz, Betzelbacher and Hauger left the Grand Prix scene to scour the inter races for 250 cc. They even took part in the races for any capacity and maintained that their little machines made life difficult for the big four-strokes. They were much more manageable than the 500 but they did lack a little power. The rules at that time forbade a machine with a capacity less than 350 cc to race in 500 cc class and according to certain technical information produced by D.K.W., a single-cylinder two-stroke with capacity greater than 350 cc could not work correctly. The three ex-riders of the Maïco factory did not know this and constructed on a low-geared Maïco 360 cc single called the Wabeha, which was said to be more powerful and supple than a 250. Since then CZ (Cz.), Husqvarna (Sw.), Jawa (Cz.), Greeves (G.B.), Suzuki (J), Montesa (Sp.), Bultaco (Sp.), all have their small 400 single-cylinder two-strokes.

The single cylinder is ideal in motocross (and in cross-country riding generally) for the follow-

Roger de Coster,
successor to Joël Robert.

In the mud, the German Franke (Zundapp).

Inset, the great champion, Sammy Miller.

ing reasons: it is light, narrow, powerful in low gear, solid and easy to look after, especially since it is a two-stroke. The laurels were divided between the CZ and Husqvarna. This superiority of Czech and Swedish material was questioned after the 1970 season with the mass arrival of the Suzukis. The Japanese now began to be interested in motocross. For some years now the Americans have developed a passion for cross-country and the Japanese have developed special bikes for this sport, the trail motorcycle. It is not the results of road racing that have popularised the trail bike but on the contrary, motocross. Suzuki has already understood this and in the future Yamaha and Kawasaki will undoubtedly follow suit.

To look at a motocross machine seems quite simple as it is very pared down and easy to construct. Yet in fact a competitive motocross machine is more difficult to make than a road racer. The Suzuki factory was already well versed in competition when it decided to make a motocross machine in 1965. However, it was only in 1969 that it was pronounced to be competitive, and then it took two years of competition for Suzuki to gain the world championship. A good motocross engine (especially a 250) is more difficult to tune than a multi-cylinder racing engine, and then there is the problem of the frame. It should be rigid, light, flexible, very strong and be equally suitable for the 500 cc (380 cc) and 250 cc. Special steel, with jealously guarded formulas is used in the construction of these frames. Much thought is given to the suspensions which must be rigid, dust and waterproof, have great clearance and be perfectly shock absorbent. On the other hand the brakes are of no particular importance, they must only be effective in every situation, and well adjusted. Once assembled, frame, suspension and engine must make a perfectly balanced indissoluble whole. For example, putting a Bultaco engine in a CZ frame produces a disastrous result, and vice versa. If the best engine and the best frame are of different makes it does not follow that by uniting them the best motocross machine is the result. The riding position on a motocross machine is very important, far more so than on a road racer. The rider must find the position in which he is least fatigued and it is different for each person. The most important qualities for a rider are: courage (he must not be afraid to throw himself into the holes and fly over the bumps); a sense of riding and balance (to know how to change direction when it is necessary and to re-establish a tangent balance all the time); and to be in excellent physical condition. This last quality is perhaps the most important. A rider who is fit and can endure a 45-min race without tiring has an immediate advantage even if he does not ride particularly well. An excellent rider who tires can lose up to 10 s a lap. To have this physical condition, the rider must have an athlete's build (the motocross champions usually have impressive physiques) and it is necessary to train regularly to keep fit. A motocross rider is at his best about twenty-three to twenty-four, but he must begin very young as his career usually ends before he is thirty.

Motocross is a complete sport where the human action plays a more important part than the mechanical. The great stars of 500 cc motocross are: Auguste Mingels, a Belgian F.N. works rider who won two European championships in 1953 and 1954. Then there are the Swedes: Bill Nilsson, Sten Lundin, Rolf Tibblin, who dominated the world championships from 1957 to 1963 and each won two titles. Then Jeff Smith, the master-rider, laid down the law for two years which were followed by the reign of Friedrichs. This East German, a policeman by profession, is a natural genius. He does not ride very well but possesses a tremendous sense of balance and above all he is indefatigable. He won successively three world championships. In the 250, the world championships were dominated by two men: the Swede, Torsten Hallman and the Belgian, Joël Robert. In 1962 and 1963 Hallman won the championship, but in 1964 twenty-year-old Joël Robert won his first title. He was beaten the following year by the Russian Arbekov. Then in 1966 and 1967, Hallman was again crowned world champion.

During these three years, Robert always finished second two points from the winner, and always because of ridiculous incidents during the race. He won again each year from 1968 to 1972. Joël Robert is a phenomenal rider, comparable to Hailwood on the track.

The English are great nature-lovers and quickly realised that the motorcycle could travel in forested areas which were impracticable for any other kind of transport. Peaceful trips soon became races where the riders tested the manoeuvrability of their machines and their riding skill. To make the game even more attractive problems of endurance (physical and material) were put into play, lengthening the duration of the trial. Just before the First World War, the English created the I.S.D.T. (International Six Days' Trial). This test was initially run with road machines, but already the rules foresaw a classification by teams composed of six competitors who rode machines made in their countries. So, for example, the English teams could only ride B.S.A., Norton or Triumph and the Germans, N.S.U., B.M.W. or Zundapp. . . . After 1970 the trophy teams of the I.S.D.T. were no longer obliged to submit to this rule. The place where the I.S.D.T. was run was most frequently in a mountainous region with very rough terrain. It changes its site and country every year. Each day, the competitors cover about 150 miles (250 km) cross-country. This distance is crossed by special timed stages, and between each of them one has to keep to a minimum speed. These "specials" are sometimes like a motocross course, sometimes a trial zone, sometimes like a hill-climb in cross-country. . . . There is even a speed trial on a road circuit. For six days no part, except tyres, may be changed on the competitors' machines which in some respects conform to the Highway Code. They are trial machines and are not limited by capacity. A team may be made up of a 50 cc, a 125 cc, a 250 cc, a 350 cc, a 750 cc. . . . It must not be thought that a 50 cc is at a disadvantage compared with a 750: on the contrary, in cross-country the lightness and handleability of the little machine overcomes the handicap in power. There, as in motocross or in trials the two-stroke engine is king.

The world fame of the I.S.D.T. makes factories more and more interested in this competition. There are official teams: Zundapp (W.G.), Jawa (Cz.), Puch (A.), Bultaco (Sp.), Ossa (Sp.), Hercules (W.G.), IZH (U.S.S.R.) and M.Z. (E.G.). This last make was incontestably the queen of the Six Days; from 1963 to 1969 they won six victories in this competition. The riders in the I.S.D.T. are for the most part trials riders or motocrossmen; but there are also specialists in this kind of competition, who are thought by the trialists and motocrossmen to be phenomenal, capable of the impossible and to be on a level with the best trial or motocross experts. The difficulties to be met in the Six Days are indescribable and unimaginable. The machines must come out of torrents more or less dry, follow mule paths on the edge of a precipice, they have to cross marshes and rivers, climb mountains to the level of the eternal snows . . . it is terrifying. Out of more than 300 participants less than half finish the course, the others have engine trouble or give up, because of physical exhaustion. The I.S.D.T., being a very special competition, takes place only once a year. Trial competitions were set up at the same time as the institution of the I.S.D.T. in England.

Here, the competitors leave at minute intervals on a marked course. This circuit varies between 30 miles (50 km) and 75 miles (120 km); (laps of 15 miles (25 km) and 37 miles (60 km) have to be completed twice) and it takes place in the country. On this track the competitors find some fifteen numbered sections. These very short sections are called non-stop zones where, as their name indicates, the competitor may not stop or put a foot on the ground. Anyone stopping gets a five-point penalty and a foot on the ground counts as one point, and two as three points. The person who, at the end of the test, has accumulated the fewest points has won. The non-stop zones are obviously very difficult to negotiate. The cyclists have to climb rocks, cross a mud-pit, climb stone steps and slalom between trees planted on a steep, slippery slope. To clear such obstacles without putting a foot on the ground, the trialists first reconnoitre the zone on foot. They take note of treacherous rolling stones, they

The International Six Days' Trial. ▶

detect roots buried in the mud, and they judge the depth of a ford. Finally, they hurl themselves into the cause, standing on the foot-rests. It is something well worth watching. The motorcyclists contort themselves on their machines to regain balance, put their weight on the back wheel to re-establish a grip. . . . The trial is a real art. Men and machines do their best to adapt themselves to the shape of nature. Once the zone is passed, they set off quickly towards the next one. They have plenty of time as the between-zones are not timed in trial and it is only necessary to respect an all-over time which is very generously calculated. It is not speed that matters in trial and therefore this sport is the least dangerous of all motorcycle sports. It is only since 1964 that a European trial championship has been organised. This sport, which is mainly for "amateurs", still involves quite a few professionals who defend the makes for whom they are competing. The best known are the German Franke (Zundapp), the Englishmen Don Smith, Farley (Montesa), Andrews (Ossa) and the Irishman Sammy Miller (Bultaco) who is as renowned in trials as Robert is in motocross.

There are no regulations about the cubic capacity of trial machines, but the 250 cc is considered to be the most suitable as it permits an ideal power-weight ratio. The 250 machines are all two-stroke singles, which are geared to some 20 hp maximum, which is amply sufficient. On the other hand, the power curve of these engines is very "flat" in low gear, since throttled down there is still plenty of horsepower. It is possible to ride at 1 mile/h (2 km/h) without touching the clutch and without stalling the engine. The single cylinder has an additional advantage in trials, it is narrow and thus runs less risk of catching the crankcase when the bike passes between large stones in a gorge. The trials chassis has its peculiarities: the frame is not necessarily very rigid, but light and narrow (for the same reason as the engine); moreover, it ensures a very important guard against the ground. It does not matter if the centre of gravity is placed high on the machine as it is not made to travel at speed. The suspensions, with great clearance (about 7 in (18 cm) in front) are shock-absorbant. The air-filter of the carburettor and the exhaust tank are built to come up almost to saddle height, which means it can cross rivers without any danger of flooding the engine. For this same reason, the small brakes are watertight. The total weight of a 250 cc trials bike does not exceed 220 lb (100 kg). Its strongly clamped back tyre is only slightly blown up (6 p.s.i.), which allows a greater carrying surface and thus an increase in grip. At the present time the Spanish industry makes the best trials machines which are the Bultaco, Montesa and Ossa.

The Japanese, too, are interested in this sport: first of all there is Yamaha, who have engaged the best rider, Mike Andrews; then there are Suzuki, Kawasaki and Honda.

grass-track and speedway

Grass-track and speedway have common origins. They were invented in 1902 by the Americans, who found it amusing and sporting to go as fast as possible round a stadium on a motorcycle. Afterwards these sports developed in different directions under the influence of the English and Australians who popularised grass-track and speedway in Europe around 1928.

Continental grass-track is usually run on 1,640 yd (1,500 m) long stadium circuits, and bends taken in an anticlockwise direction. The race is run in relays of four, where each participant has to complete four laps. On straight stretches the machines reach over 90 mile/h (150 km/h) and take the bends at more than 60 mile/h (100 km/h) sideslipping. On four laps, they attain an average of more than 75 mile/h (120 km/h) on an earth track. . . . The grass-track machines have 350 or 500 single-cylinder inverted engines. The engine, a rather antiquated design, produces at least 50 hp (for the 500) using methanol. In addition they have enormous torque, which enables them to have a gearbox with only two gears. The whole chassis of a grass-track machine is designed for sliding. There is almost no castor angle on the front fork which allows an easy control of skids. In addition this skeletal fork is ultra-light, and, in fact, damps very little. The frame of the machine is designed to twist, as too rigid a frame would not only delay the beginning of a skid, but also make the machine too heavy; it weighs about 220 lb (less than 100 kg). A tiny tank is large enough to hold fuel for four laps. The studded tyres have a distinctive appearance: the front one is very narrow and has spikes which come down very low on both sides, whereas the back one is similar to that of a motocross machine, but has the inner tube valve on the side of the tyre and not in the middle of the rim, thus it avoids catching the valve during violent acceleration. Lastly, these machines have no brakes at all as they can be slowed down by skidding. The rider's equipment is as extraordinary as the mechanics. To control a skid for example they put their left foot on the ground, and in order not to destroy the sole of the boot, they equip it with a steel shoe. To protect themselves from the dust and glancing stones, the riders wear a mask which covers their whole face. In addition they have leather clothes with well padded knee and shoulder parts, as falls in grass-track are quite frequent and do not always end happily.

Speedway and ice races are the most spectacular of motorcycle sports, and indeed the most spectacular of all existing sports. The track is usually in a football stadium and where athletics take place. It is 437 yards (400 m) long with two semicircular curves. As in grass-track, four riders starting at the same time, complete four laps, totalling 1,750 yd (1,600 m). On this short distance, the riders go all out. . . . They line up four abreast behind a starting-block, maintain their engine speed, elbows spread out, body leaning forward while pressing with all their strength on the handlebars, to prevent the bike from looping at the take-off. Then the starting signal is given and machines, men and earth spout forth in a terrible explosion. Those who have not weighted their front wheel sufficiently will see their machine rise up into the air to fall back again heavily—sometimes on top of the rider. The others, keeping their front wheel a good 4 in

(10 cm) from the ground hurl themselves into the first bend. Suddenly, like a single unit, the machines put themselves across the track, with their front wheel completely opposite-locked towards the outside of the bend. The riders, with their left foot scraping the ground and using the engine power, control the skid with great precision. Sometimes, however, in the middle of the bend, the front wheel does not touch the ground or else the bike leans sideways too far and the subsequent fall will often involve the other competitors. This is inevitable due to the fact that to present a good spectacle, riders of the same calibre, who do not slacken half a wheel's length in turning at more than 50 mile/h (80 km/h) average speed, are sent off at the same time. Speedway is a violent and often dangerous sport, but fatal accidents are very rare. In England, the popularity of speedway is quite extraordinary. Every year, Wembley Stadium in London welcomes 75,000 fanatics, who come to watch a nocturnal race which counts as the world championship. There are, however, two world championships in speedway: one for the team and one for the individual. The former dates from 1960 and there have been five Swedish victories, four Polish, and one British. The latter began in 1936, but only became official in 1949. For more than ten years, two riders dominated these championships: the New Zealander Barry Briggs, four times champion, and the Swede Ove Fundin, five times champion. Fundin won his first title in 1956 and his last in 1967; Briggs his first in 1957 and his last in 1966, and in 1969 he still finished second. The new speedway star is Ivan Mauger, a New Zealander, who has already pocketed four titles between 1968 and 1972. By comparison with grass-track machines, speedway machines vary very slightly. There is only one gear, and the engines, whose capacity is limited to 500 cc and which are fuelled with methanol, are either Jap or Eso, the latter being Czech, a subsidiary of CZ, now being used in the majority of speedway machines. The frame of a speedway machine has no rear suspension, the only major difference, due to the fact that in speedway the track is perfectly flat and no suspension is needed.

Continental long-track racing (above and previous page).

The tube valve is placed on the side of the tyre to protect it in acceleration. (p. 180)

A steel shoe protects the left foot and enhances slide. (p. 180)

Speedway riders performing a controlled skid.

ice racing

The grass-track and speedway machines are also used for races on ice, but they are fitted with special spiked tyres. An ice race (which is always 437 yds (400 m)) takes place on a rink used for Olympic skating. The rules of the races are the same as those of speedway: four riders take the starting-flag in one race and cover four laps. Just as in speedway, an ice race is a thrilling spectacle. The machines have a tendency to buck far more at the start and the back wheel skates less. Some yards before attacking the bend they throttle down a little and throw their machine sharply into the curve. Their left knee, which is used as a support, touches the ice. The end of the left handlebar is exactly 4 in (10 cm) from the ground while the bikes are inclined at an angle of almost 35°. Under the effect of the acceleration into the curve, the front wheel lifts up a little and the back makes sudden jerks, however, motorcycles on ice do not skid like speedway machines. Sometimes, after having gone too quickly into the bend, they have to extend their line and to do that they lean on the little walls of snow which border the track. As in the "wall of death" ice racing is a very dangerous sport and falls are all the more to be feared because the tyres of the bikes are bristling with sharp spikes.

The engine of the ice-racing machines is identical to that of speedway machines, a 500 Eso long stroke inverted single, but the chassis is very different. The back part of the frame is longer, which lengthens the wheelbase and allows better holding on bends. The front fork has a greater clearance, which is necessary as, after several races, the track becomes rather like a quagmire.

It also has a greater skidding angle and is equipped with a shimmy damper. All this helps to counteract the disastrous effect of the spikes which cause violent effects on steering. As on speedway machines, there are no brakes and no oscillating arm either. The handlebars are a curious shape, they are flat on the right and raised up on the left in order to give a better steering position on the bends which are all left-handed. There is only one foot-rest on these machines, which is on the right, as the left foot, shod with a steel shoe, is used for raking along the ice. The mudguards are, for safety reasons, very large and are made of solid, welded tubes. On some machines, there is a sheet of iron at the back, which comes down lower than the mudguard; this serves the purpose of a check when the motorcycle rears up on take-off. The wheels have speedway tyres with the hooks cut and the studding is different. It consists of big rivets with a hole dug out in the middle, in which the 1.1 in (28 mm) long steel spike is fixed. There are 105 of these on the back tyre and 86 on the front. The left side of the front tyre, which is the part that catches most in turning, is fitted with 65 spikes; on the right side, however, there are only 21 spikes. Before each race the points are carefully sharpened. The rider's equipment is practically the same as that in speedway, the only difference being that a piece of motor tyre protects their left leg which is used for sliding round a bend. In 1966 a world ice-racing championship was inaugurated. The Russians are undisputed masters of this sport and six titles have been won by Kadyrov.

sprinting and dragsters

With the development of the first motorcycles it was inevitable that speed and drag races should occur. Everybody with machines set out to prove that theirs was the fastest and the most efficient, and in the following years they were working towards the highest achievements in pure speed and sprint racing.

The first sprint races took place in 1923 on the promenade in Brighton. Two riders set off to cover about half a mile. The races were called "drags" and are still run in the U.S.A., where there are special strips, which enable two competitors to start off at the same time without danger. These strips are used for quarter-mile standing-start races. In Europe the term "dragging" is not acceptable and becomes "sprinting", because the rider is alone against the clock. It goes without saying that the records obtained in the U.S.A. are not recognised by the F.I.M. and vice versa. In addition, the A.M.A. and the F.I.M. have each made their own rules about the conversion of the machine and the distance covered. For a record to be accepted by the F.I.M. the race must be run in both directions, whereas in the U.S.A. one direction is enough. In the categories which are free of all restrictions, incredible monsters line up, developing 100 and 200 hp using methanol, nitromethane, or even "po" (propylene oxide, benzol and hydrazine). Because of their very explosive nature these mixtures have to be used very carefully, for example in wet or cold weather nitro is used, but "po" when it is hot. Many engines are fitted with a supercharger, which allows rates of compression going as far as 15:1. In the U.S.A. the engines that are most frequently used in dragging are of course the Harley-Davidson (1,200 cc with or without a supercharger). Elwood Sperr has even combined two 1,200 cc engines and claims a mere 300 hp. More common are the dragsters pro-

pelled by two Triumph 650 cc engines, and Ian Richardson used four 500 cc Manx Norton engines in his "Moonraker." "The Drag-Waye" from the name of its constructor, uses a tuned four-cylinder 1,300 cc Volkswagen engine, and the machine used by the "Michigan Madman", E. J. Potter, is propelled by a 5,359 cc V8 Chevrolet engine. The performance of Potter and his monster are not recognised by any federation as his machine is outside the limits of any regulations. Car-mechanics are also employed. This does not prevent him competing as a demonstration, and in January 1970 he established the absolute record for the quarter mile in 8·68 s. Some months later, the Englishman David Lecoq, who rides "Drag-Waye" gained the official record for the quarter mile with an average of 9·69 s over the course in both directions, thus bettering his previous best by 0·125 of a second. The previous record was set in 1967 by Alf Hagon, who then rode a home-made machine, a 1,260 cc Hagon Jap. Hagon also makes chassis for dragsters, which can be fitted with Bultaco, Triumph and, of course, Jap engines. The wheel-base of a motorcycle used for sprinting is very long in order to prevent the machine from rearing up at the start. The frame is simply formed by a big upper tube which holds the fuel, and a rigid rear triangle; there is no oscillating fork. The skeletal front fork is borrowed from a grass-track machine. The front wheel is like that of a moped: the back one is shod with a very large smooth tyre with a special square section. Riding a dragster needs a certain adroitness: it is necessary to know how to slip the clutch and the back wheel, and to control the weaving of the machine at the start. It is essential not to be afraid of speed, as a dragster which is capable of less than 10 s, reaches a speed of about 155 mile/h (250 km/h) at the end of the quarter mile.

An infallible recipe for making a good dragster: join together two 650 Triumph twins and fuel them with nitromethane.

197

speed records

The title of the world's fastest man on two wheels is now held by a thirty-six-year-old Californian, Don Vesco. On 28 September 1975 he broke both the A.M.A. and F.I.M. mile records at Bonneville Salt Lake, Utah, riding his 21 ft (6·4 m) long streamliner "Silver Bird", powered by two 750 cc Yamaha engines developing 1,806 hp. He averaged 303·8 mile/h (488·9 km/h) over two runs for the A.M.A. record, thus breaking the record held by Bob Leppan since 1970, by 38 mile/h (61 km/h). The difference between A.M.A. and F.I.M. records is that the A.M.A. allow two hours to elapse between the first and second run, while the F.I.M. allow only one hour. This acceptance of American timing appears to have finally closed the gap between these two federations after many years of disputes, and it is to be hoped they have finally settled their differences.

The absolute speed record is one choice, but it can only be held by one man. So to multiply the distinction the federations ratify records for different capacities over various distances, so many that until 1957 the F.I.M. record rules gave 900 solutions on how to bestow one record. This inflation was due to two things: all the distances in kilometres were doubled by those in miles, there were records over 0·6 mile (1 km), 3 (5), 6 (10), 62 (100), 310 (500), 620 (1,000), 1,242 (2,000), 1,864 (3,000), 2,485 (4,000) and 3,106 miles (5,000 km), then all the hours up to 12 hours, then the 24-hour, then the 48-hour. Even today there are 276 possibilities to break a record. It must also be said that F.I.M. recognises not only the performances of solo machines (category A) but also those of side-cars and cycle-cars (category B1,2,3) and at last it recognises the performances of special machines with three wheels. It is thus that Craig Breedlove's "Spirit of America", which went at 527·331 mile/h (848·657 km/h), saw its record recognised by the F.I.M.

In category A, reserved for solo machines, the capacity varying from 50 cc to 1,300 cc, one can challenge eleven records. However, the distance where the greatest performances are registered, is that of the flying start kilometre which must be run in both directions. In the 50 cc class the German Rudolf Kunz attained, in 1965, 130·349 miles/h (209·777 km/h) on the track at Bonneville Salt Lake on a streamlined Kreidler. The little two-stroke single was supercharged and developed 15 hp at 15,000 rev/min. The 75 cc record went in 1956 and was gained by Pasolini, who, on an Aermacchi, attained 104·041 mile/h (167·439 km/h). In reducing to 100 cc the cubic capacity of a 125 Rennfox, N.S.U. gained the record for this capacity by achieving 138·063 mile/h (222·192 km/h). The 100 cc engine, fuelled by commercial petrol, hardly developed 20 hp, which demonstrates the effectiveness of the streamlined fairing which the N.S.U. used. In the 125 category, the same year and again on Bonneville Salt Lake, an N.S.U. propelled by a Rennfox engine (20 hp at 11,000 rev/min) reached 150·129 mile/h (241·610 km/h). The 100 and 125 cc N.S.U. were ridden by the German Herman Müller. The record for the 175 has been held since 1937 by a D.K.W. at an average of 102·068 mile/h (164·264 km/h). In 1965, the American William Martin established the record for the 250 class on a 250 Yamaha, streamlined to look like a cigar. The engine of this machine was the same which at that time powered Phil Read's world championship Yamaha bike. It developed a little more than 50 hp and drove the Yamaha cigar at 174·358 mile/h (280·603 km/h). Some months later a 250 Aermacchi/Harley-Davidson had reached 177·225 mile/h (285·216 km/h) with only 35 hp at 10,000 rev/min, but this record was only recognised by the A.M.A.

In 1956 N.S.U., who had retired from circuit competition, attempted to break world records and after the 100 and 125 cc class broke the 350 and 500 cc classes, all on the track at Bonneville Salt Lake. Wilhelm Herz rode these last machines which, like the smaller capacities, were entirely streamlined. With the 350 he reached a speed of 188·611 mile/h (303·541 km/h) and with the 500, 210·080 mile/h (338·092 km/h). The engines of

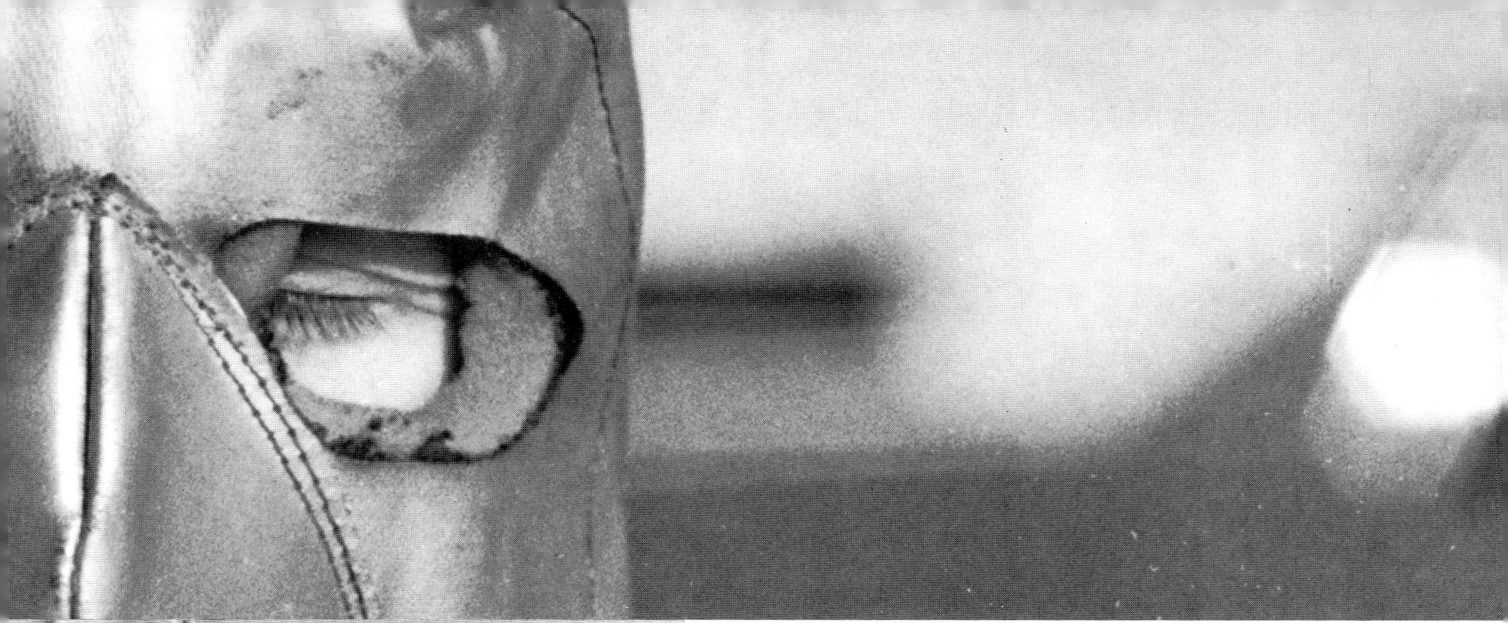

On the track at Bonneville Salt Lake: from 50 cc and 10 hp to streamlined monsters of more than 200 hp.

H DETROIT
LEX TREMULIS

GOOD/YEAR

CHASSIS BY
LOGGHE STAMPING CO.

BODY BY
V. GARDNER

STP

86
STP

these machines were derived from those of the racers, the double overhead-camshaft twins, but for the records they were tuned and developed 75 and 110 hp respectively. The record for the 750 cc class was obtained with a 667 cc tuned Triumph which developed 80 hp. This machine, ridden by the American Bill Johnson, reached 224·569 mile/h (361·410 km/h) in 1962. A Vincent H.R.D., ridden by the New Zealander Russell Wright, established the record for the 1,000 cc class by reaching 184·945 mile/h (297·640 km/h) in 1955. Lastly the record for the 1,300 cc class was recaptured by veteran George Brown in 1968, who, at fifty-eight, travelled at 182·079 mile/h (293·028 km/h) on a Vincent, bored out to 1,147 cc. This machine had a supercharger, which enabled it to compete in dragster races. If the F.I.M. recognised records ratified by the A.M.A., the title for the 1,300 cc record would go to Leppan, because the total capacity of the Gyronaut did not exceed 1,300 cc. Moreover, American 1,200 cc Harley-Davidson riders have already attained a speed of over 186 mile/h (300 km/h), and Leo Payne even achieved 196·477 mile/h (316·2 km/h) in 1970. Nowadays, challenging the flying start kilometre records is a major task, which requires careful organisation. The small-capacity N.S.U. had shown that it is not only engine power, but also a very streamlined body that is essential to attain speed records. This streamlining has to be tested in a wind-tunnel in order to achieve the most efficient shape, which, in the U.S.A. may cost up to £18 per hour and to produce a streamlined body requires at least ten hours. Likewise, the chassis is as important and has to be specially made for a speed record machine—the rider being either flat on his back as with the Gyronaut, or crouched on his stomach as on the Yamaha 250. The wheelbase of such vehicles is enormous; the Triumph ridden by Bill Johnson had an overall length of 17 ft (5·18 m). The tyres used to achieve record performances are special and therefore costly. They are usually inflated to over 44 lb (20 kg) pressure. Moreover, speeds of about 200 mile/h (320 km/h) can only be achieved at Bonneville Salt Lake, or, at a pinch, on an airfield. Breaking a record is not without dangers, like the instance of the N.S.U. 250, which was blown on to its side by a gust of wind when travelling at over 200 mile/h (320 km/h). For distances of over 6 miles (10 km) however, records are contested on the speed tracks of Monza, Montlhéry, Daytona, and the endurance records such as the 620 miles (1,000 km) 1 hour, 6 hours, 12 hours, 24 hours, require several riders. Nowadays some of these records are quite easy to beat even using touring machines. The 24-hour record for the 1,000 cc class, was set up in 1909 by Charlie Collier at an average of 32·324 mile/h (52·020 km/h).

american sports

The American idea of the motorcycle is completely different to that of the European. In America it is considered as a gadget which provides great excitement, and it is for this reason that the large-capacity machines are particularly prized. Due to necessity for speed limits, however, maximum speeds are of no importance, but on the other hand the engine must have great power in order to beat the most powerful sports cars for acceleration. In fact, as everywhere else, there are always purists who find in the motorcycle something other than its qualities as a dragster. These men travel all over Europe and America to organise meetings, the biggest of which takes place in Death Valley, California, and it is attended by 5,000 to 6,000 motorcyclists. For some years the Americans have had a passion for the cross-country motorcycle. In the beginning they used road machines which were slightly altered by accessories belonging to cross-country machines. Then these "street scramblers"; with very limited possibilities, were replaced by the trail motorcycles specially designed for cross-country riding. At the weekend they set out on their own or with trailers towards the desert. There they are in their ideal element for a journey and for competition.

In the U.S.A. there are vast desert spaces, kinds of private parks especially made for motorcycles, where cars are not allowed. At the entrance one pays to rent a bungalow in the mountains, which is reached on the motorcycle. The sporty ones prefer "Hare and Hound" to going for a ramble. One travels in a family party to the edge of the desert. While the wives and children prepare the camp, the competitors tune their machines. Then two riders disappear into the desert, and the game consists of following

202

The American ace, Gary Nixon, here skidding at 100 mile/h (160 km/h) during a flat track race.

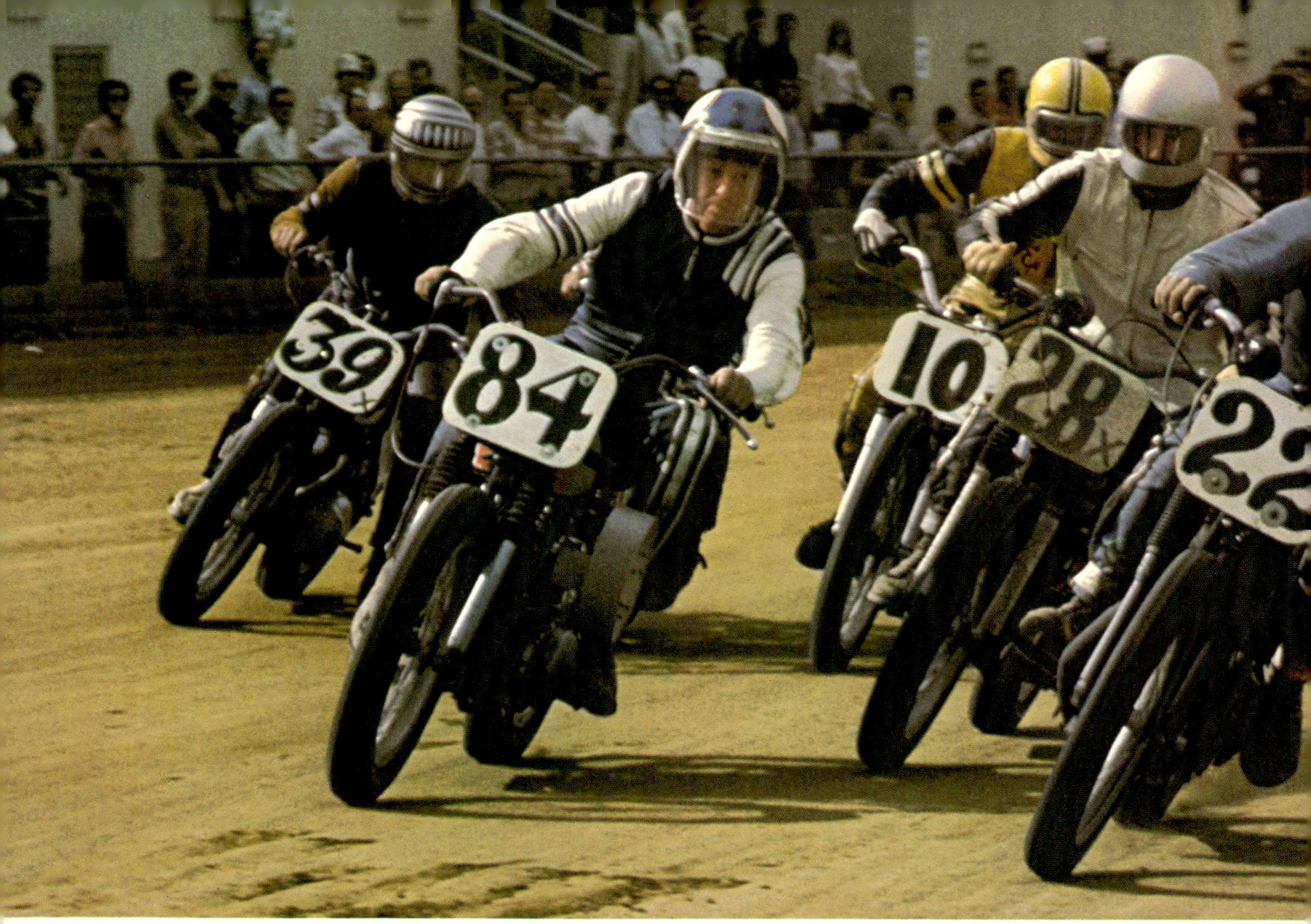
39
84
10
28
22

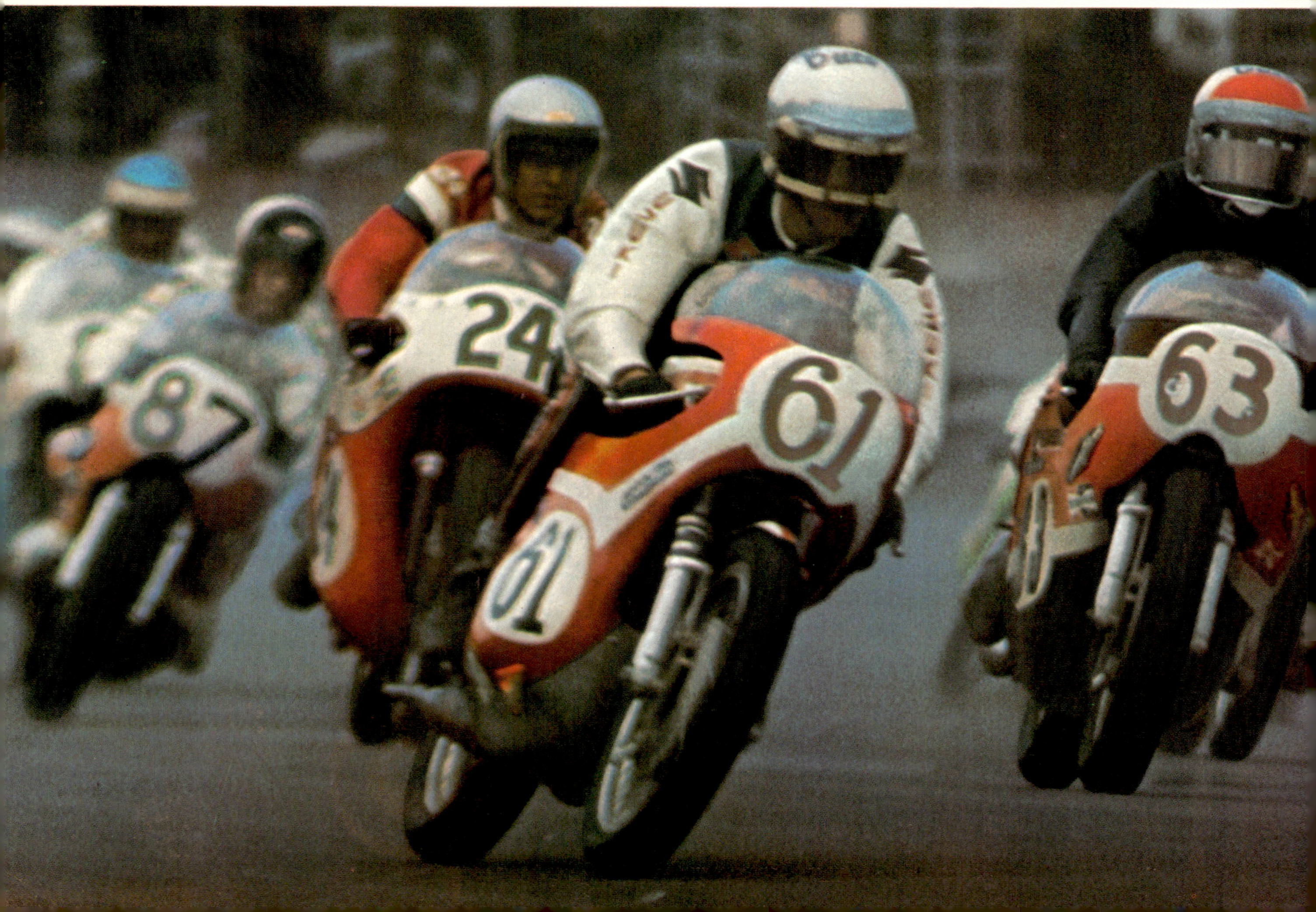
24
61
63
87

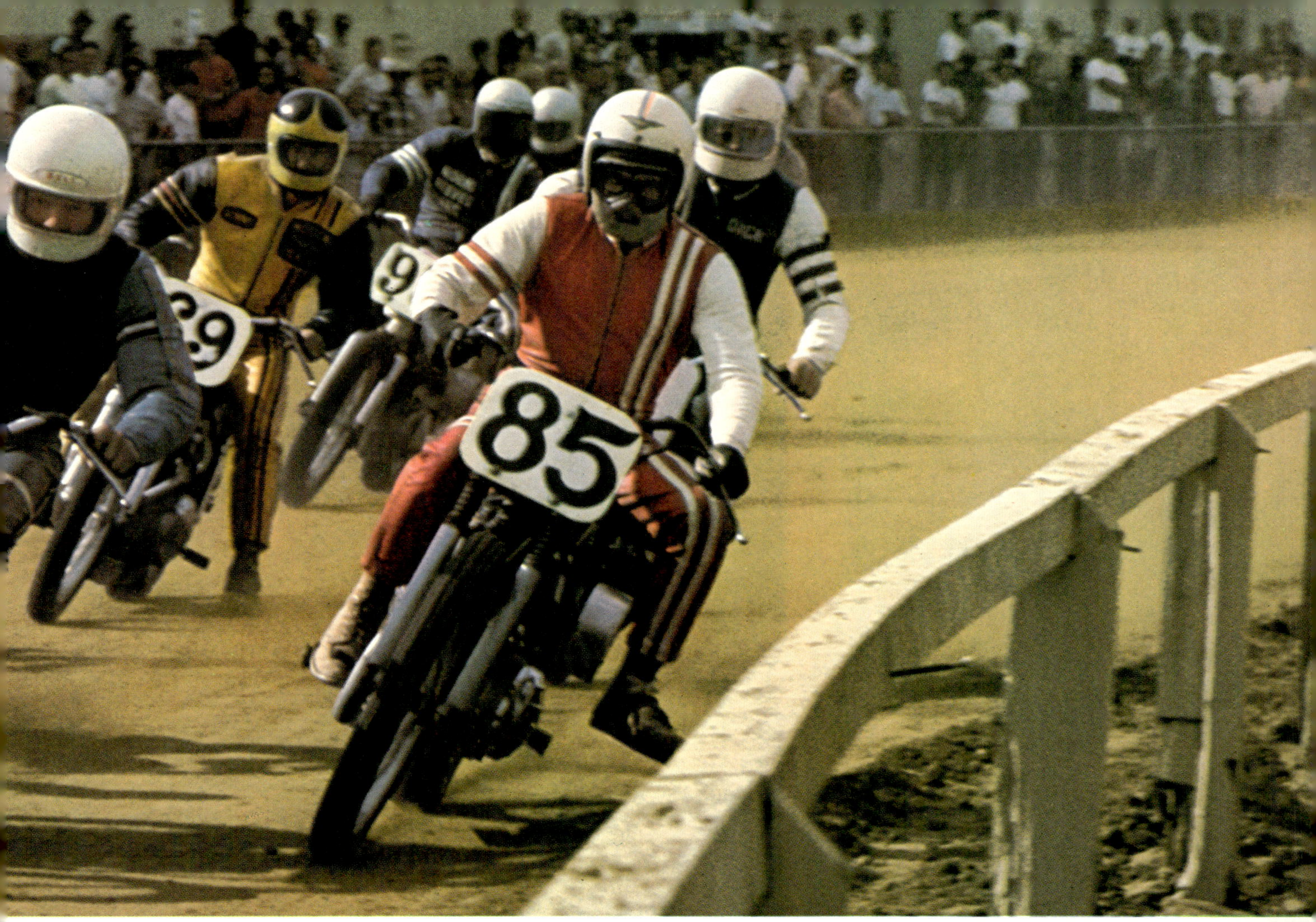
85

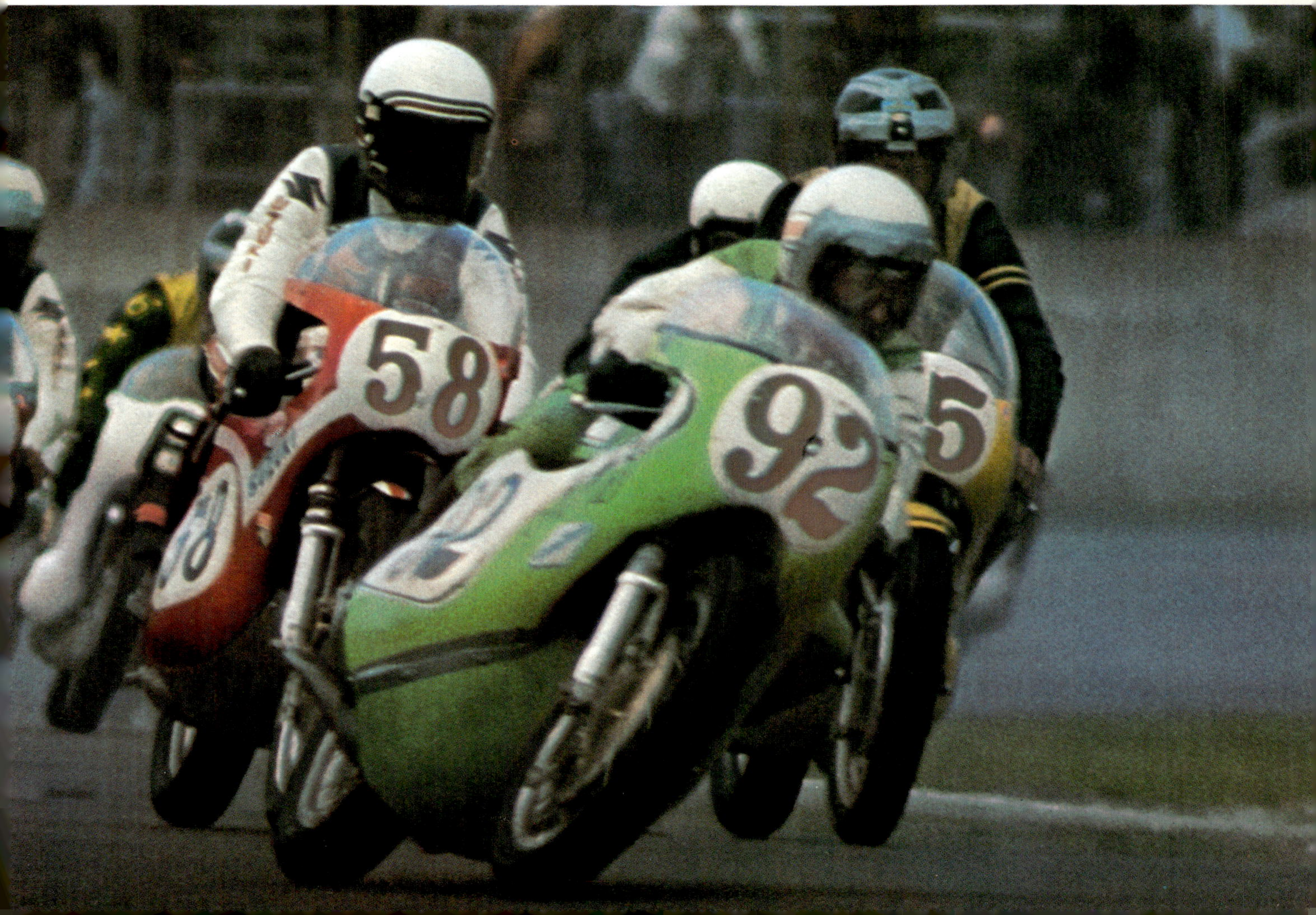
58
92

*An enduro course in
the United States*

their tracks in a kind of hunt. The Enduro races, however, are more serious and the most famous of them is the Greenhorn, where the American stars of this particular sport are to be found. Once again the competition takes place in the desert, over a minimum distance of 155 miles (250 km) which has to be covered in less than 24 hours and is usually done at an average speed of 25 mile/h (40 km/h). The Greenhorn is held under strict hourly control.

However, the hardest, the worthiest and the most unique of the endurance races is undeniably the 1,000-mile Mexican race. It consists of crossing the whole Baja peninsula in California, which is about 1,000 miles (1,600 km), in the shortest possible time. This race is also open to four-wheeled vehicles, and every year a homeric struggle takes place between the motorcycle riders and the car drivers. The motorcycles certainly have a very difficult task competing against the cars. They have one small advantage over the cars on very uneven ground, but on the other hand the cars are faster by about 20 to 30 mile/h (32 to 48 km/h). In addition, the motorcycles lose time at night because of their inferior lighting. Finally, since a single rider cannot cover 1,000 miles (1,600 km) at a stretch, a substitute rider is laid on at halfway. The difficulties of this race are incredible. First of all there is this tremendous distance to be covered, then there are the mechanical failures, the unevenness of the ground which causes loss of rhythm. Sometimes the road or the track disappears completely, and there is a danger of getting lost; or one finds oneself on a mule-track covered with holes and stones. And at the end there is only a small sum of money for the winner. Three 1,000-mile races have already been held, two of which were won by cars, and one by a 350 Honda which still holds the 24-hour speed record.

Another typical American sport is hill-climbing, in which a certain hill has to be climbed in the shortest possible time. That hill has a 490 ft (150 m) long slope and a 60° angle of climb. The competitors start off at the foot of the hill, and many never reach the top. The engines are supercharged and fuelled with nitromethane and in addition the rear wheel has a big chain that encircles the tyre. Hill-climbing is not a dangerous sport—so long as the machine does not fall backwards on top of the cyclist. In Europe, a rider, who has won most titles in his own category in one season is crowned a national champion in that category only, so there are 50, 125, 250 cc etc. road-racing champions, then motocross champions in the 250 and 500 classes, and so on. In the U.S.A. it is different. The riders are much more eclectic and the national cham-

pionship is fought out in seventeen races, which might be track or cross-country events. The Grand National championship, where expert champions take part, begins with the well-known Daytona 200. This race is about to become the most important motorcycle race in the world, and for an obvious reason. The U.S.A. absorbs most of the world production of motorcycles and a victory at Daytona gives tremendous publicity. For several years Triumph and Harley-Davidson have competed for the laurels, but now the Japanese have entered with Yamaha, Kawasaki, Suzuki and Honda. The Italian entry to be noted is Guzzi, Benelli, MV, Laverda, and they are not slow to join in the fray. So a true single race for the world championship will soon take place.

Up to the present day, European riders have not made a real impact, the reason being that a trip to the U.S.A. is rather costly. One can, however, recall two victories by Mike Hailwood on an MV in 1964 and 1965, the years that the U.S. Grand Prix was held at Daytona and Jarno Saarinen's victory in the 1973 Daytona 200. The local aces are: Gary Nixon, Art Baumann, Yvon du Hamel, Richard Hammer, Calvin Rayborn, Dick Mann, Mert Lawill . . . these are quite remarkable riders, as much at home on cinders as on macadam. After Daytona (which is a speed race on a road-racing track) they compete a flat-track race. This consists of an oval track of about 875 yd (800 m) surfaced with cinders. The machines used are large ones, either British 500 cc machines or the 750 cc side-valve Harley-Davidson. (The new rules allow 750 inverted or overhead-cam engines). By comparison with the original machine, the chassis is greatly altered. There is no longer any oscillating arm, therefore no rear suspension, no brakes, the front fork is skeletal and the tank minute. To sum it up, they have a tendency to resemble speedway machines. In consequence, the riding of flat-track bikes is as spectacular as speedway, or even more, for the speeds attained are greater. It is not rare to see Gary Nixon sliding completely, foot on the ground, turning at 95 mile/h (150 km/h). . . . Generally, these races are fought over ten or twenty laps. From flat-track they go on to speed races on the road-racing tracks; they will have to swap wide bars for clip-ons which is no problem. When the road race does not demand an excessive speed, they prefer to keep the large handlebars and ride as in the flat-track, foot on the ground. Always in the Grand National championship experts compete in a short-track race. The circuit is almost identical to the flat-track although much shorter. The maximum cubic capacity authorised in the short-track tests is 250 cc and they are run in a stadium in the evening. The third and last category of the U.S. championship is the T.T. (Tourist Trophy), which has nothing to do with the race on the Isle of Man. The 1·3 mile (2 km) long track is not uniformly flat, there are several jumps and right and left bends. The surface is partly asphalt and partly beaten earth. The bikes resemble motocross machines, but they are heavier due to the large engine and massive chassis. Riding one of these machines for 50 miles is most uncomfortable. Real motocross has interested the Americans for some time and in order to improve their knowledge of this skill they have employed the great European specialists in the subject to lay out their circuits, advise them in the choice of machines, and to educate them in the finer points of motocross. Trials and speedway are before long going to develop in the U.S.A. Mike Andrews and Sammy Miller (trials) and Ivan Mauger (speedway) are already practising this sport in America.

On most American motorways the speed limit is 62 mile/h (100 km/h), but this is not the case on the track at Salt Lake at Bonneville where during the speed week everyone can come and ride after paying quite a considerable sum of money. The money spent trying to beat the records are quite fantastic and some machines that are worth many thousands of pounds are often just used to knock a few yards off the record or else blow up in the attempt. A multitude of capacities challenge the records in their class, but no doubt the most interesting competition is that where anything is allowed to go as fast as possible. This results in

the production of extravagant monsters which are propelled by two twins of 1,300 or 1,500 cc total capacity. These engines are fuelled by nitromethane and sometimes their performance is increased by superchargers. One of the "queens" of Salt Lake is Bob Leppan's "Gyronaut X-1" which has reached 245 mile/h (395 km/h). The shape of the machine is more like a cigar than a motorcycle. It is driven by two 650 cc Triumph Bonneville engines of classical intake developing 140 hp if fuelled by methanol and 200 hp if fuelled by nitromethane. On this same track the German Rudolf Kunz ran the flying kilometre with a 50 cc tuned Kreidler at the fantastic speed of 130·4 mile/h (209·8 km/h).

The mechanical tricks and the horsepower of the dragsters are comparable to those of pure speed machines, but with those it is a question of covering the 440 yd (402 m) course with the shortest delay. At the present time, the big cubic capacities cover this distance in less than 9 s and reach a final speed of 170 mile/h (275 km/h). The world record is held by Russ Collins of California. In October 1975 he did a standing quarter mile in 7·86 s on his 3,300 cc triple-engined Honda. At the end of the run he reached 178·9 mile/h (287·9 km/h). The motorcycle jump champion is Evel Knievel of the United States. With the help of two 49 ft (15 m) long springboards he has jumped nineteen American cars lined up side by side, that is to say a total length of about 129 ft (39·3 m). . . . Imitate Icarus too closely and you break your wings—already Knievel has broken 50 bones.

Evel Knievel taking off—and heading for a bad landing.

3

the motorcyclists

the purists

There have always been the purists, the fanatics, and the aficionados in this sport. During the development of the "two-wheelers" their ranks have fluctuated, but never totally disappeared, nor will they ever disappear.

About fifteen years ago such fanatical enthusiasts were put on society's black list. They were considered unnatural to prefer a motorcycle to a car, and as they produced a lot of noise and dressed in a strange manner, they were regarded as objectionable and dangerous creatures of very doubtful morality. To complete the whole picture —add the phenomenon of the Rockers, who only went about on a motorcycle, or rather on a cycle with a motor—there was no distinction made in those days. The Press, always eager for sensational story, made much of this phenomenon and in consequence a motorcycle came to be regarded as the primary possession of a Rocker, in the same way as the bicycle chain. Foreign countries carried on the work of the Rockers in England, who had big machines and periodically ruled the quiet English seaside resorts with fear and violence. In fact, it was only a matter of very small, excited groups of people who frightened the locals with their back-firing and their slovenly appearance. During the whole of this time the true motorcyclists suffered from the adverse publicity created around this atrocious minority group. There was certainly some cause to swap a two-wheeler for something more discreet on four wheels. However, the purists held out as being exposed to ridicule by society which brought them all the closer together, and more than ever the motorcyclist world had the appearance of a fraternity. The members of this fraternity are of all ages and come from all walks of life: they are students, workers, shopkeepers, artists or directors who, in civil life, are no different from other human beings.

It is only when you speak about motorcycles with them that you discover the extraordinary side of their personality. The motorcyclist does not easily take part in this kind of conversation as he rather mistrusts the questioner who might make fun of him and his love. Moreover, in discussion the motorcyclist feels that he is exposing himself to ridicule and unveiling secrets which the uninitiated may perhaps not understand or misunderstand. Motorcyclists are independent people, not very sociable, mistrusting, but always stamped with the wisdom of people who believe in something. When actually meeting one of them on his motorcycle, in his gear, he will seem even more extraordinary. The helmet, boots, goggles, leather gloves and black jacket will give him an unattractive and almost savage air; and then there is his machine which is enormous, shining and aggressive. It is then clear why the local population distrusts such a person. However, gaining confidence from his outfit, the motorcyclist with gleaming eyes will perhaps describe his love of motorcycles. He will tell you that it is his only love. You will never see him set on fire by a football match, or a motor race.

It is also a time-consuming and expensive passion, which can cause friction in family life, especially if other members of the household do not share the motorcyclist's love. Then he will tell you:

"This morning I got up early, before it was light. I dressed myself carefully, religiously, then I went to wake up my beast. There she is, in the garage, the chrome gleaming softly in the shadows amid the perfume of cooled oil and petrol. When in the road I pull on my helmet, fix it in place and then the ceremony for starting begins: Petrol, contact, starter, one or two kicks . . . and the engine roars into life. With little revs on the throttle I keep the engine ticking over whilst I climb into the saddle.

"To mount your motorcycle is like throwing oneself into a comfortable and familiar armchair. One last inspection, one last touch to the equipment and then it is off. . . . Gently at first to warm up the engine and to listen to the revs, then faster and faster so that the engine noise is replaced by the whistling of the air. Then the rider finds a good riding position, one that avoids the motorcyclists' cramp, which affects the base of the neck and is caused by the wind pulling the head backwards. It usually lasts for hours and sometimes even days. Once these manoeuvres are finished one might think the road would become monotonous but not at all, one begins to admire the countryside. Here, there is no windscreen frame, no blind spots to block the view, and another advantage over the car is that all the scents of the countryside can be captured, the good, but also the bad.

"Furthermore, one talks to one's machine, one talks about the itinerary to follow, the roads that one will come to. One asks it to be valiant and faithful. One praises it if it goes well and blames it if it fails. All this must seem childish and ridiculous, but it has to be lived to be appreciated.

"When it is all over one feels a little sad, like at the end of an adventure."

Every motorcyclist has lived through this experience many times, as there is no shortage of occasions to give full rein to his passion—on fine days, there are the speed races and well-known rallies throughout Europe. On 14th July there is the biggest rally in France: the Chamois 2,270. This number indicates the altitude of the Col de l'Iseran, where some thousands of motorcyclists gather together, and this number is going to grow from year to year. A little later, the Madone of the Centaurs takes place in the Italian Alps. In August one goes to Norway for the Troll Rally; and in September to Belgium for the Steel Horse. These rallies are not held for competitions, but quite simply to meet other people and to give an excuse for an excursion.

In winter the motorcycle is by no means put into hibernation at the back of the garage; it is being transformed by various accessories into something even better for next season: tyres with studs, big handlebars or even a side-car. The motorcyclist prepares himself for the long-distance winter rallies, the Dragon Rally (in England), and above all: the Elefantentreffen (Elephant Rally) (in Germany). Just imagine 10,000 motorcyclists of fifteen different countries mounted on over 7,000 machines, freezing in sub-zero temperatures and gathered on the track at Nürburgring covered with several inches of snow. This is the scene at the Elephant with the most fantastic of all the international meetings, the hardest, but at the same the most beautiful, the one which attracts the pick of the enthusiasts. To complete the Elephant is a brilliant achievement, and one that is done purely for the love of the sport as there are no prizes except for a badge. As one veteran of the Elephant Rally has said:

"For us, the first week in January is unlike any other as it precedes the great rush to the Elephant and is therefore very hectic. We have to carefully prepare our equipment as this is going to protect us from sub-zero temperatures. Sometimes it is quite difficult to know what to think of next.

One fills one's boots with heat-retaining cotton, sticks stocking over one's head, covers oneself with bandages, pullovers and leather: sometimes even two layers, as one knows very well, that it is going to be very, very cold. The motorcycle also, receives a great deal of attentive care. It must be protected from the corrosion caused by salt spread on the roads, and then, if possible, a side-car must be fixed on. The side-car is ideal for the snow, even better than a well-studded vehicle. At last D-day arrives. For those who go it alone it can be tortuous. They know that on the icy patches, they run a tremendous risk of falling and perhaps damaging the bike. After about 30 miles (50 km) the cold really begins to bite. There is no longer any feeling in fingers or toes, which obviously considerably hampers the rider in his efforts to ride carefully. On the snow, the highest speed is 30 mile/h (50 km/h). One must remain very calm and not jump when a wheel momentarily skids, not move in jerks, but accelerate very gently into the skid with no braking. Always those wretched frozen hands which do not correctly respond to the manoeuvres that are demanded. One must learn to beware of the slipstream made by the oncoming lorries which would be enough to throw the machines out of control. Moreover, these lorries throw up great lumps of frozen snow, which can be very painful to the face. The banked bends are an especial fear as they always make the motorcycle slide towards the lower side. Similarly, the side winds push both rider and motorcycle to the left-hand side of the road. Always there is this terrible cold, so bad that small stinging icicles form on the nose. However, dedication prevents the rider from stopping, even to thaw himself out. Once halted one might not have the will to start again. At last, here is the "Ring" at the end of the agonising ride. What a sight, when the rider looks at himself in the mirror, dirty, exhausted, covered in salt and frozen mud, black-faced, furrowed with the marks of the helmet and the goggles, but really happy to have toiled along hundreds of miles through snow and ice, happy to have arrived. Around us, there are thousands and thousands of motorcyclists, from all over Europe. Everyone is dressed in leather, bundled up in jackets, with dirty, unshaven faces, but still attractive. Everybody knows everybody else without having ever met them. They do not speak the same language but can make themselves understood by sign language. This phenomenal gathering began about fifteen years ago. Some owners of Russian-type Zundapps, nicknamed "Green Elephants", met during one winter in the Black Forest. Their machines were particularly suited to this long excursion and in fact had been

used in the Russian campaign during the last war. Every winter more and more Green Elephants gathered in the Black Forest and soon they had to move on and settle in the Eifel on the Nürburgring circuit.

"Now in front of the stands, motorcycle folklore is in full swing, with local costume, leather and barbour jackets. All the machines are neatly drawn up waiting for the night, which will be the scene of the greatest fit of madness ever witnessed. Some hundreds of machines are waiting on the starting line of the circuit with engines stopped and lights out. Only the resin torches held by the passengers feebly light up the gathering. This impression of an open-air cabaret, these helmeted silhouettes and this silence has something supernatural. Then, suddenly, all the engines start up at once, get under way and rush into the night for a tour round the circuit. At the beginning, everyone rides in an orderly manner one behind the other, and it is a most beautiful sight to see the long ribbon of lights. Then the spirit of competition is awakened, the riders begin to rush forward. Snow flies, wheels skid, engines roar, someone falls, gets up and rides off with renewed vigour. Three side-cars have broken loose in front and turn into a bend, two go on, the third goes off. . . . In front, a red light suddenly turns white as some of the best riders skid round. On a side-turning everything is at sixes and sevens. Some side-cars do not climb, but slip on the banking and are pushed out onto the outside edge of the curve. There are gesticulations, shouts, pushing, pulling, leaning on the back wheel with all force in order to free it. And a few miles further on there is great panic. . . . At least fifty side-cars have crashed into each other; but there is more fear and mechanical damage than real harm.

"As the circuit is ended, everybody is found sitting around with glasses of beer or scalding coffee, and there they talk about the problems of the trip, in all its technical details. . . . An Englishman, rather broader than tall, the Elephant of the Elephants, is downcast—someone has stolen his badges. He cares nothing for the jacket on which they were sewn—but the badges which represent his whole career as a motorcyclist! On the other hand the Norwegian Berger Paulsen, well known from the great rallies, is enthralled with the idea of doing a 600 mile (1,000 km) in the snow the next day, and his grand-daughter, who is with him, shares his pleasure. At a neighbouring table, a splendid bearded fellow tells how he has tricked the German police; he is wearing a fur hat decorated with a red star, and has thus passed himself off as a Russian diplomat . . . on a Harley-Davidson.

"The woods are lit up by immense camp fires round which gathers a crowd of picturesque figures. Some sing hymns, others ribald songs accompanied by the guitar. Further on a sheep, grilled on skewers, is being eaten, and alongside tea, strongly laced with alcohol, is being drunk. This is the best way for the campers to keep warm and endure the freezing cold at the Elephants, and for those who do not have tents, there are always some huts in the woods scattered around the circuit, or even better the benches on the stands.

"Next day is the great departure. The Elephants have only lasted one night. Everyone returns to their respective countries, feeling sad, but knowing full well they will all come back next year. Perhaps the appeal of the Elephants lies in the journey where it is a lone battle with the rider and the elements, in the pleasure of winning, without reward and the desire to be a hero.

"It is not only in rallies that motorcyclists can meet each other, talk, and exchange points of view. There are also clubs, open to everyone on payment of an annual subscription. In France there are hundreds of these clubs. They are divided into two broad categories: sports clubs and touring clubs. The latter are content to organise one or two monthly meetings and to offer their members an outing almost every Sunday. These outings are often a small national meeting. The sporting clubs are more active. They organise motocross meetings, trials, or races, and sometimes also rallies. The clubs which have both a sporting and a touring side, are very rare.

"Apart from the clubs in the main cities provincial motorcyclists have little opportunity to meet as there are not enough enthusiasts to form a club. In the provinces the motorcycle is not yet truly accepted, which means that the French club is very limited in its scope. The two sections into which it has fallen is detrimental and above all the young do not find it satisfying, as the following shows:

"There were three of us and a hundred of them. They palavered on and on about the organisation of the next New Year's Eve banquet, and about future activities, in which we would all go on an organised visit to the gypsum quarries at Cormeilles-en-Parisis (near Pontoise). It was not exactly a thrilling programme, for the few young men like us who like to ride far and fast! So we prefer to meet every Friday night at the 'Bouquet', at the Place d'Alésia, to plan our own outings. So, every week-end, and in all weather, our little group startles the little sleepy villages in the country as it passes through. During the racing season the main goal for our members is the Grand Prix circuits, and we will travel 600 miles and more to see the champions race for three hours. These trips take us into Italy, Spain, Belgium, Germany. . . . Sometimes we will meet up with a young motorcyclist on the road. To do 40 miles at 30 mile/h behind a President who preaches the Highway Code, with the sole aim of being present before a well-laden table in a restaurant at the prize-giving of the super club of Triffouillis-les-Oies. And what prizes! A set of ultra-hot sparking plugs, a tin of pâté, a glass ashtray which takes the place of a cup. So, every week without fail we line up outside the 'Bouquet'. There are ten, fifteen or twenty polished bikes, personified by sports equipment, handlebars, racing tyres, aluminium mudguards and vividly coloured fairings, enough to excite the most blasé motorcyclist. Interested people examine the machines, join the conversation and end up in our company for the evening. This is how our group soon grows to fantastic proportions. Our group is, however, subdivided into the foundation members, purists, and the occasional motorcyclists who have some difficulty in joining the first group because they cannot produce their credentials: experience in fast, long distance riding. From 9 o'clock in the evening onwards the surrounding area is the scene of incessant activity. All makes are represented, from the smallest to the largest, the slowest to the fastest, the cleanest to the dirtiest, which makes the butcher in the corner groan as he sees the front of his shop stained with spots of oil.

"The police are also displeased and insist on enforcing the law which maintains that pavements are places for pedestrians, not bikes, as there are always about a dozen machines drawn up on these pavements. Then there are quarrels about the motorcyclists being persecuted as they are mistaken for Rockers. Already it is 10 o'clock. Conversation is flowing, untiringly bound up with the vast subject: the motorcycle. Previous races and new productions are discussed, and the motorcyclists boast of the performances of their machine and its legendary strength, forgetting of course the little troubles which make every owner of a high-speed machine a nervous wreck. Their last fall is recalled as a great memory and there are even those who make it a point of honour to boast as many injury-free falls as possible; but there are always some crutches among the black leather jackets and helmets heaped casually on the chairs of the cafés. Great peals of laughter from a neighbouring table: one of the lads is imitating an exhaust noise; there are specialists in noises, even baritones for the singles and sopranos for the multis. At midnight there are shouts of 'Cheerio Puch, cheerio Tri-

umph, cheerio Honda'—it is easier to remember the make of a friend's machine than his name. The tables are empty, bills are scattered around, scrawled with sketches of new machines or mechanical components. . . . Every true motorcyclist must have at his finger-tips all the mechanisms of a motorcycle, and has to be able to repair it himself. A last touch to the goggles, a few kicks and a black silhouette followed by a red light disappears in a clap of thunder. On the macadam of the pavement, spots of oil spread out slowly, to be absorbed until next Friday."

That was six years ago. Since then, the club has known its ups and downs. 1968 was its heyday with more than 300 youths meeting there on Friday nights. However, this did not please the residents who brought in the police to get rid of these unwelcome intruders. Therefore, with rigorous law enforcements and heavy fines, the police cleared the Alésia. So they had to meet elsewhere and the Place de la Bastille was chosen. However, they were again expelled because of the noise. Now they were wondering where to go next. A solution was found in the East End of London where the headquarters of a club was set up in 1959. This club is now one of the most important in the world: about 15,000 members meet there coming from all over England and even from abroad. It was set up by a clergyman who was a tremendous motorcycling enthusiast, who had realised that the greater part of the young English motorcyclists did not know too much about handling their bikes. To start with he gave them a place where they could meet, a disused church in Paddington Green. There, all the motorcyclists could meet to talk about motorcycles without disturbing anybody and without fearing expulsion by the police. Then, little by little, an organisation was formed with group excursions and traditional motorcycle rallies as their aim.

In certain aspects the motorcycle can be used for educative and even rehabilitation purposes. In Paris, for instance, there is a young people's home which concerns itself particularly with young delinquents who have been set free. This home has several different sports departments (judo, underwater swimming, just to mention two) and one concerns itself with the motorcycle. It has also been noted that these young men were more interested in the skill of riding than in any other sport. They developed a real love of the two-wheeler and its mechanics and this was enough to help them back to a mental stability. The work of teachers might be greatly simplified if the parents of delinquents were not so furiously opposed to their sons having motorcycles.

the show bike (or chopper)

The new rise of the motorcycle is partly due to the fact that motorcycling has become fashionable. The machines themselves were attractive articles, particularly the Japanese ones with their chrome and vivid colours. In Europe, two American films were made about motorcyclists called *Hell's Angels* and *Savage Angels*. The films both describe the sad adventures of neo-Nazi gangs of hooligans, who spread terror everywhere they go and inevitably these gangs go about on motorcycles—and what motorcycles! . . . big Harleys altered so much they are hardly recognisable. It should be pointed out, however, that the number of Hell's Angels is deceiving, there are comparatively few—just 2,000—of them in the U.S.A. while there are 9,000,000 ordinary motorcyclists. So, for Europeans the above-mentioned films were a revelation, not because they were works of art, far from that, nor because the contents were absorbing, but simply because the machines themselves gained an unheard-of success.

Soon motorcycles were specially constructed for French film stars and famous singers and in this way the fashion for the "show bike" was launched. When thinking of a "show bike" a stream of fashionable adjectives come to mind, such as "entrancing, crazy, sensational, fabulous, terrible, magnificent, brilliant". How is one to describe a thing which is more like a Christmas tree than a motorcycle, a machine on which the exhaust pipes stick up almost 7 ft (2 m) in the air, and equipped with handlebars which are level with the rider's ears. It is completely chromed and painted in luminous mauves, yellows and greens. Anything is allowed as there are no conventions, the most brilliant and shiny are regarded to be the most beautiful; in fact, the more psychedelic it becomes the better.

The clientele for this kind of motorcycle is a very specialised one as it is not really interested in the motorcycle as such, but rather in exhibitionism. For the most part it is young people who prefer this machine to a more discreet car and wealthy playboys in need of a novelty to draw attention to themselves. It goes without saying that the use of the "show bike" is very restricted: it is all right for use in a city or at the most to cover a short distance from hotel to beach. There is, of course, no question of going great distances on this model, unless one is prepared to ride stoically at 40 miles/h (70 km/h) in great discomfort. Riding a "show bike" is perhaps spectacular, if not exactly fast. However, when talking to an owner, he will maintain that he frequently travels at more than 100 mile/h (160 km/h).

In spite of a false idea of things, these motorcycle snobs serve the cause of the motorcycle very well as they are not people who draw attention to themselves by being badly dressed, remaining elegant on their machines. Also they make great efforts to be known and to share their "new passion". For some this interest in the "show bike" may be only transitory, but others will continue and develop their interest. Their "have you seen me" side will gradually disappear to give place to a much more sober and conventional motorcycle enthusiasm.

This type of person is not a purist and does not worship the motorcycle any more than he is a slave of fashion. He is part of that growing crowd of people, who have just discovered, or rediscovered, the usefulness and the pleasure of a two-wheeler. Quite often they already possess a car and think of their motorcycle as a leisure object which at the same time gives them a splendid service. Usually they buy a new or almost new machine to avoid eventual mechanical hitches, because for them a motorcycle should more or less look after itself. In the morning it must start without trouble at the first kick or pressing of the starter. It is also essential that it is not subject to oil loss and that it is not too noisy. In fact, to sum up, it must be a civilised machine, always ready for use, otherwise the convert will soon be displeased.

Chopped motorcycles have taken
bike engineering into the realms of
three-dimensional art, yet this 750 cc
Harley Davidson is still regularly
ridden on the road.

Harley Davidson 74—1200 cc's of
ultimate customs motorcycle, the
ideal of the American biker and the
dream of the chopper enthusiast the
world over.

The ''elephants''. ▶

World Championship Results
riders and constructors

50 cc

Year	Rider	Constructor
1949	Not contested	
1950	Not contested	
1951	Not contested	
1952	Not contested	
1953	Not contested	
1954	Not contested	
1955	Not contested	
1956	Not contested	
1957	Not contested	
1958	Not contested	
1959	Not contested	
1960	Not contested	
1961	Not contested	
1962	Ernst Degner (W.G.)	Suzuki
1963	Hugh Anderson (N.Z.)	Suzuki
1964	Hugh Anderson (N.Z.)	Suzuki
1965	Ralph Bryans (Irl.)	Honda 2
1966	Hans-Georg Anscheidt (W.G.) (Suzuki 2)	Honda 2
1967	Hans-Georg Anscheidt (W.G.)	Suzuki 2
1968	Hans-Georg Anscheidt (W.G.)	Suzuki 2
1969	Angel Nieto (Sp.)	Derbi
1970	Angel Nieto (Sp.)	Derbi
1971	Jan de Vries (H)	Kreidler
1972	Angel Nieto (Sp.)	Derbi
1973	Jan de Vries (H)	Kreidler
1974	Henk van Kessel (H)	Kreidler
1975	Angel Nieto (Sp.)	Kreidler

125 cc

Year	Rider	Constructor
1949	Nello Pagani (Italy)	F.B. Mondial
1950	Bruno Ruffo (Italy)	F.B. Mondial
1951	Carlo Ubbiali (Italy)	F.B. Mondial
1952	Cecil Sandford (G.B.)	MV Agusta
1953	Werner Haas (W.G.) (N.S.U.)	MV Agusta
1954	Rupert Hollaus (Austria)	N.S.U.
1955	Carlo Ubbiali (Italy)	MV Agusta
1956	Carlo Ubbiali (Italy)	MV Agusta
1957	Tarquinio Provini (Italy)	F.B. Mondial
1958	Carlo Ubbiali (Italy)	MV Agusta
1959	Carlo Ubbiali (Italy)	MV Agusta
1960	Carlo Ubbiali (Italy)	MV Agusta
1961	Tom Phillis (Australia)	Honda
1962	Luigi Taveri (Switz.)	Honda 2
1963	Hugh Anderson (N.Z.)	Suzuki 2
1964	Luigi Taveri (Switz.)	Honda 4
1965	Hugh Anderson (N.Z.)	Suzuki 2
1966	Luigi Taveri (Switz.)	Honda 5
1967	Bill Ivy (G.B.)	Yamaha 4
1968	Phil Read (G.B.)	Yamaha 4
1969	Dave Simmonds (G.B.)	Kawasaki 2
1970	Dieter Braun (W.G.)	Suzuki 2
1971	Angel Nieto (Sp.)	Derbi
1972	Angel Nieto (Sp.)	Derbi
1973	Kent Andersson (Swe.)	Yamaha 2
1974	Kent Andersson (Swe.)	Yamaha 2
1975	Paolo Pileri (Italy)	Morbidelli2

350 cc

Year	Rider	Constructor
1949	Freddie Frith (G.B.)	Velocette
1950	Bob Foster (G.B.)	Velocette
1951	Geoff Duke (G.B.)	Norton
1952	Geoff Duke (G.B.)	Norton
1953	Fergus Anderson (G.B.)	Moto Guzzi
1954	Fergus Anderson (G.B.)	Moto Guzzi
1955	Bill Lomas (G.B.)	Moto Guzzi
1956	Bill Lomas (G.B.)	Moto Guzzi
1957	Keith Campbell (Australia) (Moto Guzzi)	Gilera 4
1958	John Surtees (G.B.)	MV Agusta 4
1959	John Surtees (G.B.)	MV Agusta 4
1960	John Surtees (G.B.)	MV Agusta 4
1961	Gary Hocking (Rhod.)	MV Agusta 4
1962	Jim Redman (Rhod.)	Honda 4
1963	Jim Redman (Rhod.)	Honda 4
1964	Jim Redman (Rhod.)	Honda 4
1965	Jim Redman (Rhod.)	Honda 4
1966	Mike Hailwood (G.B.)	Honda 4
1967	Mike Hailwood (G.B.)	Honda 6
1968	Giacomo Agostini (Italy)	MV Agusta 3
1969	Giacomo Agostini (Italy)	MV Agusta 3
1970	Giacomo Agostini (Italy)	MV Agusta 3
1971	Giacomo Agostini (Italy)	MV Agusta 4
1972	Giacomo Agostini (Italy)	MV Agusta 4
1973	Giacomo Agostini (Italy) (MV Agusta 4)	Yamaha 2
1974	Giacomo Agostini (Italy)	Yamaha 2
1975	Johnny Cecotto (Venez.)	Yamaha 2

500 cc

Year	Rider	Constructor
1949	Leslie Graham (G.B.)	AJS 2
1950	Umberto Masetti (Italy) (Gilera 4)	Norton
1951	Geoff Duke (G.B.)	Norton
1952	Umberto Masetti (Italy)	Gilera 4
1953	Geoff Duke (G.B.)	Gilera 4
1954	Geoff Duke (G.B.)	Gilera 4
1955	Geoff Duke (G.B.)	Gilera 4
1956	John Surtees (G.B.)	MV Agusta 4
1957	Libero Liberati (Italy)	Gilera 4
1958	John Surtees (G.B.)	MV Agusta 4
1959	John Surtees (G.B.)	MV Agusta 4
1960	John Surtees (G.B.)	MV Agusta 4
1961	Gary Hocking (Rhod.)	MV Agusta 4
1962	Mike Hailwood (G.B.)	MV Agusta 4
1963	Mike Hailwood (G.B.)	MV Agusta 4
1964	Mike Hailwood (G.B.)	MV Agusta 4
1965	Mike Hailwood (G.B.)	MV Agusta 4
1966	Giacomo Agostini (Italy) (MV Agusta 3)	Honda 4
1967	Giacomo Agostini (Italy)	MV Agusta 3
1968	Giacomo Agostini (Italy)	MV Agusta 3
1969	Giacomo Agostini (Italy)	MV Agusta 3
1970	Giacomo Agostini (Italy)	MV Agusta 3
1971	Giacomo Agostini (Italy)	MV Agusta 3
1972	Giacomo Agostini (Italy)	MV Agusta 3
1973	Phil Read (G.B.)	MV Agusta 4
1974	Phil Read (G.B.) (MV Agusta 4)	Yamaha 4
1975	Giacomo Agostini (Italy)	Yamaha 4

250 cc

Year	Rider	Constructor
1949	Bruno Ruffo (Italy)	Moto Guzzi
1950	Dario Ambrosini (Italy)	Benelli
1951	Bruno Ruffo (Italy)	Moto Guzzi
1952	Enrico Lorenzetti (Italy	Moto Guzzi
1953	Werner Haas (W.G.)	N.S.U. 2
1954	Werner Haas (W.G.)	N.S.U. 2
1955	Herman Müller (W.G.) (N.S.U. 2)	MV Agusta
1956	Carlo Ubbiali (Italy)	MV Agusta
1957	Cecil Sandford (G.B.)	F.B. Mondial
1958	Tarquinio Provini (Italy)	MV Agusta
1959	Carlo Ubbiali (Italy)	MV Agusta
1960	Carlo Ubbiali (Italy)	MV Agusta
1961	Mike Hailwood (G.B.)	Honda 4
1962	Jim Redman (Rhod.)	Honda 4
1963	Jim Redman (Rhod.)	Honda 4
1964	Phil Read (G.B.)	Yamaha 2
1965	Phil Read (G.B.)	Yamaha 2
1966	Mike Hailwood (G.B.)	Honda 6
1967	Mike Hailwood (G.B.)	Honda 6
1968	Phil Read (G.B.)	Yamaha 4
1969	Kel Carruthers (Australia)	Benelli 4
1970	Rod Gould (G.B.)	Yamaha 2
1971	Phil Read (G.B.)	Yamaha 2
1972	Jarno Saarinen (Finland)	Yamaha 2
1973	Dieter Braun (W.G.)	Yamaha 2
1974	Walter Villa (Italy) (Harley-Davidson 2)	Yamaha 2
1975	Walter Villa (Italy)	Harley-Davidson 2

Side-cars

Year	Rider	Constructor
1949	Eric Oliver (G.B.)	Norton
1950	Eric Oliver (G.B.)	Norton
1951	Eric Oliver (G.B.)	Norton
1952	Cyril Smith (G.B.)	Norton
1953	Eric Oliver (G.B.)	Norton
1954	Wilhelm Noll (W.G.)	B.M.W. 2
1955	Wilhelm Faust (W.G.)	B.M.W. 2
1956	Wilhelm Noll (W.G.)	B.M.W. 2
1957	Fritz Hillebrand (W.G.)	B.M.W. 2
1958	Walter Schneider (W.G.)	B.M.W. 2
1959	Walter Schneider (W.G.)	B.M.W. 2
1960	Helmut Fath (W.G.)	B.M.W. 2
1961	Max Deubel (W.G.)	B.M.W. 2
1962	Max Deubel (W.G.)	B.M.W. 2
1963	Max Deubel (W.G.)	B.M.W. 2
1964	Max Deubel (W.G.)	B.M.W. 2
1965	Fritz Scheidegger (Switz.)	B.M.W. 2
1966	Fritz Scheidegger (Switz.)	B.M.W. 2
1967	Klaus Enders (W.G.)	B.M.W. 2
1968	Helmut Fath (W.G.) (U.R.S. 4)	B.M.W. 2
1969	Klaus Enders (W.G.)	B.M.W. 2
1970	Klaus Enders (W.G.)	B.M.W. 2
1971	Horst Owesle (W.G.) (Münch 4)	B.M.W. 2
1972	Klaus Enders (W.G.)	B.M.W. 2
1973	Klaus Enders (W.G.)	B.M.W. 2
1974	Klaus Enders (W.G.)	B.M.W. 2
1975	Rolf Steinhausen (W.G.)	König 2

Motocross 250 and 500 cc

Motocross 500 cc

Year	Champions (nat.)	Make
1957	Bill Nilsson (Swe.)	A.J.S. Crescent
1958	René Baeten (Bel.)	F.N. d'Herstal
1959	Sten Lundin (Swe.)	Monark
1960	Bill Nilsson (Swe.)	Husqvarna
1961	Sten Lundin (Swe.)	Lito
1962	Rolf Tibblin (Swe.)	Husqvarna
1963	Rolf Tibblin (Swe.)	Husqvarna
1964	Jeff Smith (G.B.)	B.S.A. 420 cc
1965	Jeff Smith (G.B.)	B.S.A. 440 cc
1966	Paul Friedrichs (E.G.)	CZ 360 cc
1967	Paul Friedrichs (E.G.)	CZ 380 cc
1968	Paul Friedrichs (E.G.)	CZ 420 cc
1969	Bengt Aberg (Swe.)	Husqvarna
1970	Bengt Aberg (Swe.)	Husqvarna
1971	Roger de Coster (Bel.)	Suzuki
1972	Roger de Coster (Bel.)	Suzuki
1973	Roger de Coster (Bel.)	Suzuki
1974	Heikki Mikkola (Fin.)	Husqvarana
1975	Roger de Coster (Bel.)	Suzuki

Motocross 250 cc

Year	Champion (nat.)	Make
	European Championships	
1957	Fritz Betzelbacher (W.G.)	Maico
1958	Jaromïr Cizek (Cz.)	Jawa
1959	Rolf Tibblin (Swe.)	Husqvarna
1960	Dave Bickers (G.B.)	Greeves
1961	Dave Bickers (G.B.)	Greeves
	World Championships	
1962	Torsten Hallman (Swe.)	Husqvarna
1963	Torsten Hallman (Swe.)	Husqvarna
1964	Joël Robert (Bel.)	CZ
1965	Victor Arbekov (U.S.S.R.)	CZ
1966	Torsten Hallman (Swe.)	Husqvarna
1967	Torsten Hallman (Swe.)	Husqvarna
1968	Joël Robert (Bel.)	CZ
1969	Joël Robert (Bel.)	CZ
1970	Joël Robert (Bel.)	Suzuki
1971	Joël Robert (Bel.)	Suzuki
1972	Joël Robert (Bel.)	Suzuki
1973	Hakan Andersson (Swe.)	Yamaha
1974	Gennadiy Moisseev (U.S.S.R.)	KTM
1975	Harry Everts (Bel.)	Puch

The least conventional looking machine is considered to be the best-looking motorcycle

Career World Championship Wins by Class (to end of 1975)

50 cc

A. Nieto (Spain)	19	(1969–)
H.-G. Anscheidt (W.G.)	14	(1962–68)
J. de Vries (Neth.)	14	(1970–)
H. R. Anderson (N.Z.)	8	(1962–65)
R. Bryans (G.B.)	8	(1964-66)
E. D. Degner (W.G.)	7	(1962–65)

125 cc

C. Ubbiali (Italy)	26	(1950–60)
L. Taveri (Switz.)	22	(1955–66)
H. R. Anderson (N.Z.)	17	(1962–65)
A. Nieto (Spain)	16	(1970–)
W. D. Ivy (G.B.)	14	(1966–68)
K. Andersson (Swe.)	14	(1972–)
P. W. Read (G.B.)	10	(1965–)
D. A. Simmonds (G.B.)	10	(1969–71)
E. D. Degner (W.G.)	8	(1959–65)

250 cc

P. W. Read (G.B.)	27	(1964–)
S. M. B. Hailwood (G.B.)	21	(1961–67)
J. A. Redman (Rhod.)	18	(1961–65)
T. Provini (Itay)	14	(1957–65)
C. Ubbiali (Italy)	13	(1955–60)
R. A. Gould (G.B.)	10	(1970–72)
W. Villa (Italy)	9	(1974–)
J. Saarinen (Finland)	8	(1971–73)
W. Haas (W.G.)	7	(1953–54)
W. D. Ivy (G.B.)	7	(1967–68)
K. Carruthers (Australia)	7	(1969–)

350 cc

G. Agostini (Italy)	53	(1965–)
J. A. Redman (Rhod.)	22	(1962–65)
S. M. B. Hailwood (G.B.)	16	(1962–67)
J. Surtees (G.B.)	15	(1956–60)
G. E. Duke (G.B.)	11	(1950–58)
F. K. Anderson (G.B.)	7	(1953–54)
W. A. Lomas (G.B.)	7	(1955–56)

500 cc

G. Agostini (Italy)	67	(1965–)
S. M. B. Hailwood (G.B.)	37	(1961–67)
G. E. Duke (G.B.)	22	(1950–58)
J. Surtees (G.B.)	22	(1956–60)
P. W. Read (G.B.)	11	(1964–)
G. Hocking (Rhod.)	8	(1961–62)

Side-car

K. Enders (W.G.)	27	(1967–74)
E. S. Oliver (G.B.)	17	(1949–54)
F. Scheidegger (Switz.)	16	(1959–66)
M. Deubel (W.G.)	12	(1961–65)
H. Fath (W.G.)	10	(1960–69)
S. Schauzu (W.G.)	9	(1967–)
W. Noll (W.G.)	8	(1954–56)
F. Camathias (Switz.)	8	(1958–65)
W. Schneider (W.G.)	7	(1955–59)

Career total

G. Agostini (Italy)	120	(1965–)
S. M. B. Hailwood (G.B.)	76	(1959–67)
P. W. Read (G.B.)	52	(1961–)
J. A. Redman (Rhod.)	46	(1961–66)
C. Ubbiali (Italy)	39	(1950–60)
J. Surtees (G.B.)	38	(1955–60)
A. Nieto (Spain)	35	(1969–)
G. E. Duke (G.B.)	33	(1950–58)
L. Taveri (Switz.)	30	(1955–66)
K. Enders (W.G.)	27	(1967–74)
H. R. Anderson (N.Z.)	25	(1962–65)
W. D. Ivy (G.B.)	21	(1966–68)
T. Provini (Italy)	20	(1954–65)
G. Hocking (Rhod.)	19	(1959–62)
K. Andersson (Swe.)	18	(1969–)
E. S. Oliver (G.B.)	17	(1949–54)
F. Scheidegger (Switz.)	16	(1959–66)
E. D. Degner (W.G.)	15	(1959–65)
J. Saarinen (Finland)	15	(1971–73)
H.-G. Anscheidt (W.G.)	14	(1962–68)
J. de Vries (Neth.)	14	(1970–)
D. Braun (W.G.)	13	(1969–)
F. K. Anderson (G.B.)	12	(1951–54)
M. Deubel (W.G.)	12	(1961–65)
W. Haas (W.G.)	11	(1952–54)
R. Bryans (G.B.)	11	(1964–67)
D. A. Simmonds (G.B.)	11	(1969–71)

Giacomo Agostini on his MV3

Luigi Taveri.

Mike Hailwood on his Honda.

Phil Read.

C. Lacombe.

Photos:
C. Lacombe,
Motorcycling Monthly (p. 227)
Motor Cycle News (pp. 235–6)

Layout:
Jean-Claude Jouannet

Printed:
Mussot, Paris, France, 1976